The Select Series:
Microsoft® Word 2002
Brief Volume

Yvonne Johnson

Prentice
Hall

Upper Saddle River, New Jersey

Publisher and Vice President: Natalie E. Anderson
Executive Acquisitions Editor: Jodi McPherson
Managing Editor: Monica Stipanov
Assistant Editor: Jennifer Cappello
Editorial Assistant: Dayna Hilinsky
Development Editors: Christy Parrish and Samantha Penrod
Media Project Manager: Cathleen Profitko
Marketing Manager: Emily Williams Knight
Production Manager: Gail Steier De Acevedo
Project Manager: Tim Tate
Associate Director, Manufacturing: Vincent Scelta
Manufacturing Buyer: Natacha St. Hill Moore
Design Manager: Pat Smythe
Interior Design: Lorraine Castellano and Proof Positive/Farrowlyne Associates, Inc.
Cover Design: Lorraine Castellano
Full-Service Composition: Proof Positive/Farrowlyne Associates, Inc.
Printer/Binder: Banta Book Group, Menasha

10 9 8 7 6 5 4 3 2 1
ISBN 0-13-008850-1

THE SELECT SERIES: MICROSOFT® OFFICE XP

Series Authors

Pamela R. Toliver and Yvonne Johnson

Volume I

Volume II

Brief

Getting Started

Volume I

Volume II

Comprehensive

Brief

Dedication

This book is dedicated to my new daughter-in-law, Rebecca Ann Patrick Johnson, who is a welcome addition to our family and holds a very special place in my heart.

Acknowledgments

This is the third edition of this book that my coauthor and I have written. Each edition has had its own challenges, but this one, in particular, presented some thorny obstacles. I would like to thank all those people, some whose names I don't even know, who worked diligently to see this book published. Although I cannot list everyone who has contributed to the making of this book, I would like to recognize the efforts of my coauthor, Pam Toliver, as well as Christy Parrish, the Developmental Editor, Monica Stipanov, Managing Editor, and Jennifer Cappello, Assistant Editor. Finally, I would like to express my gratitude to Jodi McPherson, Executive Editor, for her strong leadership and the direction that she has given to the series.

Yvonne

Preface

About this Series

The Select Series uses a class-tested, highly visual, project-based approach that teaches students through tasks using step-by-step instructions. You will find extensive full-color figures and screen captures that guide learners through the basic skills and procedures necessary to demonstrate proficiency in their use of each software application.

The Select Series introduces an all-new design for Microsoft Office XP. The easy-to-follow design now has larger screen shots with steps listed on the left side of the accompanying screen. This unique design program, along with the use of bold color, helps reduce distraction and keeps students focused and interested as they work. In addition, selectively placed Tip boxes and Other Ways boxes enhance student learning by explaining various ways to complete a task.

Our approach to learning is designed to provide the necessary visual guidance in a project-oriented setting. Each project concludes with a review section that includes a Summary, Key Terms & Skills, Study Questions, Guided Exercises, and On Your Own exercises. This extensive end-of-project section provides students with the opportunity to practice and gain further experience with the tasks covered in each project.

What's New in the Select Series for Office XP

The entire Select Series has been revised to include the new features found in the Office XP suite, which contains Word 2002, Excel 2002, Access 2002, PowerPoint 2002, Publisher 2002, FrontPage 2002, and Outlook 2002.

The Select Series provides students with clear, concise instruction supported by its new design, which includes bigger screen captures. Steps are now located in the margin for ease of use and readability. This instruction is further enhanced by graded exercises in the end-of-project material.

Another exciting update is that every project begins with a Running Case from Selections, Inc., a department store that has opened shop online as e-Selections.com. Students are put in an e-commerce–based business environment so that they can relate what they are learning in Office XP to a real world situation. Everything is within a scenario that puts them in the department store where they perform tasks that relate to a particular division of the store or Web site.

About the Book

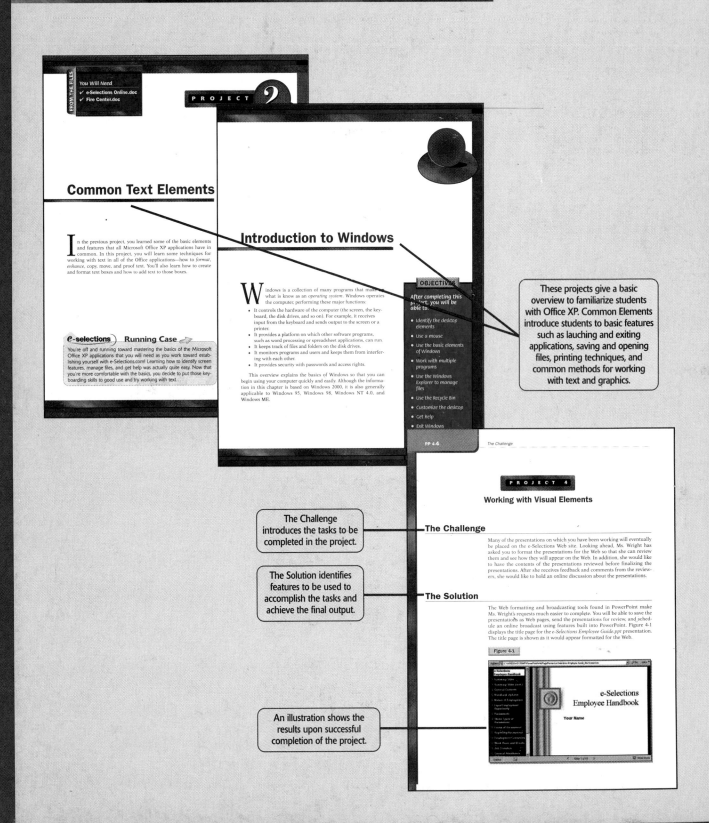

You Will Need
FROM THE FILES:
- ✓ e-Selections Online.doc
- ✓ Fire Center.doc

PROJECT 9

Common Text Elements

In the previous project, you learned some of the basic elements and features that all Microsoft Office XP applications have in common. In this project, you will learn some techniques for working with text in all of the Office applications—how to *format*, *enhance*, copy, move, and proof text. You'll also learn how to create and format text boxes and how to add text to those boxes.

Introduction to Windows

Windows is a collection of many programs that make up what is know as an *operating system*. Windows operates the computer, performing these major functions:

- It controls the hardware of the computer (the screen, the keyboard, the disk drives, and so on). For example, it receives input from the keyboard and sends output to the screen or a printer.
- It provides a platform on which other software programs, such as word processing or spreadsheet applications, can run.
- It keeps track of files and folders on the disk drives.
- It monitors programs and users and keeps them from interfering with each other.
- It provides security with passwords and access rights.

This overview explains the basics of Windows so that you can begin using your computer quickly and easily. Although the information in this chapter is based on Windows 2000, it is also generally applicable to Windows 95, Windows 98, Windows NT 4.0, and Windows ME.

e-selections   **Running Case**

You're off and running toward mastering the basics of the Microsoft Office XP applications that you will need as you work toward establishing yourself with e-Selections.com! Learning how to identify screen features, manage files, and get help was actually quite easy. Now that you're more comfortable with the basics, you decide to put those keyboarding skills to good use and try working with text...

OBJECTIVES

After completing this project, you will be able to:

- Identify the desktop elements
- Use a mouse
- Use the basic elements of Windows
- Work with multiple programs
- Use the Windows Explorer to manage files
- Use the Recycle Bin
- Customize the desktop
- Get help
- Exit Windows

> These projects give a basic overview to familiarize students with Office XP. Common Elements introduce students to basic features such as lauching and exiting applications, saving and opening files, printing techniques, and common methods for working with text and graphics.

PP 4-4   The Challenge

PROJECT 4

Working with Visual Elements

The Challenge

Many of the presentations on which you have been working will eventually be placed on the e-Selections Web site. Looking ahead, Ms. Wright has asked you to format the presentations for the Web so that she can review them and see how they will appear on the Web. In addition, she would like to have the contents of the presentations reviewed before finalizing the presentations. After she receives feedback and comments from the reviewers, she would like to hold an online discussion about the presentations.

The Solution

The Web formatting and broadcasting tools found in PowerPoint make Ms. Wright's requests much easier to complete. You will be able to save the presentations as Web pages, send the presentations for review, and schedule an online broadcast using features built into PowerPoint. Figure 4-1 displays the title page for the *e-Selections Employee Guide.ppt* presentation. The title page is shown as it would appear formatted for the Web.

Figure 4-1

e-Selections
Employee Handbook

Your Name

> The Challenge introduces the tasks to be completed in the project.

> The Solution identifies features to be used to accomplish the tasks and achieve the final output.

> An illustration shows the results upon successful completion of the project.

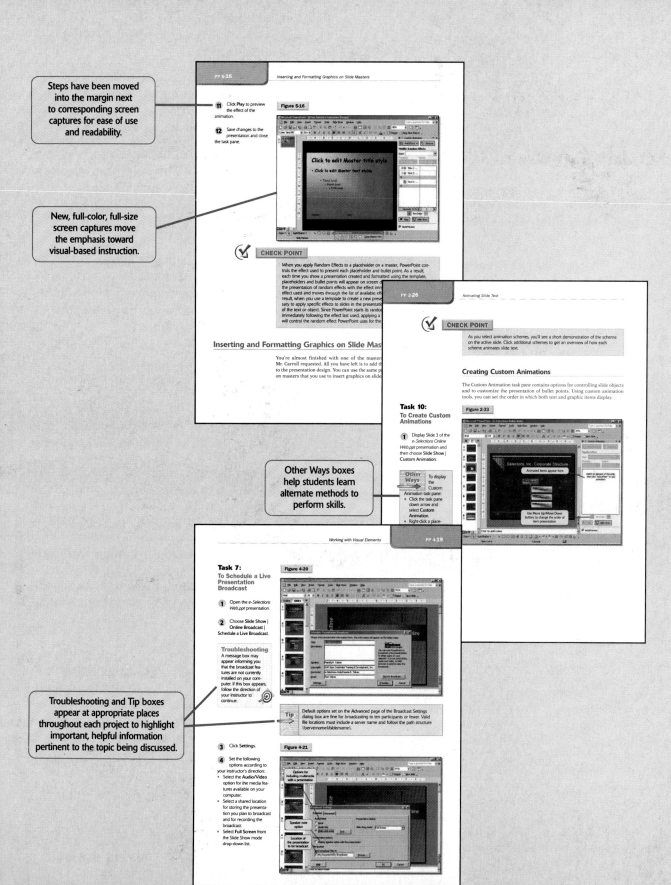

Steps have been moved into the margin next to corresponding screen captures for ease of use and readability.

New, full-color, full-size screen captures move the emphasis toward visual-based instruction.

Other Ways boxes help students learn alternate methods to perform skills.

Troubleshooting and Tip boxes appear at appropriate places throughout each project to highlight important, helpful information pertinent to the topic being discussed.

Organization of the Select Series for Office XP

The new Select Series for Office XP includes four combined Office XP texts from which to choose:

- **Microsoft Office XP Volume I** is MOUS certified in each of the major applications in the Office suite (Word, Excel, Access, and PowerPoint). Four additional supplementary modules (Introduction to Internet Explorer, Introduction to Windows, Introduction to Outlook, and Common Elements) are also included. In addition, three integrated projects are included which integrate files and data among Word, Excel, Access, and PowerPoint.
- **Microsoft Office XP Volume II** picks up where Volume I leaves off, covering advanced topics for the individual applications.
- **Microsoft Office XP Brief** provides less coverage of the individual applications than Volume I (a total of four projects as opposed to six). The supplementary modules are also included.
- A new volume, **Getting Started with Microsoft Office XP,** contains the Introduction and first chapter from each application (Word, Excel, Access, and PowerPoint) plus the Common Elements modules.

Individual texts for Word 2002, Excel 2002, Access 2002, and PowerPoint 2002 provide complete coverage of each application and are MOUS certified. They are available in Volume I and Volume II texts and also as Comprehensive texts.

This series of books has been approved by Microsoft to be used in preparation for Microsoft Office User Specialist exams.

APPROVED COURSEWARE

The Microsoft Office User Specialist (MOUS) program is globally recognized as the standard for demonstrating desktop skills with the Microsoft Office suite of business productivity applications (Microsoft Word, Microsoft Excel, Microsoft PowerPoint, Microsoft Access, and Microsoft Outlook). With MOUS certification, thousands of people have demonstrated increased productivity and have proved their ability to utilize the advanced functionality of these Microsoft applications.

Customize the Select Series with Prentice Hall's Custom Binding program. The Select Series is part of the Custom Binding Program, enabling instructors to create their own texts by selecting projects from Office XP to suit the needs of a specific course. An instructor could, for example, create a custom text consisting of the specific projects that he or she would like to cover from the entire suite of products. The Select Series is part of PHit's Value Pack program in which multiple books can be shrink-wrapped together at substantial savings to the student. A value pack is ideal in courses that require complete coverage of multiple applications.

Instructor and Student Resources

Instructor's Resource CD-ROM

The **Instructor's Resource CD-ROM** that is available with the Select Office XP Series contains:

- Student data files
- Solutions to all exercises and problems
- PowerPoint lectures
- Instructor's manuals in Word format that enable the instructor to annotate portions of the instructor manual for distribution to the class
- A Windows-based test manager and the associated test bank in Word format

MyPHLIP www.prenhall.com/select

This text is accompanied by a companion Web site at ***www.prenhall.com/select*** that is supported by MyPHLIP. PHLIP stands for Prentice Hall's Learning on the Internet Partnership. This enhancement brings you and your students a richer, more interactive Web experience.

Features of this new site include the ability for you to customize your homepage with real-time news headlines, current events, exercises, an interactive study guide, student data files, and downloadable supplements. This site is designed to take learning Microsoft Office XP with the Select Series to the next level.

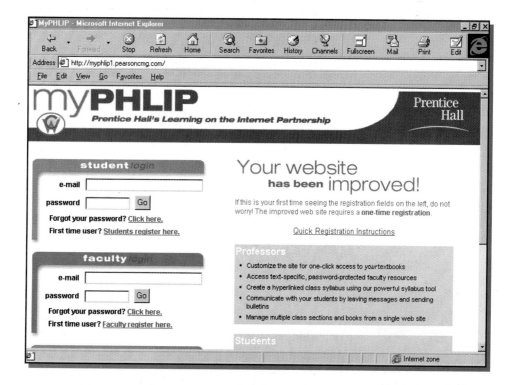

Now you have the freedom to personalize your own online course materials! Prentice Hall provides the content and support you need to create and manage your own online course in WebCT, Blackboard, or Prentice Hall's own Course Compass. Choose "Standard" content to enhance the material from this text or "Premium" content, which provides you with even more lecture material, interactive exercises, and projects.

Training and Assessment www.prenhall.com/phit

Prentice Hall offers Performance Based Training and Assessment in one product, Train&Assess IT. The Training component offers computer-based training that a student can use to preview, learn, and review Microsoft Office application skills. Web or CD-ROM delivered, Train IT offers interactive, multimedia, computer-based training to augment classroom learning. Built-in prescriptive testing suggests a study path based not only on student test results but also on the specific textbook chosen for the course.

The Assessment component offers computer-based testing that shares the same uscr interface as Train IT and is used to evaluate a student's knowledge about specific topics in Word, Excel, Access, PowerPoint, Windows, Outlook, and the Internet. It does this in a task-oriented environment to demonstrate proficiency as well as comprehension of the topics by the students. More extensive than the testing in Train IT, Assess IT offers more administrative features for the instructor and additional questions for the student.

Assess IT also allows professors to test students out of a course, place students in appropriate courses, and evaluate skill sets.

CourseCompass www.coursecompass.com

CourseCompass is a dynamic, interactive online course-management tool powered exclusively for Pearson Education by Blackboard. This exciting product allows you to teach market-leading Pearson Education content in an easy-to-use, customizable format.

BlackBoard www.prenhall.com/blackboard

Prentice Hall's abundant online content, combined with Blackboard's popular tools and interface, result in robust Web-based courses that are easy to implement, manage, and use—taking your courses to new heights in student interaction and learning.

WebCT www.prenhall.com/webct

Course-management tools within WebCT include page tracking, progress tracking, class and student management, gradebook, communication, calendar, reporting tools, and more. GOLD LEVEL CUSTOMER SUPPORT, available exclusively to adopters of Prentice Hall courses, is provided free-of-charge upon adoption and provides you with priority assistance, training discounts, and dedicated technical support.

Brief Table of Contents

Table of Contents

PROJECT 1

Basic Common Elements

One of the greatest advantages of using the ever-popular Microsoft Office suite is the number of features common to all programs that make up the Office suite. Microsoft Office XP takes full advantage of many common elements. The large number of common elements means that techniques you learn in one Office XP application can be used to accomplish the same task in other Office XP applications. This section introduces you to many of the features common to Office XP applications and describes some of the unique twists you'll find with these common features as you move from application to application in Microsoft Office XP.

OBJECTIVES

After completing this project, you will be able to:

- Launch applications
- Work with screen elements
- Perform basic file management tasks
- Use Help
- Preview and print files
- Exit applications

e-selections) Running Case

You have recently been hired as a part-time office clerk for e-Selections.com, the online branch of Selections, Inc. Your goals are to advance in the company as you advance in your college studies and to position yourself for an upper-level position after you graduate. Because you are new to the office and unfamiliar with the software applications that are used, you decide to begin by exploring the software installed on your computer. e-Selections.com uses the most recent release of Microsoft Office.

Basic Common Elements

The Challenge

Microsoft Office applications contain numerous features that are common to the four primary Office applications. You have been asked to identify basic elements that are common to Word, Excel, Access, and PowerPoint and to develop the skills necessary for performing tasks associated with these common features.

The Solution

Because the features you have been asked to identify are common to the four primary Office applications, it's a great idea to learn the basics that apply to all applications in one centralized location. Then, when you start using each of the Microsoft Office applications, you can focus on their unique features.

Overview of Office XP Applications

Microsoft Office XP contains a number of different applications. Each application is designed to make the process of creating electronic files that contain different types of data and information more efficient. The Microsoft Office XP applications addressed in this text are listed and described in Table 1-1.

Table 1-1	Microsoft Office XP Applications and Their Uses
Application	**Description**
Microsoft Word 2002	The word processing program used to create, format, and save letters, manuscripts, newsletters, and other documents.
Microsoft Excel 2002	The spreadsheet program used to create, format, and save columnar data and display it graphically.
Microsoft Access 2002	The database program used to create, format, and save volumes of information (data) related to specific subjects or purposes.
Microsoft PowerPoint 2002	The presentation program used to create visual slides that present summaries of data used to enhance oral presentations.
Microsoft Outlook 2002	The e-mail, calendar, and address program used to create and store e-mail messages, list appointment and meeting dates and times, and record the names and addresses of associates.

Launching Applications

Office XP offers a variety of techniques for launching applications. The procedure you use will depend on how Office XP is installed on your computer and your personal preferences.

To *launch* Office XP applications, use one of the following procedures:

- Choose **Start | Programs,** and then select the Office XP application you want to launch.

Figure 1-1

Troubleshooting
If shortcuts to the Office XP applications do not appear on your Programs list, click the arrow button at the bottom of the Programs list and scroll until the applications appear.

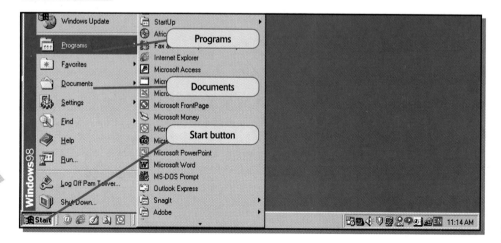

- Choose **Start | New Office Document,** and then double-click the **Blank** file type for the application you want to launch—the application required to create that type of file launches.

Figure 1-2

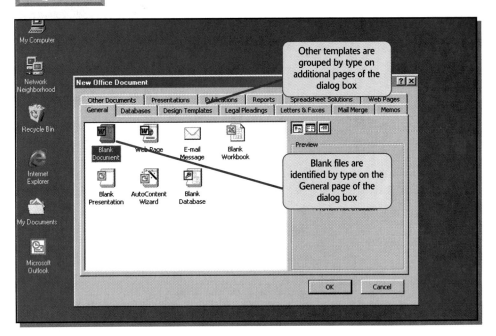

CHECK POINT

Office XP offers a series of professionally designed file formats called templates that you can choose to create a variety of different files. Click the tab for the type of file you want to create (e.g., Memos), click a template name, and view the template preview in the lower right corner of the dialog box. The templates listed depend on those installed on your computer. As a result, your templates may appear different from those listed here.

- Double-click the application shortcut icon on the desktop.
- Click the application icon on the Microsoft Office bar, if it is installed on your computer. When it is installed, the Microsoft Office bar usually appears on the right side of the computer screen. The arrangement of buttons on the bar may be different due to customizations.

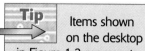

Tip Items shown on the desktop in Figure 1-3 represent program icons that generally appear when Microsoft Office XP is installed on a computer running Windows 95 or Windows 98 that has no additional program shortcuts placed on the desktop. Program icons and other features found on your desktop will be different from those shown here because of system customizations.

Figure 1-3

Tip The Documents list shows files from all applications—not just Microsoft Office files. The icon beside each file identifies the application used to create or edit the files.

- Choose **Start | Documents** and select a recently used file to open. The application used to create the file launches. The Documents list holds the last 15 documents accessed. It may contain few items when you first start using the computer, but the list grows as you complete activities.
- Open **My Computer** or **Windows Explorer**, open the folder containing the file you want to open, and double-click the file. The application used to create the file launches.

Depending on the application you launch, the initial screen will differ:

- Word, Excel, and PowerPoint display new files: Word displays a new blank document, Excel displays a new blank workbook, and PowerPoint creates a new blank presentation.
- Access displays an empty screen and the New File task pane with a palette of tools for creating a new file or opening an existing file.

Because accessing and using most of the common elements covered in this section is easiest in Word, it will be used to introduce many common features. The procedures for launching Word 2002 described here should be accessible from all computers on which Office XP is installed.

Identifying Screen Elements

Screen elements common to all Microsoft Office XP applications are identified in Figure 1-4 and described in Table 1-2.

Task 1:
Launching Microsoft Word 2002

1 Choose **Start** | **Programs**.

2 Scroll to the bottom of the Programs list, if necessary.

3 Select Microsoft Word to launch Word.

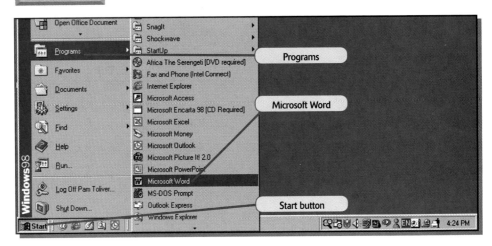

Figure 1-4

Troubleshooting The icons that appear at the right end of the task bar on your computer may be different from those shown in Figure 1-4. They represent programs that are running in the background on the active computer.

4 Review screen elements identified in Figure 1-5.

Tip Because installations and setups vary from computer to computer and set up changes from user to user, screen elements may vary from those shown here.

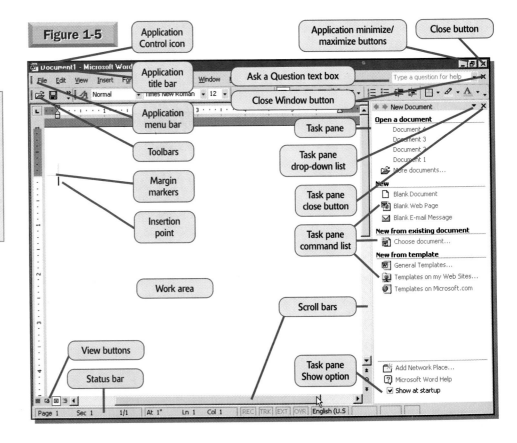

Figure 1-5

Table 1-2   Word Screen Features

Feature	Description
Application title bar	Identifies the program and file that is open.
Application menu bar	Groups task commands by type.
Application Control icon	Displays options for maximizing, minimizing, resizing, and closing the application window.
Toolbars	Provide single-click access to frequently performed tasks.
Work area	Provides room to type text.
Status bar	Identifies active application features and the insertion point position.
Insertion point	Identifies the typing position.
Application minimize/ maximize buttons	Control window size.
Close button	Exits the application.
Close Window button	Closes the active file and leaves the application running.
Scroll bars	Display different areas of the file on screen.
Task pane	Displays tools for creating and opening files and tools for performing special tasks.
Task pane Close button	Closes the task pane.
Ask a question text box	Accesses help about the topic entered.
Margin markers	Identify margin positions on screen.
Task pane command list	Displays a grouped list from which you can access the Office Clipboard and the program search feature, select a command, create a new document, open a recently edited document, or create a formatted document.
View buttons	Change the appearance of the document on screen.
Task pane drop-down list	Presents a list of different elements and features that can be displayed on the Task Pane.
Task pane Show option	Controls whether the task pane appears each time you start Word.

Working with Screen Elements

Many of the screen elements seen in Microsoft Word are common to other Office XP applications. As a result, once you learn how to navigate the screen elements in one Office application, you can apply the techniques to comparable features in other Office XP applications.

Using the Task Pane

The *task pane* is a new feature in Microsoft Office. It provides access to some of the most basic file management tools you will need as you progress through each application. You can close the task pane to increase the work area in a program and then redisplay it as needed.

The task pane is divided into distinct sections identified by the tasks to be performed. Options for performing tasks appear in blue text below each section heading. Options followed by ellipses are options that open dialog boxes; options that have no ellipses carry out a command. Task pane tools are also found on menus and *toolbars*.

Task 2:

To Close and Open the Task Pane

1 Click the task pane **Close X** button. The task pane closes.

2 Choose **View | Task Pane**. The task pane opens.

Figure 1-6

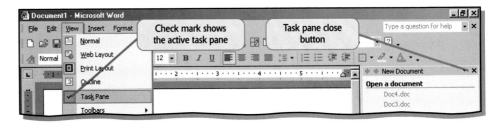

Other Ways
You can also display the task pane by pointing to a toolbar, right-clicking, and selecting **Task Pane** or by choosing **View | Toolbars | Task Pane**. To prevent the task pane from opening each time you launch Word, clear the **Show at startup** option at the bottom of the task pane.

Hiding and Displaying Toolbars

A variety of different toolbars can be displayed in Office XP applications, each designed to assist with specific tasks. In each application, the Standard and Formatting toolbars contain buttons for performing the most frequently completed tasks. Other toolbars appear automatically as you perform specific tasks. There will be times as you work in the different applications when you will want to display additional toolbars.

Tip
To identify the name of a toolbar button, position the mouse pointer on the button and pause. A Screen Tip will tell you what the name of the button is.

Task 3:
To Display and Hide Toolbars

1 Choose **View | Toolbars** to display a list of available toolbars.

2 Select **Formatting**. The Formatting toolbar is hidden.

Figure 1-7

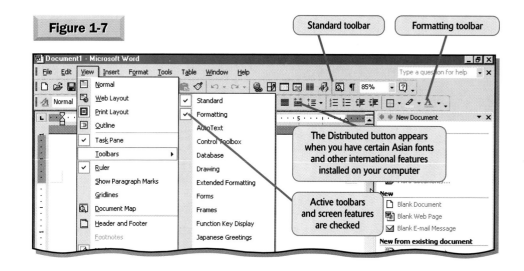

3 Point to the Standard toolbar and right-click. A list of available toolbars appears.

4 Select **Formatting**. The Formatting toolbar appears on screen in its original position.

Figure 1-8

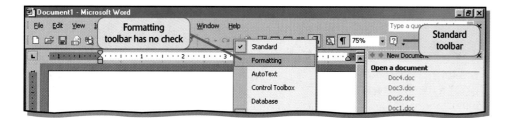

CHECK POINT

Selections, Inc., in an effort to accommodate clients worldwide through its e-Selections Online Division, has a number of International fonts, such as Asian, Japanese, and so forth, installed on some of the computers at its corporate offices. As a result, additional features are available to those who use the international workstations. You will notice additional buttons on toolbars, added menu commands, and other extra features as you work with Office XP. These features are designed to help those who develop materials for the international market to access the tools more efficiently.

Displaying and Hiding the Language Bar

The *Language bar*, when it is installed and displayed, appears as a floating toolbar in all Office XP applications. It contains tools related to the language features that are built in to Office XP. When the Language bar is closed, it appears as an icon on the taskbar tray so that it is easy to call up when you need it.

Task 4:
To Display and Hide the Language Bar

1 Click the **Language** EN button on the Windows taskbar tray and select **Show Language Bar** to open the toolbar.

2 Click the Language bar **Minimize** button. A message box displays information about how to redisplay the Language bar.

3 Click **OK**. The Language button appears on the tray of the Windows taskbar.

Troubleshooting
If the Language bar is closed, open it by choosing **Start | Settings | Control Panel | Text Services** to open the Text Services dialog box. Then click the Language Bar button and select the Show the Language bar on the desktop option. Then click OK twice and close the Control Panel dialog box.

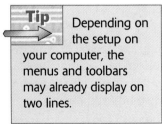

Tip Depending on the setup on your computer, the menus and toolbars may already display on two lines.

Figure 1-9

Figure 1-9

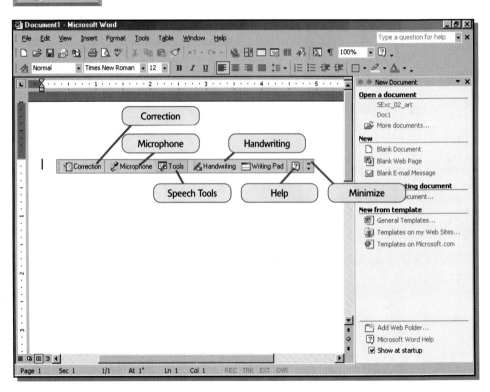

Figure 1-10

Resetting Menus and Toolbars

Menus and toolbars in Office XP are set to auto-customize as you work. Here's how they work:

- When menus in Office XP applications are displayed, only the most frequently used commands appear on the initial menu. After the menu is displayed for a few seconds, the extended menu shows additional menu commands.
- When you select a menu command from the extended menu, the command is placed on the initial menu in its standard position so that it is more readily available the next time you need it.
- The Standard and Formatting toolbars are initially displayed on one line to increase the work area on screen. Buttons for additional commands appear on a Toolbar Options drop-down list at the right end of displayed toolbars.

- When you select a button from the Toolbar Options drop-down palette, the button is placed at its standard location on the appropriate toolbar.

So that the steps presented in this book are accurate for each class working on lab computers, it is necessary to turn off this auto-customization feature.

Task 5:
To Turn Off Auto-Customization Features

1 Choose **Tools | Customize**. The Customize dialog box opens.

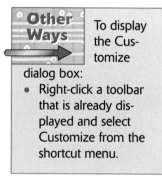

Other Ways

To display the Customize dialog box:
- Right-click a toolbar that is already displayed and select Customize from the shortcut menu.

Figure 1-11

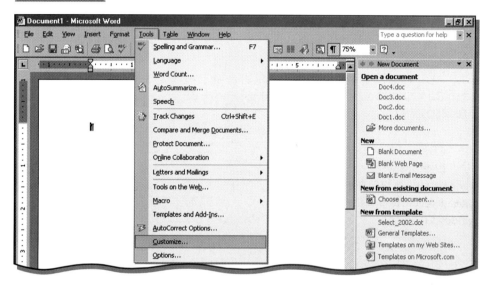

2 Click the **Options** tab, if necessary.

3 Select the **Show Standard and Formatting toolbars on two rows** option to display the full Standard and Formatting toolbars on separate rows.

4 Select the **Always show full menus** option, if necessary.

5 Click **Close**.

Figure 1-12

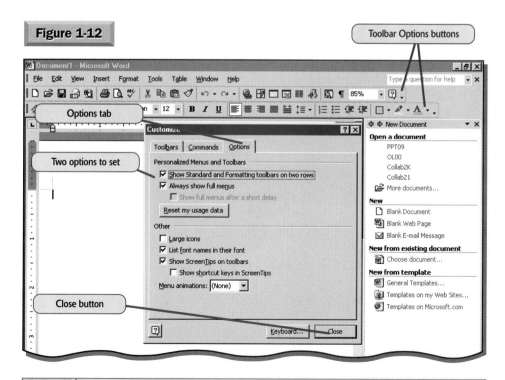

Tip

To toggle toolbars between one- and two-line displays, click the Toolbar Options button that appears as a down arrow at the end of each toolbar and select **Show Buttons on Two (or One) Row(s)**.

Changing Zoom Settings

The *Zoom* setting controls the portion of a file that appears on screen and can be used to make file text easier to read. After the auto-customization feature is turned off and the Standard and Formatting toolbars appear on separate rows, the Zoom control tool appears on the Standard toolbar.

Troubleshooting The list of Zoom values changes depending on the application and current view.

Task 6:
To Set Zoom Control

  1 Click the **Zoom** `100%` ▼ down arrow on the Standard toolbar. A list of available sizing options appears.

2 Select **50%**. The document shifts on screen.

3 Click in the **Zoom** box on the Standard menu.

4 Type **100** and press Enter. The document size is restored.

Figure 1-13

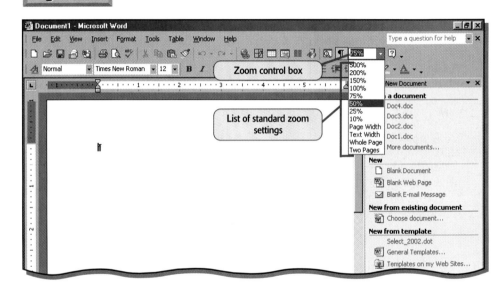

Performing Basic File Management Tasks

Basic file management tasks include opening files, creating new files, saving files, and editing file properties. The procedures for accomplishing these tasks are similar in all Office XP applications.

Opening Files

Office XP provides a number of different procedures that you can use to open an existing document, workbook, presentation, or database. The Open dialog box has been redesigned in Office XP and presents a Web-like look that even contains links to Web servers. To open a file, do one of the following:

- Choose **File | Open.**
- Click the **Open** button on the Standard toolbar.
- Press Ctrl + O.
- Choose **Start | Open Office Document.**
- Click **More Documents** in the **Open a document** area of the task pane.

Regardless of which procedure you use to open a file, an Open dialog box similar to the one shown in Figure1-14 appears. Features of the Open dialog box are described in Table 1-3.

Tip A folder in Windows can contain files or additional folders.

Figure 1-14

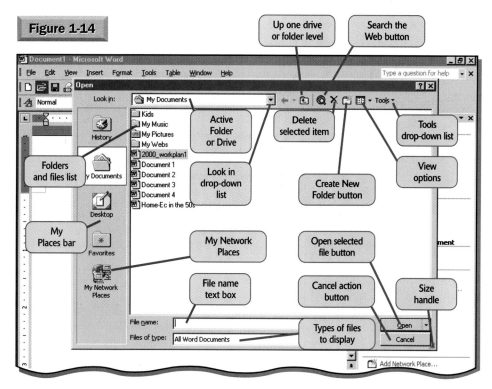

Table 1-3   Open dialog box elements

Feature	Description
Look in drop-down list	Identifies the current drive and/or folder.
Up One Level button	Accesses the "parent" folder when a folder is active; My Computer when a drive is active; and Desktop when the My Documents folder is open.
Search the Web button	Launches Internet Explorer 5.5, or your default Web browser, to the Microsoft Homepage so that you can perform a search for the document to open.
Delete button	Removes the selected document or folder.
Create New Folder button	Creates a new folder within the active drive or folder.
View drop-down list	Displays a list of options that change the way files and folders are displayed in the dialog box.
Tools drop-down list	Contains commands that enable you to find and delete files and folders, print files, and identify properties of files and folders.
My Places bar	Contains links to folders and file storage locations so that you can open them quickly, and it can be customized to hold the folders you use most frequently.
My Network Places	Displays links to Web sites and other Network Places that you have designated on networked computers to which you have access.
Dialog box size handle	Can be dragged to change the size and shape of the dialog box.
File name text box	Enables you to type the name of the document to open.
Files of type text box	Identifies the types of files displayed. You can display other types of files by altering the file type selected.
Folders and Files list	Shows all folders and files in the active folder or on the active drive for the active application.
Open button	Opens the selected (highlighted) file or folder. It contains a drop-down list that enables you to open a copy of the file, open the file in Read-Only mode, Open and Repair, or open a Web document in a browser.
Cancel button	Closes the dialog box without opening a file or folder.

CHECK POINT

By default, the last four files opened in that application on your computer appear at the bottom of the File menu. In addition, the last fifteen files accessed appear on the Documents list displayed from the Start menu. As a result, two alternative procedures can be used to open files.

- Select the file from the bottom of the File menu.

- Choose **Start | Documents** and select the recently edited file to open.

You can change the number of files that appear at the bottom of the File menu for any application using the **Tools | Options** command and then setting the Recently used file list on the **General** page of the Options dialog box.

Task 7:

To Open a Copy of a Document

1 Launch Word, if necessary, close the task pane, and choose **File | Open**. The Open dialog box opens.

Figure 1-15

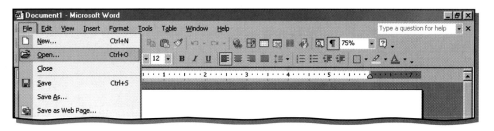

2 Click the **Look in** down arrow and open the disk drive and/or folder containing the *e-Selections.doc* file. The disk drive and/or folder name appears in the Look in text box.

Figure 1-16

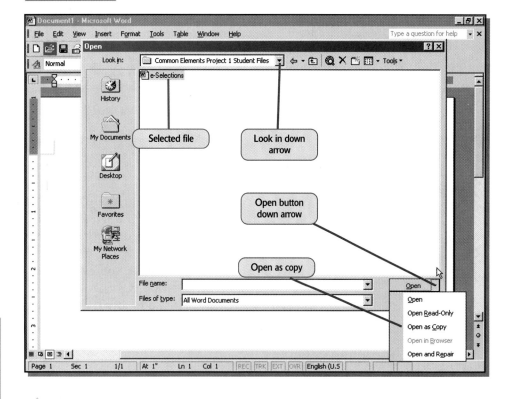

3 Select the *e-Selections.doc* file. The file name appears highlighted.

4 Click the drop-down list arrow on the **Open** button and select **Open as Copy**.

Tip You can also open a read-only copy of a document to preserve the original file. When you open a read-only copy of a document, make changes to the file, and want to save the changes, you must save the file using a new file name.

Troubleshooting The current settings on your computer control the appearance of the document on your screen. As a result, your screen may be different from the screen pictured in Figure 1-17.

5   Review the document.

> **Tip** Opening a copy of an existing document leaves the original intact so that you can use it later, if necessary.

Figure 1-17

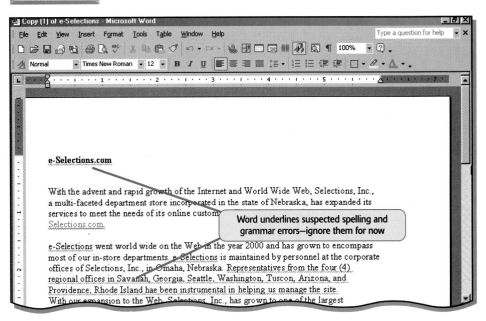

Creating New Files

As you discovered with opening files, Microsoft Office XP offers a variety of different techniques for performing tasks. Take creating new files for example; a new document appears when you launch Word, a new blank workbook is created each time you launch Excel, and a new blank presentation is created when you start PowerPoint. As you explore all Office XP applications, you'll find that options for creating and opening files are presented when you launch Access. To create a new file in any Office XP application after it is launched, you can use one of the following procedures:

- Click the **New** button on the Standard toolbar of any Office XP application. A new blank file appears if you are working in Word, Excel, and PowerPoint. In Access, clicking the New button displays the New File task pane so that you can create a blank database or a database using a template.
- Press Ctrl + N. A new blank file appears in Word, Excel, or PowerPoint. In Access, the New File task pane opens so that you can select the type of database you want to create.
- Choose **File | New**. The New dialog box opens and displays a list of templates—professionally designed, preformatted file formats specific to the application you're using—that you can use to create a specific type of file.
- Click the option for a new file from the task pane:
  - **New Blank Document** to create a new blank file;
  - **New from existing *file* | Choose *File*** to open the New from Existing File dialog box;
  - **New from template** to display the same list of templates shown using the **File | New** command.

Task 8:

To Create New Files

1 Launch Word, if necessary, and click the **New** 🗋 button on the Standard toolbar to create a new blank document.

2 Display the task pane and click **Blank Document** on the task pane. Document3 appears and another document button appears on the taskbar.

3 Point to the bottom of the screen, if necessary, to display the taskbar.

Tip 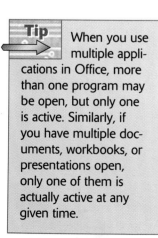 In addition to buttons representing different document files that are open, you may see taskbar buttons for other programs—such as e-mail programs—that are running on your computer.

Tip When you use multiple applications in Office, more than one program may be open, but only one is active. Similarly, if you have multiple documents, workbooks, or presentations open, only one of them is actually active at any given time.

Figure 1-18

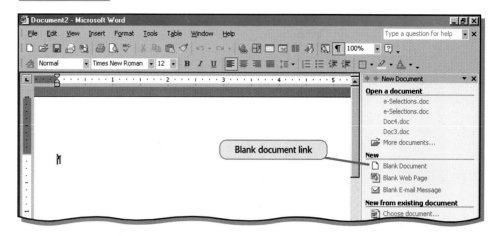

Blank document link

Figure 1-19

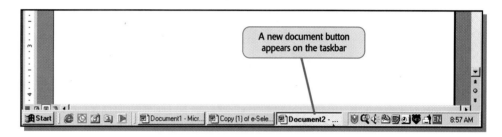

A new document button appears on the taskbar

Switching Among Open Files

Word, Excel, and PowerPoint enable you to open or create multiple files without closing files that are already open. These three applications place a file button on the Windows taskbar for each file you have open. To switch from one open file to another, you can:

- Click the **Windows taskbar** button for the open file you want to access.
- Press Ctrl + F6 to browse open files for the active application.
- Press Ctrl + Shift + F6 to move backward among open files for the active application.
- Click the file name in the task pane.
- Press Alt + Tab to switch among programs and files from all open applications.
- Choose the **Window** menu and then select the file you want to access from the bottom of the menu.

Closing Files

Office XP applications provide a variety of techniques for closing files. To close the active file:

- Click the file **Close** Window **X** button at the right end of the menu bar.
- Right-click the Windows taskbar button for the file you want to close and select **Close**.
- Choose **File | Close**.
- Press Ctrl + F4.

>
> **Troubleshooting** When only one file is open in Word, Excel, or Powerpoint, a Close button also appears at the right end of the title bar. This button enables you to exit the application, so be sure you click the correct Close button.

Task 9:

To Close a File

1 Switch to Document3, if necessary.

2 Click the **Close Window X** button.

3 Display Document2, if necessary.

4 Choose **File | Close**. The Copy of *e-Selections* appears on screen. Leave it open for the next task.

Figure 1-20

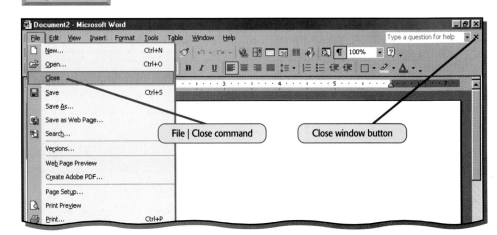

Saving Files

Each new document you create, each copy of an existing document you open, and each document you edit needs to be saved. You'll find a number of different Save commands listed on the File menu of Office XP applications. Knowing the difference between the Save commands is important. Here's how they work:

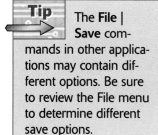

Tip The **File | Save** commands in other applications may contain different options. Be sure to review the File menu to determine different save options.

Table 1-4	Save Commands
Command	**Description**
Save	Automatically overwrites previously saved files that you open and edit. Opens the Save As dialog box the first time a document is saved so that you can name and select a storage location for new files. The dialog box contains text boxes where you can type a file name and select a save format.
	Saves copies of existing files that you open using the Open as Copy command in the same folder of the same disk using the filename *Copy (#) of xx.doc*.
	In Access, Save enables you to save a database object.
Save As	In Word, Excel, and PowerPoint, this command opens the Save As dialog box, which you can use to save an existing file using a different file name, save the active file in a different drive or folder, or save a file as a different file type.
	In Access, Save As enables you to export a selected database object to create another specific database object only.
Save as Web Page	Opens the Save As dialog box, automatically activates **Web Page** as the Save as type, and adds a page title using the first line of text in the file.

Tip Folders you create in other applications such as Windows Explorer are available for storing files from Microsoft Office XP applications.

To initiate the Save command, you can use one of the following techniques:

- Click the **Save** 🖫 button on the Standard toolbar.
- Press ⌨Ctrl + ⌨S.
- Choose **File | Save**.
- Choose **File | Save As**.

Creating Folders. Because file management is so important, Office applications streamline the process by enabling you to create new folders "on the fly" from the Open and Save As dialog boxes. In addition, you can embed fonts as you save documents to ensure that the document will look the way you intended when it is opened on a different computer.

Task 10:

To Save a Copy of a File with Embedded Fonts in a New Folder

1 Click the title bar of the *Copy (1) of e-Selections.doc* file to make it active, if necessary. Active windows usually have a darker title bar than inactive windows.

2 Choose **File | Save As** to open the Save As dialog box.

Figure 1-21

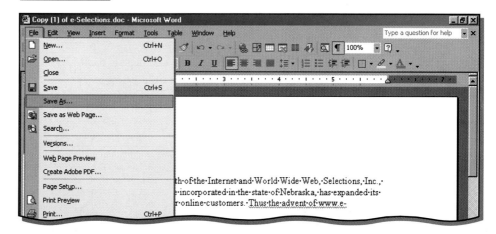

3 Click the **Save in** down arrow, select the disk drive on which you want to create a new folder, and click the **Create New Folder** button.

Figure 1-22

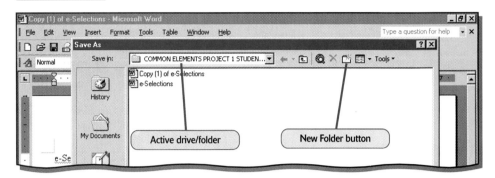

Active drive/folder   New Folder button

4 Type *Your Initials* followed by *Your Class Name* in the **Name** text box and click **OK**. The new folder opens and appears in the Save in text box at the top of the Save As dialog box.

Figure 1-23

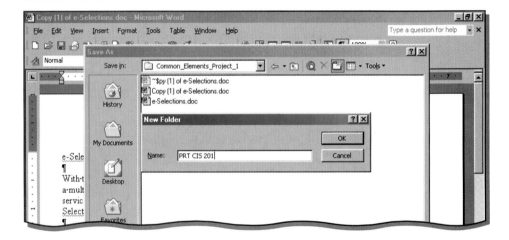

 Troubleshooting If you want to create a subfolder, you must open the folder in which you want to place the subfolder.

5 Click the **Tools** down arrow and select **Save Options** to open the Save dialog box that contains save options.

Figure 1-24

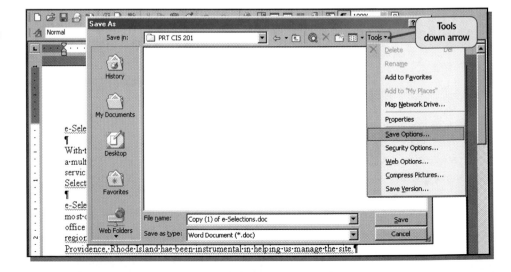

Tools down arrow

6 Select the **Embed TrueType fonts** and the **Do not embed common system fonts** options.

7 Click **OK**.

8 Click **Save**. The new file named *Copy (1) of e-Selections.doc* appears in the new folder, and the file name also appears in the title bar of the document.

Tip Be sure to review options that appear in the Save dialog box. Knowing what options are available may come in handy sometime in the future.

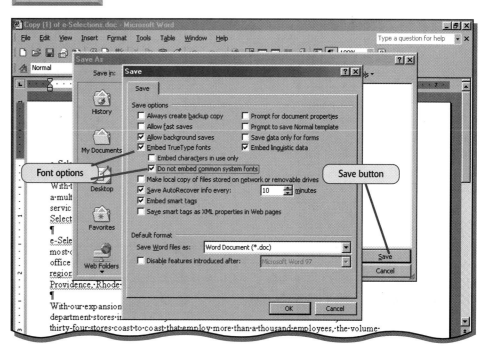

Figure 1-25

WEB TIP

You can save a Web page using the same basic save techniques used to save files in Office XP applications. Simply display the Web page in the browser and choose **File | Save As**, open the folder in which to store the file, type a file name for the file, and click **OK**.

Customizing the My Places Bar and Sizing Dialog Boxes

The *My Places bar* contains a default set of folders, Web sites, and files for the user to access—the default places on the bar may or may not be locations that you would want to access. As a result, the My Places bar can be customized to hold the folders and sites you visit most. Now that you have created a folder to hold your work, you can add the folder to My Places bar to make it more accessible.

Task 11:

To Add a Folder to the My Places Bar and Size a Dialog Box

1 Launch Word, if necessary, close the task pane, and click the **Open** button on the Standard toolbar. The Open dialog box opens.

2 Locate the personal folder you created in Task 10 and select it (but don't open it).

3 Click the **Tools** drop-down list on the dialog box toolbar and select **Add to "My Places"**.

4 Click the down arrow at the bottom of the Places bar. The new folder appears.

5 Drag the dialog box size handle to increase the size of the dialog box so that all the folders are visible. The down-arrow button disappears.

6 Click **Cancel** to close the dialog box.

Tip Adding a folder or site to the My Places bar of one dialog box adds it to all dialog boxes in all Office XP applications.

Figure 1-26

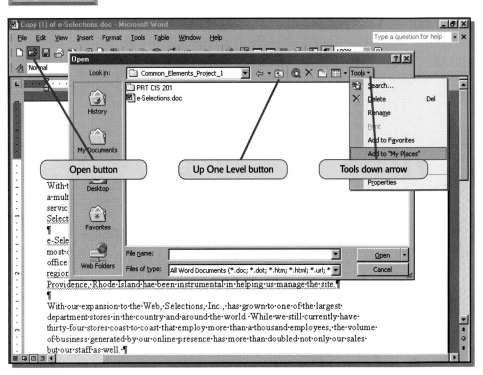

Open button   Up One Level button   Tools down arrow

Figure 1-27

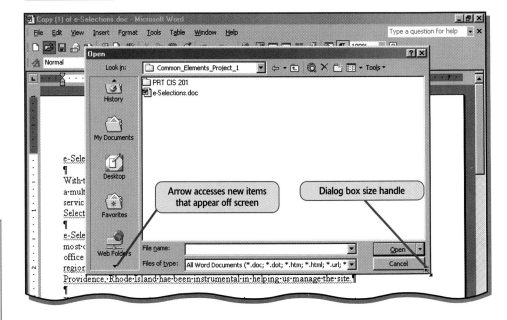

Arrow accesses new items that appear off screen   Dialog box size handle

Troubleshooting Because your personal folder was the last folder you used, it may appear in the **Look in** box at the top of the dialog box and the folder will be open. Click the **Up One Level** button on the dialog box toolbar to close the folder and then select it.

Saving and Previewing Web Pages

Each Office XP application can be used to save files as Web pages and to view those files as they would appear in a Web browser. Whereas the specific steps required to save files as Web pages vary from application to application within Office XP, the basic steps for initiating the process and for viewing the files is the same for all applications.

Task 12:
To Save a File as a Web Page and View the Web File

1 Open your *Copy (1) of e-Selections.doc,* if necessary.

2 Choose **File | Save as Web Page**.

3 Click your folder in the Places bar to open the folder, if necessary.

4 Click the **Change Title** button. The Set Page Title dialog box opens.

> **Troubleshooting**
> Changing the page title has no impact on the file name or document text. The Page Title appears in the title bar of the browser when you display the document in the browser window.

5 Type *Your Initials* First Web Page in the **Page title** text box and then click **OK**.

Figure 1-28

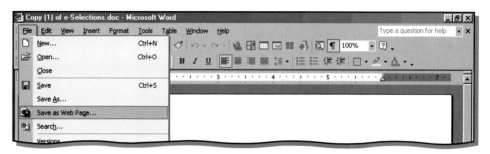

Figure 1-29

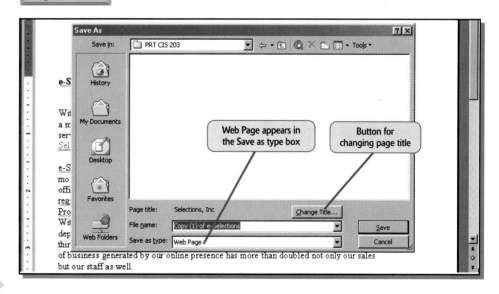

Web Page appears in the Save as type box

Button for changing page title

Figure 1-30

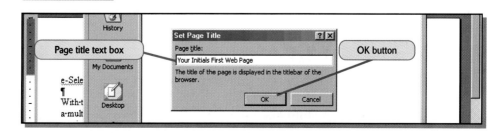

Page title text box

OK button

6 Type *Your Initials* First Web Page in the **File name** text box.

7 Click **Save**. The file is saved as a Web page and the Web Layout View becomes active.

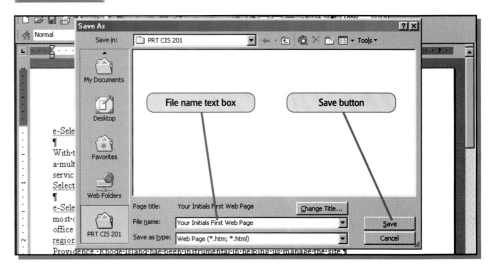

Figure 1-31

File name text box

Save button

8 Choose **File | Web Page Preview**. Your Web browser application will open and enable you to view the document as a Web page.

Troubleshooting
The settings on your browser may be different from those shown here because of programs and other features installed on your computer.

9 Click the browser application **Close** button.

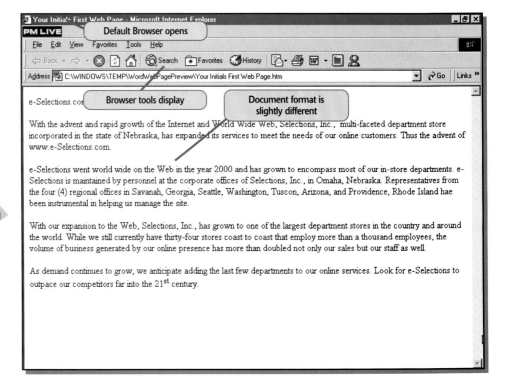

Figure 1-32

Default Browser opens

Browser tools display

Document format is slightly different

Changing File Properties

Properties, the term used to describe important information about a file, are automatically stored with each Office XP file you save. Properties are grouped into different categories and provide detailed information about the file, such as the date on which the file was created, the date on which it was last edited, the author's name, the author's company, the file size, and other application-specific information (e.g., the number of words in a Word document). In addition, the Office XP application used to create the file assigns a title for the file based on the file name assigned to the file. You can edit and check existing file information or add additional bits of information about the file.

Task 13:
To Edit File Properties

1 Choose **File | Properties** to open the Properties dialog box.

Tip In Access, the name of this command on the File menu is Database Properties.

2 Select the word *first* in the Title text box.

3 Type e-Selections to replace *first*. The title now appears as *Your Initials e-Selections Web Page.*

4 Click **OK and close the file**.

Figure 1-33

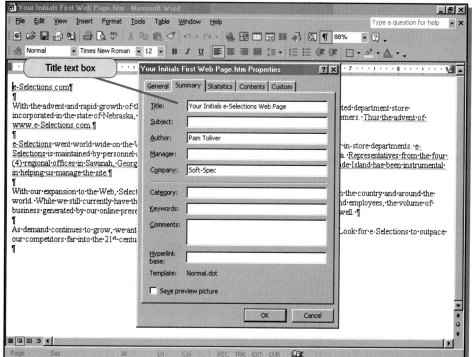

CHECK POINT

Because of the need for privacy in transmitting documents electronically, Office XP has implemented a procedure for removing personal information from a file on save. To set this option so that personal information is not transmitted with your files, follow these quick steps:

1. Choose **Tools | Options | Security.**

2. Select the **Remove personal information from this file on save** option.

3. Click **OK.**

Setting this option and then saving files prevents your name and other personal information from appearing in the Properties dialog box. It does NOT, however, prevent information about the document, such as creation date, edit date, and your company name, from appearing in the Properties dialog box.

Getting Help

In the Windows section, you learned how to use Windows Help and how to locate information about specific topics. Each Office XP application comes equipped with a variety of help features that will have you getting help from all over the world—right on your computer as you work!

Asking Questions

A new *Ask a Question* tool has been added to the right end of the menu bar. Using the Ask a Question text box, you can simply enter a question and receive a list of possible topics related to answering the question.

Task 14:
To Ask a Question

1 Create a new blank document, click the **Ask a Question** text box on the menu bar to position the insertion point in the box.

2 Type **How do I display the Office Assistant?** and press Enter.

3 Click **Display tips and messages through the Office Assistant.**

4 Click the **Show** button on the Help window toolbar to display other help associated with the topic.

5 Click the Help window **Close X** button. The Help window closes and Word resizes to screen size.

Troubleshooting
Because the help files are updated frequently, the list you see when you search for help may be different from the lists shown in Tasks 14 and 15.

Figure 1-34

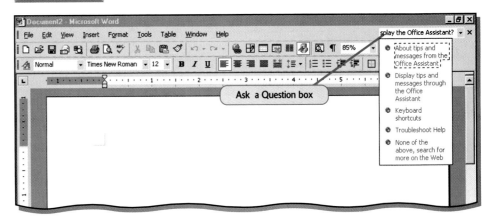

Ask a Question box

Figure 1-35

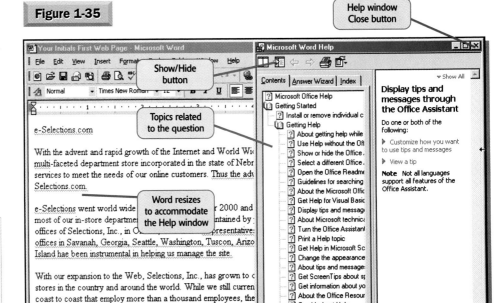

Help window Close button

Show/Hide button

Topics related to the question

Word resizes to accommodate the Help window

Using the Office Assistant

The *Office Assistant* is a help feature that is growing in popularity. The Office Assistant is easy to use, is personally animated, and provides a focused list of help topics related to questions you "ask."

If the Assistant was displayed the last time one of the Office applications was used, it will appear on screen when you launch an application. When closed, the Assistant waits on the Standard toolbar and appears when you call it to look up information about topics for which you need help. After you start the Office Assistant in one application, it remains on screen until you close it—even when you open another Office application. The information it provides when you ask it a question relates to the application that is active at the time you ask a question—regardless of what application was active when you started the Office Assistant.

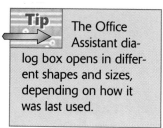

Tip While Clippit is the default Office Assistant, Microsoft Office applications come with a gallery of different Office Assistant shapes you can select. Search the Help files to learn how to change the Office Assistant.

Task 15:

To Use the Office Assistant

1 Launch Excel using the same techniques you used to launch Word.

2 Choose **Help | Show the Office Assistant**.

3 Click the **Office Assistant**.

Tip The Office Assistant dialog box opens in different shapes and sizes, depending on how it was last used.

Figure 1-36

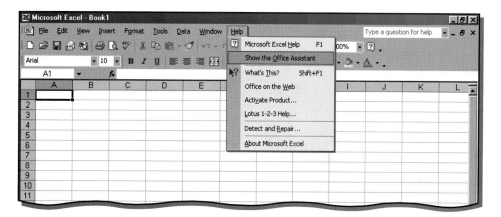

Figure 1-37

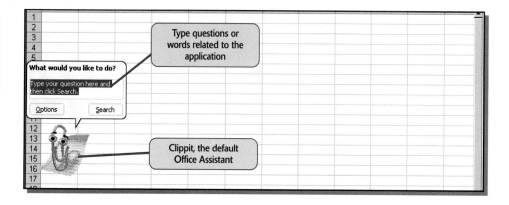

4 Type **How do I print a worksheet?** The Office Assistant takes notes as you type.

5 Click **Search** to locate associated help topics and then select **About printing**. Information and topics containing information about printing worksheets appears.

6 Close the **Help** window. The Excel window resizes to its original size.

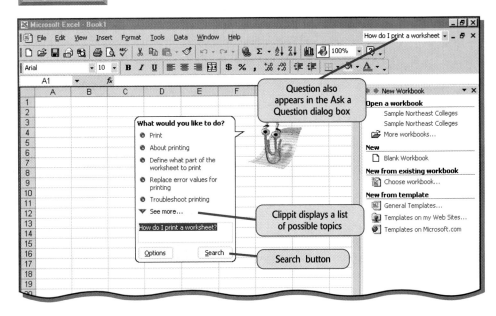

Figure 1-38

7 Right-click the **Office Assistant** and select **Hide**. The Office Assistant disappears and waits to be called again.

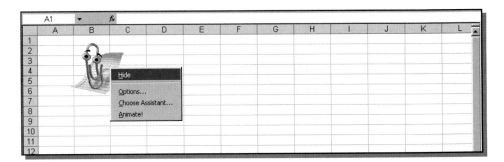

Figure 1-39

Troubleshooting After you select Hide several times, a dialog box will appear asking if you want to deactivate the Office Assistant. Read the options carefully and select the option that best represents how you want to use the Office Assistant.

Tip As you work with Help, you'll discover that the format of information displayed after you select a topic varies. In some cases, a list of step-by-step instructions appears in the Help window, and at other times, a list of further topics related to the subject you selected appears.

CHECK POINT

A number of features are available in Office XP to help you recover files. Each of these features is described in Table 1-5.

Table 1-5 Recovery Features

Feature	Description
Save on Crash	Word, Excel, and PowerPoint files that are open when a crash occurs are automatically saved so that they can be recovered after the system is restored.
Timed recovery save (AutoRecover)	An option set in Word, Excel, and PowerPoint to automatically save open files at regular intervals so that they can be recovered in case of power outages and Save on Crash failure.
Document Recovery task pane	An application pane that opens on the left side of an application window after a crash or improper shutdown, if recovery files are available. Users can choose to view both the recovery file and the original file to determine which file to use.
Hang Manager	A feature designed to "break" into a nonresponding application so that a Save on Crash action can be performed. You'll find this feature by choosing **Start	Programs	Microsoft Office Tools	Microsoft Office Application Recovery**.
Corrupt document recovery	An explicit corrupt document tool for recovering or repairing Word and Excel files. Simply select **Open and Repair** from the Open drop-down list as you open the file.
Office Safe Mode	Office-specific tools designed to fix and troubleshoot failed application startups. When an Office application fails to launch, a prompt should appear explaining the error and presenting start alternatives.

WEB TIP

If you're connected to the Internet, you can access one of several Web sites maintained by Microsoft to provide up-to-the-minute help online. The Web provides information directly from Microsoft support team members as well as information and helpful hints from other Office users. To access the Microsoft Web site directly from an Office XP application, choose **Help | Office on the Web**. Your default Web browser launches and displays the Office XP Update page.

Previewing and Printing

While each Office XP application has printing features that are specific to the application, printing basics are the same for all applications. In addition, each application has features that enable you to preview your files before printing them.

Previewing Pages

Even though most applications display files in WYSIWYG (*what you see is what you get*) format, sometimes what you see on paper is not quite what you expected. It is always a good idea to preview pages before sending them to the printer so that you can prevent some of these surprises. Each Office XP application has some type of Print Preview feature that enables you to see what the file will look like when it's printed.

- For all applications, you can display the preview by choosing **File | Print Preview,** or by clicking the **Print Preview** button on the Standard toolbar.
- In PowerPoint, you can display each slide on screen by choosing **View | Slide Show**, by pressing F5, by choosing **Slide Show | View Show**, or by clicking the **Slide Show** button at the bottom of the presentation window.

Task 16:

To Preview a File

1 Launch Word, if necessary, and open your *Copy (1) of e-Selections* file.

2 Click the **Print Preview** button on the Standard toolbar.

Figure 1-40

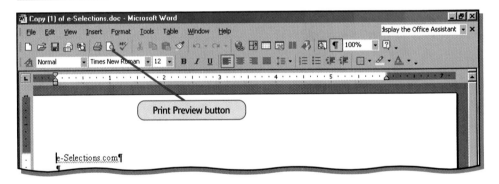

Print Preview button

3 Click the **Close** button on the Preview toolbar.

Figure 1-41

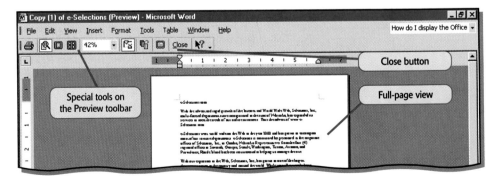

Special tools on the Preview toolbar

Close button

Full-page view

Setting Print Options and Printing

There are three basic methods for printing documents:

- Choose **File | Print** to display the Print dialog box and set print options.
- Click the **Print** button on the Standard toolbar to print the active file using default settings.
- Press Ctrl + P to display the Print dialog box and set print options.

The options displayed in the Print dialog box vary among Office applications. There are a number of options, however, that are common to the Print dialog boxes of all the applications.

 Troubleshooting If the printer you want to use is not installed on your computer, check with your instructor or the lab assistant to obtain the necessary information and disks to install the printer.

Task 17:

To Set Print Options and Print a File

1 Choose **File | Print**.

2 Review print options and then click **OK**.

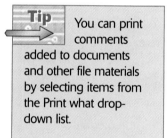 **Tip** You can print comments added to documents and other file materials by selecting items from the Print what drop-down list.

Figure 1-42

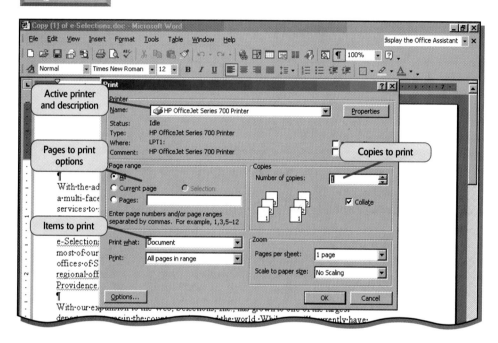

Exiting Applications

Before you exit Office XP applications, you should save work that you want to keep and close the files you have open. If you exit an application without saving changes to open files, the Office XP application prompts you to save changes to the file. Be sure to read these prompts carefully to ensure that you take the action you intend and avoid unnecessary loss of data.

To exit Office XP applications, use one of the following procedures:

- Click the application **Close** ✖ button.
- Choose **File | Exit**. If multiple files are open in the application, all files close as you exit the application.
- Click the **Application Control** icon at the left end of the title bar, and select **Close**.
- Press Alt + F4.
- Right-click the **application** button on the Windows taskbar and select **Close**.

SUMMARY AND EXERCISES

SUMMARY

- The many common elements of Office XP enable you to use techniques learned in one application to accomplish the same task in other applications.

- Applications can be launched in a variety of ways, based on your preferences and how Office XP is installed on your computer.

- Screen elements appear each time you open an Office XP application; they are designed to control the way files appear in the application window, to aid in file management tasks, and to provide easy access to commonly performed tasks.

- File management tasks include opening files, creating new files, saving files, and editing file properties.

- Documents can be opened as a copy or as a read-only file to ensure that your original remains intact.

- New documents can be created as blank files or by using a pre-designed template.

- Word, Excel, and PowerPoint enable you to open or create multiple files without closing files that are already open.

- When you elect to close a file that has been edited, regardless of which procedure you use, the application will prompt you to save the file.

- Files from all applications can be saved in a format recognized by the Web.

- Files saved as Web pages can be previewed from Office XP applications.

- The My Places bar, which appears in the Open and Save As dialog boxes, can be customized to hold folders and files you access frequently.

- The Open and Save As dialog boxes can be sized to display more information.

- File properties are automatically stored with each file you save unless you set options to prevent personal information from being saved with the file.

- Numerous help features are available. The Office Assistant and the Ask a Question features enable you to ask questions about the active application.

- Printing basics, such as previewing and setting print options, are basically the same for all Office XP applications.

KEY TERMS & SKILLS

KEY TERMS

corrupt document (p. 1-29)
embedded fonts (p. 1-19)
Hang Manager (p. 1-29)
Language bar (p. 1-9)
launch (p. 1-3)
My Places bar (p. 1-14)
Office Assistant (p. 1-27)
Office Safe mode (p. 1-29)

properties (p. 1-24)
Status bar (p. 1-7)
task pane (p. 1-7)
templates (p. 1-4)
toolbar (p. 1-7)
View buttons (p. 1-7)
Zoom (p. 1-12)

SKILLS

Add a folder to the My Places bar
  (p. 1-22)
Close a file (p. 1-18)
Close and open the task pane
  (p. 1-8)
Create new files (p. 1-16)
Create new folders (p. 1-19)
Display and hide toolbars (p. 1-9)
Edit file properties (p. 1-25)
Exit applications (p. 1-31)
Hide and display the Language
  bar (p. 1-9)
Launch applications (p. 1-3)
Launch Microsoft Word (p. 1-6)
Obtain help online (p. 1-29)
Open a copy of a document (p. 1-15)
Open a file (p. 1-13)

Preview pages (p. 1-30)
Print (p. 1-31)
Recover files (p. 1-29)
Remove personal information
  from a file on save (p. 1-25)
Save a copy of a file (p. 1-19)
Save a file (p. 1-18)
Save a file as a Web page (p. 1-21)
Set print options (p. 1-30)
Set Zoom control (p. 1-12)
Size a dialog box (p. 1-21)
Switch among open files (p. 1-17)
Turn off auto-customization features
  for menus and toolbars (p. 1-11)
Use Ask a Question (p. 1-26)
Use the Office Assistant (p. 1-27)
View the Web file (p. 1-23)

STUDY QUESTIONS

MULTIPLE CHOICE

1. Which procedures for accomplishing tasks are basically the same in all Office XP applications?
  a. presentation design
  b. file management
  c. data management
  d. toolbar options

2. Which are three options for initiating commands in Office XP?
  a. toolbar buttons, keystrokes, and mouse options
  b. taskbar buttons, menu commands, and keystrokes
  c. menu commands, keystrokes, and toolbar buttons
  d. both b and c

3. Which of the following procedures is *not* an option to open an existing document, workbook, presentation, or database?
  a. choose **Start | Open Office Document**
  b. choose **File | Open**
  c. press Ctrl + P
  d. click the **Open** button

4. The programs that display new files when you launch them are
  a. Access, PowerPoint, and Word.
  b. Excel, Access, and PowerPoint.
  c. Access and Excel.
  d. Word, Excel, and PowerPoint.

5. To change the portion of the file that appears on screen, adjust the
  a. task pane.
  b. Zoom control.
  c. toolbars.
  d. status bar.

6. Save commands include all the following *except*
  a. Save.
  b. Save As.
  c. Save as HTML.
  d. Save as Web Page.

7. To create a new file after an application is launched,
  a. press Ctrl + N.
  b. click the **New** button on the Standard toolbar.
  c. choose **File | New**.
  d. all of the above

8. The Ask a Question text box appears on the
  a. title bar.
  b. menu bar.
  c. toolbar.
  d. task pane.

9. Techniques for recovering files in Office XP include
  a. AutoRecover.
  b. recovering corrupt files.
  c. saving on crash.
  d. all of the above

SHORT ANSWER

1. List three different ways you can launch an application.
2. Identify several different ways to exit an application.
3. How do you open and close the task pane?
4. Regardless of the procedure you are using, what features will help prevent unwanted loss of data, and when will this option be presented to you?
5. How can you turn off the Office Assistant?
6. What is the difference between Save and Save As and when would you use each command?
7. What is Office Safe mode and when will it be used?
8. When would you remove personal information from files?
9. What are embedded fonts?
10. How do you resize a dialog box?

FILL IN THE BLANK

1. When you want to leave the original file intact but also want to use the file as a basis for a new file, you can open a(n) _____ of the original file and save it as a new file.
2. The _____ appears down the left side of the Open and Save As dialog boxes.
3. _____ is the default Office Assistant.
4. Click the _____ button to switch to a different open file.
5. _____ enables you to see what your printout will look like before you print it.
6. Display a list of toolbars by choosing the _____ command on the _____ menu.
7. The _____ setting controls the portion of a file that appears on screen.
8. Files saved for Web use are saved with a(n) _____ extension.
9. The _____ toolbar appears to float on screen when it is active in an Office XP application.
10. Options for turning off the auto-customization feature appear in the _____ dialog box.

FOR DISCUSSION

1. Briefly discuss when, how, and why you would use the Office Assistant.
2. Discuss the different ways to save a document and explain when and why you might choose each particular option.
3. The Word screen on one computer in the lab looks different from the Word screen on another computer in the lab. Explain the possible reasons why.
4. How do you add a folder to the My Places bar and why would you want to?

GUIDED EXERCISES

1 LAUNCHING APPLICATIONS

A good way to test the capacity of your computer system is to launch multiple applications and see if the performance speed keeps pace. You already have Word and Excel running. To test your system, you will launch various applications using a variety of different techniques.

1 Choose **Start | Programs | Accessories | Windows Explorer**.

2 Choose **Start | Programs | Accessories | Calculator**.

3 Choose **Start | Programs | Internet Explorer**.

2 SWITCHING AND EXITING APPLICATIONS

Now that you have examined the capacity of your computer, you can close all the open applications except Word.

1 Switch to Calculator and click the **Close** button.

2 Switch to Windows Explorer and choose **File | Close**.

3 Switch to Internet Explorer and press $\boxed{\text{Alt}}$ + $\boxed{\text{F4}}$.

4 Right-click the **Excel** button on the taskbar and select **Close**.

3 PRINTING AND SAVING FILES

The e-Selections file that you opened and saved can be printed and then saved using a different file name.

1 Switch to the *Copy of e-Selections.doc* file, if necessary.

2 Choose **File | Print**, review print options and close the Print dialog box.

3 Click the **Print** button to print the file using default settings.

4 Choose **File | Save As** and open your personal folder on the My Places bar.

5 Type *Your Initials* e-Selections in the **File name** text box and press $\boxed{\text{Enter}}$.

4 CREATING A NEW FILE

The main purpose for creating new documents is to type text in the document work area. It's time to create your first document and type some text.

1 Switch to Word, if necessary.

2 Create a new document using the procedure you prefer.

3 Type the text shown here at the top of the document—it's okay if you make mistakes—and don't worry if your lines break at different spots from those shown here in this text.

An apple or two for lunch on Monday is an excellent antidote to a weekend of overeating. Besides all this, the apple comes in its own packaging, travels well, and keeps indefinitely. What could be simpler?

4 Save your document in your personal folder, naming the file *An Apple on Monday*.

5 Follow your instructor's direction for placing your name on the document. Then print a copy of the document.

ON YOUR OWN

The difficulty of these case studies varies:
are the least difficult; are more difficult; and are the most difficult.

1 LAUNCHING APPLICATIONS AND WORKING WITH TOOLBARS

Launch Microsoft Excel 2002 and display the Picture toolbar. Record the names of each of the tools contained on the toolbar and identify when you would use the toolbar. Hide the toolbar.

2 CHANGING THE ZOOM SETTING

Change the Zoom setting for the blank Excel workbook to Selection using the Zoom dialog box. Record how the workbook appears. Then change the Zoom setting to 50% using the Zoom drop-down list on the Standard toolbar and record how the workbook appears on screen. Change the Zoom settings back to 100% using the preferred procedure.

3 OPENING AND SAVING AN EXCEL FILE

Open the *Sample Northeast Colleges.xls* file that you downloaded from the Prentice Hall Web site. Type **Your Name** in the active location. Then save your file as a new file in your personal folder. Name the file *Your Initials Sample Colleges*.

4 PREVIEWING AND PRINTING EXCEL FILES

Preview your *Sample Colleges* Excel file to see how it will print. Print a copy of the file.

5 SAVING, PREVIEWING, AND PRINTING AN EXCEL FILE AS A WEB PAGE

Save your *Sample Colleges* worksheet as a Web page, storing it in your personal folder. Preview the file in your default Web browser. Print a copy of the file from the Web browser.

Common Text Elements

I n the previous project, you learned some of the basic elements and features that all Microsoft Office XP applications have in common. In this project, you will learn some techniques for working with text in all of the Office applications—how to *format*, *enhance*, copy, move, and proof text. You'll also learn how to create and format text boxes and how to add text to those boxes.

OBJECTIVES

After completing this project, you will be able to:

- Navigate documents

- Select text

- Insert, delete, and replace text

- Enhance, format, and align text

- Move and copy text and text format

- Use the Office Clipboard

- Undo and redo changes

- Use Office proofing tools

- Use A...

e-selections) Running Case

You're off and running toward mastering the basics of the Microsoft Office XP applications that you will need as you work toward establishing yourself with e-Selections.com! Learning how to identify screen features, manage files, and get help was actually quite easy. Now that you're more comfortable with the basics, you decide to put those keyboarding skills to good use and try working with text...

PROJECT 2

Common Text Elements

The Setup

In Common Elements Project 1, you learned a number of screen features and other tools that control the way documents appear on screen. As you worked with these screen features, the figures in the text changed to reflect screen changes. Before starting Common Elements Projects 2 and 3, it is important that you check some of those screen settings to ensure that your screen matches the figures in the projects. The settings shown in Table 2-1 will be used in both Projects 2 and 3.

Table 2-1	Common Elements Projects 2 and 3 Screen Settings
Feature	**Setting**
Office Assistant	Hide the Office Assistant.
Toolbars and Menus	Set the toolbars to appear on two lines and set the Always show full menus option. Hide all toolbars except Standard and Formatting.
Task pane	Close the task pane.

Troubleshooting Because screen settings and installation options vary, you may see differences between your screens and those shown in this text.

The Challenge

Typing and formatting text is a skill required for working in all Office XP applications. The *e-Selections Online* document needs to be dressed up a bit. Formatting and text enhancements can be applied to create the document shown in Figure 2-1.

Figure 2-1

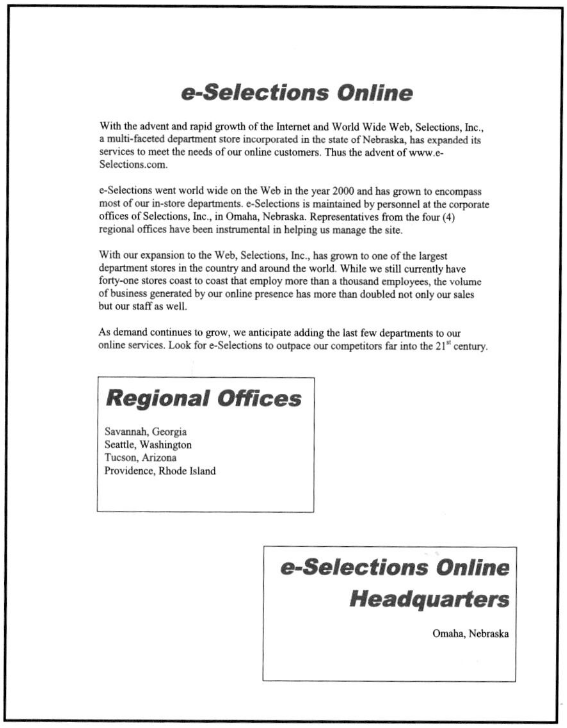

Figure 2-1

e-Selections Online

With the advent and rapid growth of the Internet and World Wide Web, Selections, Inc., a multi-faceted department store incorporated in the state of Nebraska, has expanded its services to meet the needs of our online customers. Thus the advent of www.e-Selections.com.

e-Selections went world wide on the Web in the year 2000 and has grown to encompass most of our in-store departments. e-Selections is maintained by personnel at the corporate offices of Selections, Inc., in Omaha, Nebraska. Representatives from the four (4) regional offices have been instrumental in helping us manage the site.

With our expansion to the Web, Selections, Inc., has grown to one of the largest department stores in the country and around the world. While we still currently have forty-one stores coast to coast that employ more than a thousand employees, the volume of business generated by our online presence has more than doubled not only our sales but our staff as well.

As demand continues to grow, we anticipate adding the last few departments to our online services. Look for e-Selections to outpace our competitors far into the 21st century.

Regional Offices

Savannah, Georgia
Seattle, Washington
Tucson, Arizona
Providence, Rhode Island

e-Selections Online Headquarters

Omaha, Nebraska

The Solution

Using Word, you will apply text formatting features that are common to all Office XP applications—exceptions will be noted.

Working with Text

Whether you're typing a letter in Word, entering values in an Excel worksheet, adding data to an Access table, or creating slides in PowerPoint, you'll type and edit text. Learning how to navigate, edit, enhance, format, *align*, move, and copy text now will make working with text in each application easier.

Navigating Text

Navigating text simply means moving from character to character, paragraph to paragraph, screen to screen, or page to page in a file. You can use both the keyboard and the mouse to move the insertion point within a file. Mouse techniques that are common to all Office applications include using scroll bars to display different parts of a file and clicking to position the insertion point in the paragraph, cell, or field you want to edit. Table 2-2 identifies navigation keystrokes common to Word, Excel, PowerPoint, and Access.

Table 2-2	Navigation Keystrokes
Press	**To Move**
←	Left one character or column
→	Right one character or column
↓	Down one line or row
↑	Up one line or row
Page Up	Up one screen
PageDown	Down one screen
Home	To the beginning of a line or row
End	To the end of a line or row
Ctrl + End	To the end of a file
Ctrl + Home	To the beginning of a file

As you work with each application, you'll discover additional keystrokes specific to that application. For example: in Excel, you'll learn to move from worksheet to worksheet in a workbook; in PowerPoint, you'll learn to display presentation slides; and in Access, you'll learn to move among records in forms using the navigation controls.

Inserting, Deleting, and Typing Over Text

All Office **XP** applications are set with *Insert mode* active so that you simply position the insertion point where you want to insert text and start typing. Existing text moves over to make room for the new text. To *replace* existing text with new text, you can select text that you want to replace (see Table 2-3) and type the new text in its place.

> **Tip**
> In Word, you can also switch to *Overtype mode* by pressing Insert on the keyboard or by double-clicking the OVR area of the status bar.

The technique used to *delete* text depends on the position of the insertion point:

- Position the insertion point immediately before the text you want to delete and press Delete once for each character and space you want to delete.
- Position the insertion point immediately after the text you want to delete and press Bksp once for each character and space you want to delete.

You can also use text selection techniques to select text and replace it with other text. Techniques for selecting text vary somewhat from application to application, but some basics are common to all applications. Table 2-3 summarizes common text selection techniques.

Table 2-3 Common Text Selection Techniques	
Action	**To Select**
Double-click a word	The word
Triple-click a word	The paragraph or table cell
Press Shift **+ arrow keys**	Characters, lines, or rows from the insertion point

Text appears highlighted—white text on a black background—when it is selected. Text you type and keyboard keys you press while text is selected replace selected text.

Tip The task pane also contains formatting features that are explored more thoroughly in the Microsoft Word 2002 book and the Word section of the Microsoft Office XP book.

Enhancing and Formatting Text

Word, Excel, PowerPoint, and Access datasheets share common methods for changing the appearance of text. Special features enable you to enhance and format text by changing the text *font*—the shape and size of text characters—as well as changing text *attributes*—how text characters appear. Changes you make to text that has already been typed affect the selected text only. However, you can "turn on" an enhancement or change font characteristics before typing text and it will remain active until you turn the enhancement "off" or change the font again when you are finished. Tools on the Formatting toolbar, menu commands on the Format menu, and dialog boxes can all be used to format text.

Task 1:

To Navigate, Select, Enhance, and Format Text

1 Open the document *e-Selections Online.doc.*

2 Select the title *e-Selections Online.* The text appears highlighted.

3 Click the **Bold B** button on the Formatting toolbar to make the text appear in bold letters.

Figure 2-2

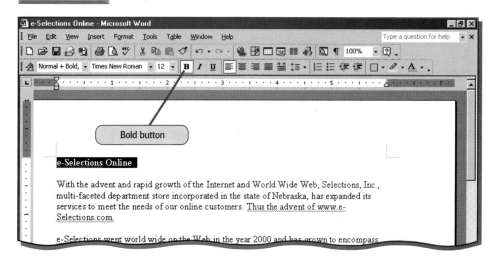

4 Click the **Font** down arrow.

5 Select **Arial Black**. The selected text reformats with the new font.

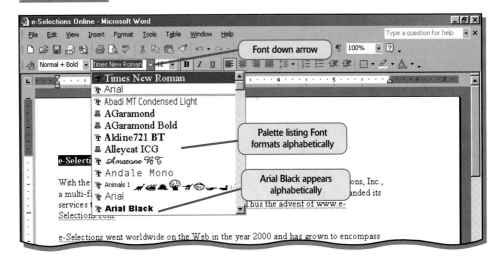

Figure 2-3

6 Click the **Font Size** down arrow. A list of numbers appears on a palette, with the current font size highlighted.

7 Select **24**. The title appears much larger.

8 Click the **Italic** button on the Formatting toolbar. The title appears slanted and the Italic button is white.

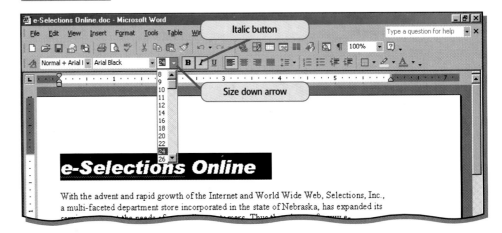

Figure 2-4

Troubleshooting The fonts installed on your computer and the printer that you are using control, to some extent, the fonts that you see listed. The fonts you see may be different from those shown here.

If Arial Black is unavailable on your font list, select a similar font or follow the direction of your instructor.

9 Choose **Format | Font** to open the Font dialog box.

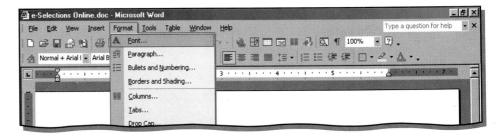

Figure 2-5

10 Click the **Font color** down arrow. A palette of colors appears.

11 Click **Blue** and click **OK**. The title text is reformatted in blue print.

Tip Notice the special effects listed in the Font dialog box. As you become more comfortable applying standard enhancements to text, you may want to try applying some of these special effects and explore options contained on other pages of this dialog box.

Figure 2-6

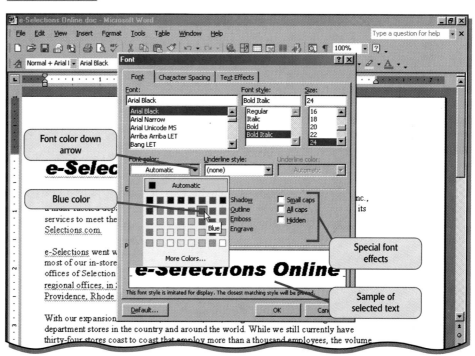

12 Press Ctrl + End to position the insertion point at the bottom of the document.

13 Choose **File | Save As** and save the file using the file name *Your Initials e-Selections Online.*

Other Ways To apply font color:

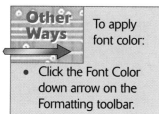

- Click the Font Color down arrow on the Formatting toolbar.

Figure 2-7

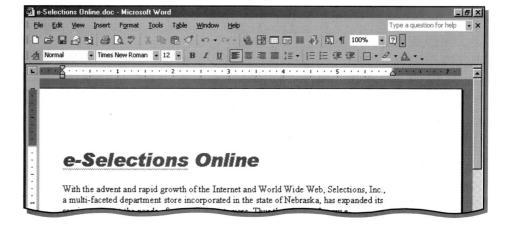

WEB TIP

Additional fonts are available online from a variety of different companies. Search the Internet for fonts to see what's available.

Copying and Moving Text

The *Cut* command is used to remove text from its current position. The *Copy* command leaves text at its current position. Office XP offers three different techniques for moving and copying text:

- Click the **Cut** ✂ , **Copy** 📋, or **Paste** 📋 buttons on the Standard toolbar.
- Choose **Edit | Cut/Copy/Paste**.
- Press Ctrl + X to Cut; Ctrl + C to Copy; or Ctrl + V to Paste.

When you use the Cut command to move text or the Copy command to copy text, Office XP applications place the selected text or information on the Clipboard, where it stays until you *paste* it where you want it.

Although other Windows applications store only one snippet of information on the Clipboard, Office XP contains a special feature that enables you to store multiple snippets of information (up to 24) from all types of Office applications on a special Office Clipboard. You can then choose the snippet or snippets to place when you paste. The Office Clipboard appears in the task pane when it is active.

Task 2:

To Display the Office Clipboard

1 Choose **Edit | Office Clipboard**. The task pane opens and displays the Office Clipboard.

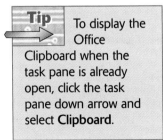

Tip To display the Office Clipboard when the task pane is already open, click the task pane down arrow and select **Clipboard**.

Figure 2-8

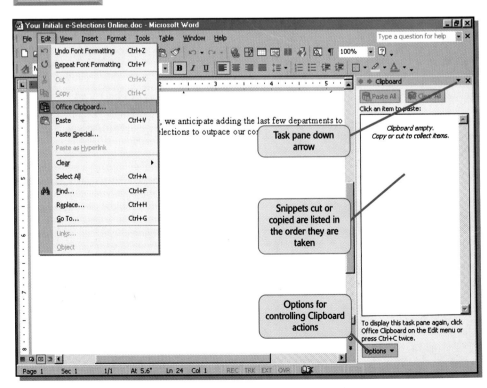

CHECK POINT

The Office Clipboard may appear automatically as you work when you cut or copy multiple snippets of information in one or more Office XP applications. Normally, items are added to the Office Clipboard only when it is active. Options that control the way the Office Clipboard acts are found on the Options drop-down list that appears at the bottom of the Clipboard task pane. These options are described in Table 2-4.

Table 2-4 Options for Controlling the Office Clipboard	
Select the Option	**To**
Show Office Clipboard Automatically	Activate the Office Clipboard when you cut or copy the second snippet.
Collect Without Showing Office Clipboard	Places items on the Office Clipboard even when it is not open.
Show Office Clipboard Icon on Taskbar	Places an Office Clipboard icon on the tray of the Taskbar so that you can access the Office Clipboard more easily.
Show Status Near Taskbar When Copying	Displays a screen tip above the tray on the Taskbar each time you copy something to the Clipboard. The tip lets you know how many items are currently on the Office Clipboard.

In addition, you can display the Office Clipboard by pressing Ctrl + C twice. The icons that appear beside snippets on the Office Clipboard identify the application from which the snippet was taken. You can paste all snippets at the current cursor location by clicking the Paste All button. You can also click an individual snippet to insert it at the insertion point.

Task 3:
To Copy and Move Text

1 Position the insertion point at the bottom of the document, if necessary.

2 Click the **Bold** **B** button and type **Regional Offices.**

3 Click the **Bold** **B** button to turn bold off and then press Enter twice.

Figure 2-9

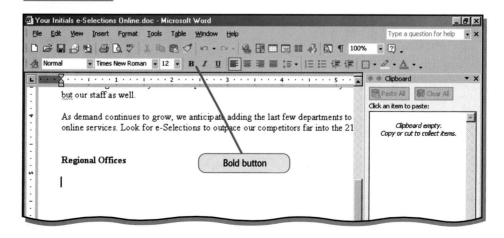

4 Select the text *Savanah, Georgia* in the second paragraph and click the **Cut** ✂ button to remove selected text from its current position and place it on the clipboard.

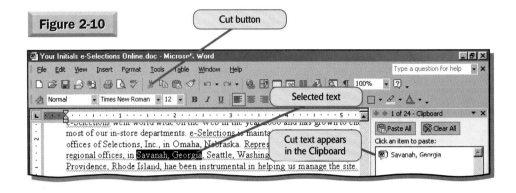

Figure 2-10

5 Move to the end of the document and click the **Paste** 📋 button to place text from the clipboard at the end of the document.

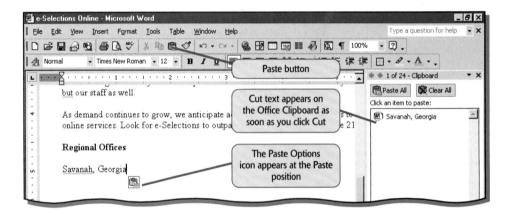

Figure 2-11

6 Click the **Paste Options** icon next to the pasted text and review the options that appear.

7 Select **Keep Source Formatting** to close the option list and then press ⏎.

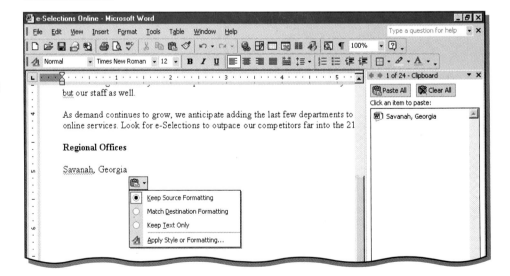

Figure 2-12

Tip

Selecting the Keep Source Formatting option tells Word to include any enhancements and special formatting that were originally applied to the text when you paste the text in the new location. To drop special formatting from the original text so that text is formatted to follow font characteristics of the paragraph in which you paste the text, you would select Match Destination Formatting from the Past Options list.

8 Repeat the procedures in Steps 4–6 to move the cities and states for the other three regional offices so that they appear as shown in Figure 2-13.

9 Select the text, *in , , ,* *and,* that is highlighted in Figure 2-13 and delete it.

10 Save changes to the document.

Tip Snippets of information are collected on the Clipboard task pane in the order in which you cut or copy them. The most recently cut or copied snippet appears at the top of the task pane for easy access.

Figure 2-13

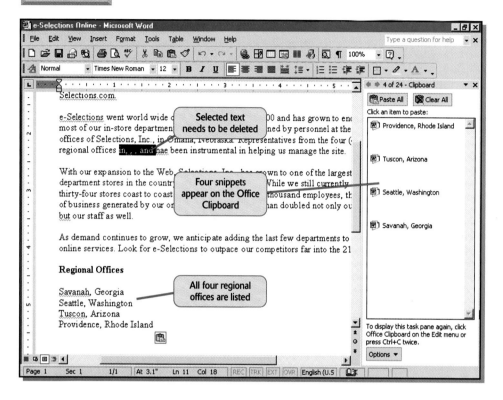

Copying Text Formats

Formatting text by applying enhancements, color, and font styles can be tedious—especially when you want to format text in several different locations and maintain consistency of format. You're in luck! Office XP applications are equipped with a *Format Painter* that's designed to help you copy text format and apply the format to other text. Using the Format Painter to copy format is basically a three-step process:

Tip Double-click the Format Painter button to copy format to multiple locations. When you're finished painting all the text with the copied format, click the Format Painter button again to turn it off.

1 Select the text with the format that you want to copy.

2 Click the **Format Painter** button.

3 "Paint" the format onto the text you want to format.

Task 4:
To Copy Text Formats Using the Format Painter

1 Close the Office Clipboard and then select the formatted title text, *e-Selections Online*.

2 Click the **Format Painter** button on the Standard toolbar to copy the format of the selected text.

3 Scroll to the bottom of the document page until the *Regional Offices* text appears on the screen.

4 Click and drag the paintbrush across the text *Regional Offices* to paint the copied format onto the text.

5 Click anywhere in the document to deselect the text.

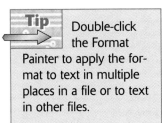

Tip Double-click the Format Painter to apply the format to text in multiple places in a file or to text in other files.

Figure 2-14

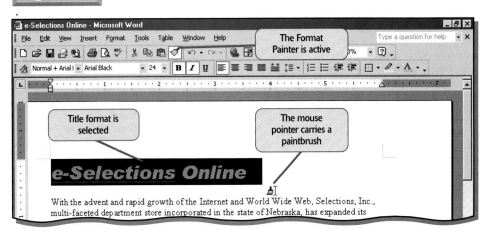

The Format Painter is active

Title format is selected

The mouse pointer carries a paintbrush

Figure 2-15

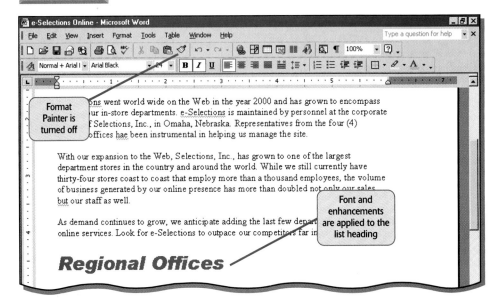

Format Painter is turned off

Font and enhancements are applied to the list heading

Troubleshooting Positioning the insertion point in a word is usually sufficient to copy the text format, but when multiple fonts and character settings are contained in a paragraph or in a word select the character that contains the format you want to copy.

Using Undo and Redo

The *Undo* feature in all Office XP applications reverses actions; the *Redo* feature restores actions that were reversed. Using Undo and Redo is quite simple. Office XP applications offer keyboard, mouse, and menu procedures for these two features, as shown in Table 2-5.

Table 2-5	Undo/Redo Procedures		
Command	**Mouse**	**Keyboard**	**Menu**
Undo	Click the **Undo** ↩ button on the Standard toolbar.	Press Ctrl + Z	Choose **Edit | Undo**
Redo	Click the **Redo** ↪ button on the Standard toolbar.	Press Ctrl + Y	Choose **Edit | Redo**

Each of these actions reverses the last action, but Office XP applications enable you to reverse numerous actions in succession. In addition, you can click the down arrow beside the Undo or Redo buttons and select the action you want to reverse. All actions down to and including the action you select can be reversed.

Aligning Text

Among the buttons you'll find on the Formatting toolbars in Word, Excel, PowerPoint, and on Access Forms are buttons that control text alignment. You can use these alignment buttons to adjust the position of text in document paragraphs, table or worksheet cells, database forms, and presentation slides. You can also access alignment commands using the keyboard. The menu commands for setting alignment vary among the applications. Table 2-6 identifies common procedures for aligning text in Word, Excel, PowerPoint, and on Access Forms.

Table 2-6	Alignment Commands	
Command	**Mouse**	**Keyboard**
Align Left	Click the **Align Left** ≣ button on the Formatting toolbar.	Press Ctrl + L
Center	Click the **Center** ≣ button on the Formatting toolbar.	Press Ctrl + E
Align Right	Click the **Align Right** ≣ button on the Formatting toolbar.	Press Ctrl + R
Justify	Click the **Justify** ≣ button on the Formatting toolbar.	Press Ctrl + J

Task 5:
To Align Text and Use Undo and Redo

1 Position the insertion point in the title of your *e-Selections Online.doc* document.

2 Click the **Align Right** button on the Formatting toolbar.

3 Undo the action to reposition the text at the left margin.

4 Center the title.

5 Save changes to the document.

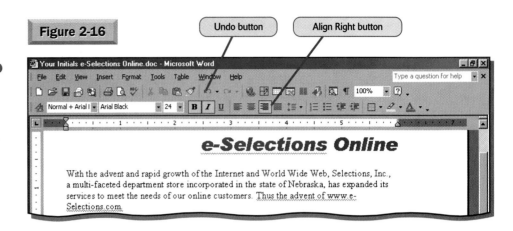

Figure 2-16

Undo button   Align Right button

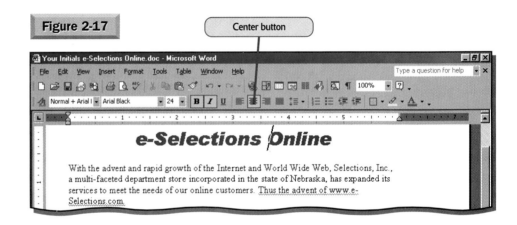

Figure 2-17

Center button

Tip

If special fonts required to develop documents in different languages such as Japanese have been installed on your computer, you may see a special Distributed alignment button on the Formatting toolbar. Try aligning text using the Distributed alignment and view the results.

Using Proofing Tools

Proofing tools built into Office XP applications make it easy to locate text, replace text, and check the spelling in your files. There is also a tool that is shared by Word, Excel, Access, and PowerPoint that enables you to enter frequently mistyped text and have the Office application automatically correct your error! The procedures for using these tools are consistent among all Office XP applications.

Running the Spelling Checker

When you first opened *e-Selections Online.doc*, you saw red, wavy underlines below misspelled words in the document. Unless the spell-as-you-go feature is turned off, the *spelling checker* feature runs continuously as you work in Office XP applications. The spelling checker feature locates words that don't appear in the Office XP dictionary and highlights them for you so that you can determine whether they are correct or need to be changed.

> **Tip**
>
> Words that are underlined as you work can be corrected quite easily. Simply point to the misspelled word and right-click. A list of suggested spellings for the word that is not recognized appears at the top of the shortcut menu. Select the correct spelling of the word, click **Ignore All**, or click **Add** to add the word to the dictionary.

Task 6:
To Use Spelling Checker on a File

1 Press Ctrl + Home to move to the beginning of the document and then click the **Spelling** button on the Standard toolbar.

2 Click **Ignore Rule**—this text appears as you want it to appear. Word locates the next possible error and highlights it.

Figure 2-18

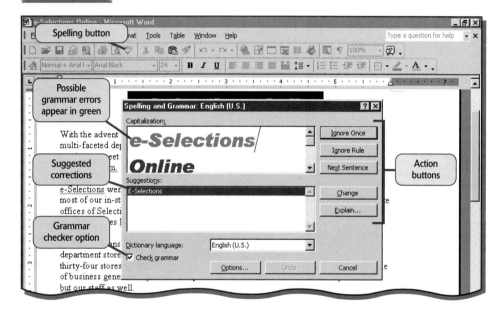

3 Click **Ignore Once**. The next possible error is highlighted.

4 Click **Ignore Rule** to ignore this rule, too.

Troubleshooting
If you start the spelling checker in the middle of a document, a different message window may appear that asks if you want to continue proofing the document from the beginning. Click **Yes** and continue until the spelling checker is complete.

Figure 2-19

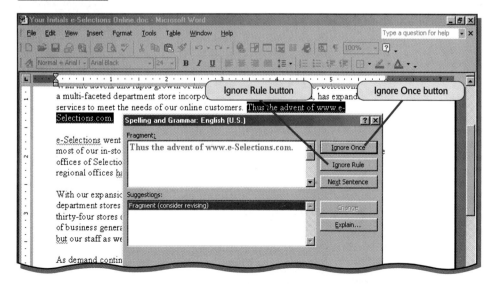

5 Select *have* from the **Suggestions** list and click **Change**. Word highlights the next possible error.

6 Continue checking the file, correcting errors that appear, until Word tells you the spelling and grammar check is complete.

Figure 2-20

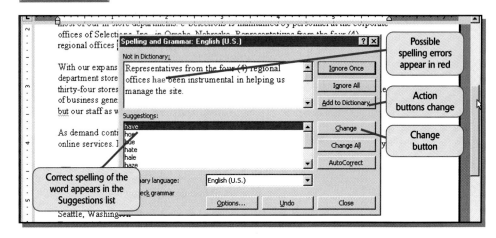

Possible spelling errors appear in red

Action buttons change

Change button

Correct spelling of the word appears in the Suggestions list

Tip If Word fails to present the correct spelling in the list of suggested words, you can correct the spelling of the word in the Not in Document area of the Spelling and Grammar dialog box and then click Change.

7 Click **OK** and save changes to the file.

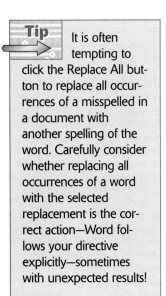

Tip It is often tempting to click the Replace All button to replace all occurrences of a misspelled in a document with another spelling of the word. Carefully consider whether replacing all occurrences of a word with the selected replacement is the correct action—Word follows your directive explicitly—sometimes with unexpected results!

Figure 2-21

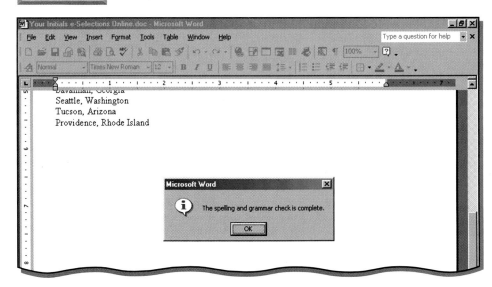

Finding and Replacing Text

The Find and Replace features enable you to locate text if it appears in a file and replace text with substitute text. These features are powerful tools for navigating and editing large files.

Task 7:

To Find and Replace Text

1 Press ⌈Ctrl⌉ + ⌈Home⌉ to position the insertion point at the top of the document and then choose **Edit | Find**. The Find and Replace dialog box opens.

2 Type thirty-four in the **Find what** text box and click **Find Next**.

Troubleshooting
Word searches the document for the phrase beginning at the insertion point. As a result, you may find a different occurrence of the phrase.

3 Click the **Replace** tab.

4 Type forty-one in the **Replace with** text box and click **Replace All**. Word replaces all occurrences of the number thirty-four with the number forty-one. A message window tells you how many replacements were made.

Figure 2-22

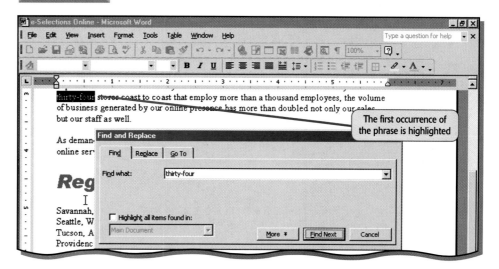

The first occurrence of the phrase is highlighted

Troubleshooting   In Access, the Find command is available only when an object is open. Find does not appear on the Edit menu when the database window is active.

Figure 2-23

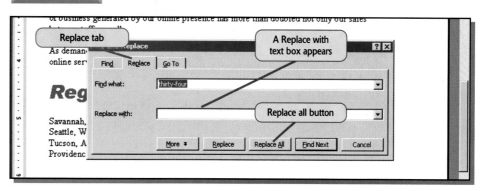

Replace tab

A Replace with text box appears

Replace all button

5 Click **OK**, close the dialog box, and save your changes to the document.

Figure 2-24

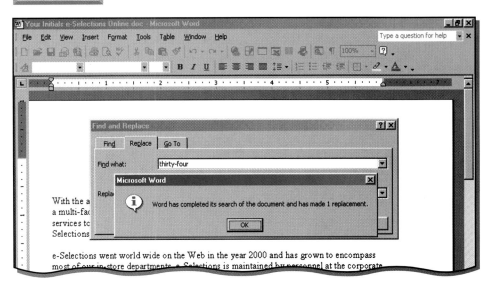

 CHECK POINT

The Find command is a useful tool for locating text in the active document. But what about those times when you want to locate information contained in another file or in an e-mail message?

The **Search** command is a feature new to Office XP applications. It makes it possible to locate text contained in files stored on your computer (including all disk drives), on a network, or in an e-mail message. When you become more comfortable with the basic Find and Replace functions, you'll want to explore this new Search feature using the Microsoft documentation and online Help features.

Creating and Using AutoCorrect Entries

Each of the Office XP applications comes equipped with an *AutoCorrect* feature that is designed to automatically correct the most frequently misspelled or mistyped words. When you type *t-e-h* or *a-h-v-e*, for example, the Office application automatically changes the words to *t-h-e* and *h-a-v-e* to correct the spelling. Office comes with a built-in set of commonly mistyped words that can be edited. You can also add the words *you* most frequently mistype to the AutoCorrect list and use AutoCorrect to create entries that will substitute frequently used phrases for abbreviations. Mistyped or abbreviated text is replaced after you press the spacebar, an end-of-sentence punctuation mark, or Enter.

Task 8:
To Create AutoCorrect Entries

1 Open *e-Selections Online.doc*, if necessary.

2 Select the word *e-Selections*.

3 Choose **Tools | AutoCorrect Options** to open the AutoCorrect dialog box.

> **Troubleshooting**
> The AutoCorrect entries you see may be different from those shown here.

4 Type esel in the **Replace** text box.

5 Click **Add**. The entry *esel* appears alphabetically on the AutoCorrect list.

6 Click **OK**. The dialog box closes.

> **Tip** Other options that appear on the AutoCorrect page of the AutoCorrect dialog box control how Word corrects typing errors as your work. For example, you can ensure that Word automatically capitalizes the days of the week when you forget to capitalize them, have Word correct two initial capital letters at the beginning of a word, or capitalize the first letter of each sentence when you fail to do so.

Figure 2-25

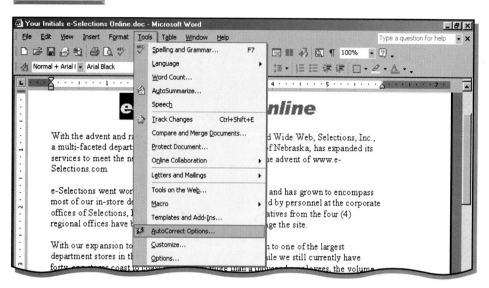

Figure 2-26

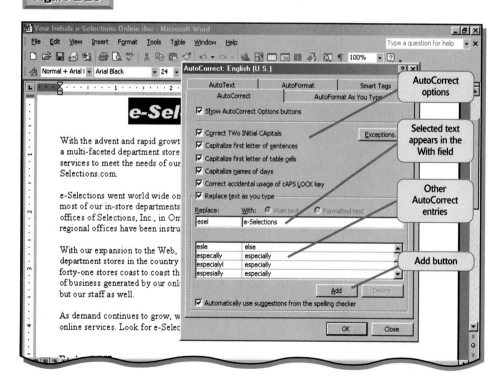

7 Move to the end of the document, press Enter twice, type **esel**, and press Spacebar. AutoCorrect expands the text and substitutes e-Selections for the abbreviation.

Figure 2-27

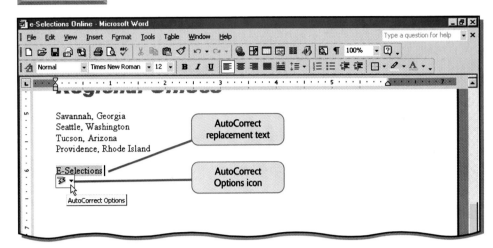

8 Point to the replacement text. A small blue rectangle appears below the first character of the replacement text.

9 Point to the blue rectangle.

Troubleshooting   The AutoCorrect Options button appears only when you point to the blue rectangle.

10 Click the **AutoCorrect Options** icon.

Figure 2-28

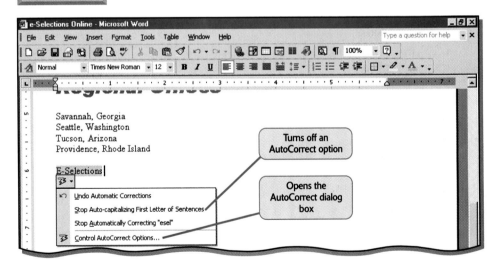

11 Press Esc to close the AutoCorrect Options list.

12 Delete the line added using AutoCorrect and then save the changes to the file.

Tip   Options displayed on the AutoCorrect Options list enable you to undo an AutoCorrect action, turn off the AutoCorrect entry you just typed, or set AutoCorrect Options. Additional options appear on the AutoCorrect Options list when Word takes an AutoCorrect action such as capitalizing the first word of a sentence or correcting two initial capital letters in a word.

Creating Text Boxes

Most text added to Office XP files appears within the basic file structure; between margins of documents, within cells of spreadsheets, within place-holders of presentation slides, and within database objects. Text boxes enable you to add text outside the parameters of the file structure. Text boxes are drawn on screen and text is typed within the text box. Text boxes can be repositioned within the file as needed.

Task 9:

To Create a Text Box

1 Open *e-Selections Online.doc,* if necessary, and position the insertion point at the end of the document.

2 Click the **Drawing** button on the Standard toolbar to open the Drawing toolbar at the bottom of the window.

3 Select the *Regional Offices* title and list text at the bottom of the document.

4 Click the **Text Box** tool on the Drawing toolbar. The mouse pointer changes to a crosshair pointer that looks like a plus (+) sign.

> **Tip** The crosshair pointer is used to draw text boxes and other shapes identified in Common Elements Project 3. The center of the crosshair pointer marks the position of the box or object start point.

Figure 2-29

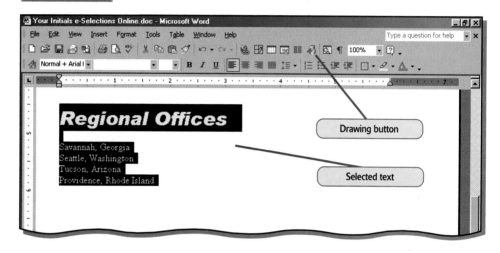

Figure 2-30

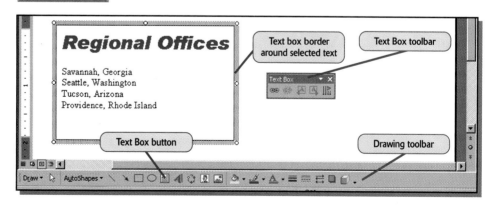

Troubleshooting   In Word, a Drawing Canvas appears if you click the Text Box tool before selecting text. You can draw the text box anywhere on the document, either inside or outside the Drawing Canvas, or press [Esc] to close the Drawing Canvas.

Adding Text to Text Boxes and Repositioning the Text Box

You can also create a new text box and type text directly into the text box. Then change the shape and format of the text box and reposition the text box wherever you want it in the document. Document text will automatically adjust to appear around the text box.

Task 10:
To Add Text to Text Boxes

1   Scroll to the bottom of the document and position the insertion point to the right of the existing text box.

2   Click the **Text Box** [A] tool and then press [Esc] to close the Drawing Canvas, if necessary.

3   Position the mouse pointer on the document page where the upper left corner of the text box should be and drag the mouse diagonally to draw a second text box beside the existing text box.

Figure 2-31

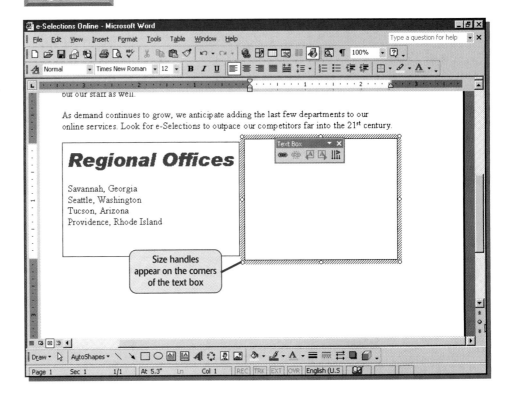

4 Type the text shown in Figure 2-32 in the new text box.

Tip Typing text in text boxes requires basically the same skills used to type text in the document outside the text boxes. Text wraps within the confines of the text box. Press Enter to start new lines when necessary.

Figure 2-32

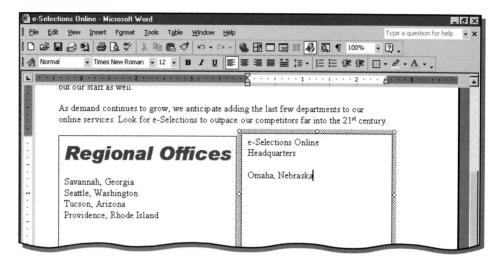

5 Copy the format from the *Regional Offices* title to the *e-Selections Online Headquarters* title using the Format Painter.

Troubleshooting
If you paint the format onto the city and state shown in the text box, undo the action and try again.

Figure 2-33

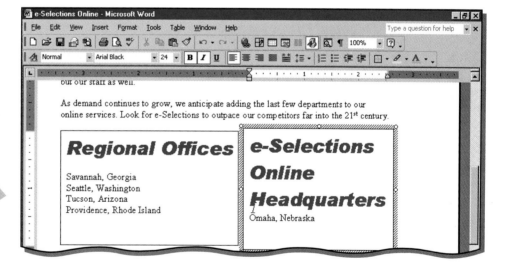

6 Select the new text box, position the mouse pointer on the lower right corner size handle, and then click and drag the handle to resize the text box as shown in Figure 2-34.

Troubleshooting
If you accidentally drag the side of the text box off the page, you can undo the action and try again. It often takes several tries to get the hang of box sizing.

Figure 2-34

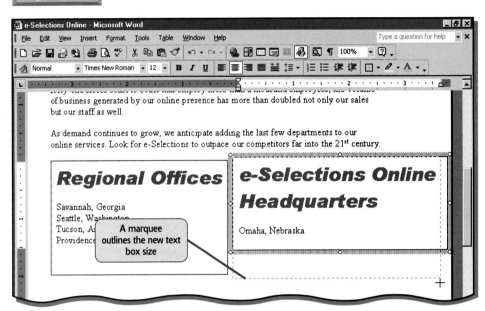

A marquee outlines the new text box size

7 Press [Shift] and click the text box, position the insertion point on a border of the text box until you see a four-headed mouse pointer, and then click and drag the new text box to position it as shown in Figure 2-35.

Tip Pressing [Shift] while clicking drawn objects selects the whole object rather than positioning the insertion point in the text within the text box.

8 Right align text in the new text box and then save changes and close the file.

Figure 2-35

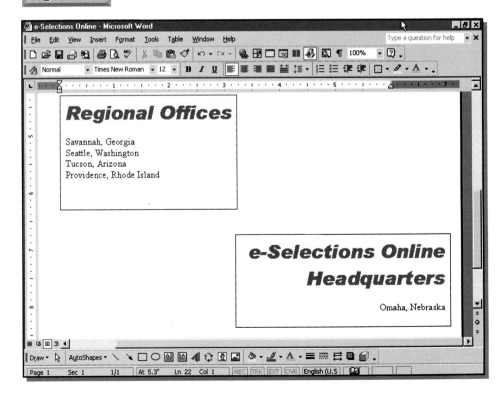

SUMMARY

- Navigating text enables you to move from character to character, paragraph to paragraph, screen to screen, or page to page.

- By selecting text, you can apply enhancements to text, change fonts, or move and copy text.

- Inserting and deleting text is the same in all Office XP applications. Word enables you to switch to Overtype mode to replace text as you type.

- Enhancing and formatting text is made easy using the buttons on the Formatting toolbar.

- Text can be cut, copied, and moved within or among all Office XP applications.

- The Office Clipboard can hold up to 24 snippets of information and can be displayed at any time an Office application is open.

- Office XP makes it easy to maintain text format consistency by using Format Painter.

- Using the Undo feature enables you to reverse the last action, and using the Redo feature enables you to restore actions that were reversed using the Undo feature. In Office XP you can also reverse multiple actions.

- Text can be aligned left or right, centered, or justified on the left or right.

- Proofing tools are used to locate text, replace text, and check the spelling of text in files.

- The AutoCorrect feature corrects commonly misspelled words and enables you to enter your own words to be automatically corrected.

- Text boxes can be drawn on screen and can be used to hold text and position the text more precisely in a file.

KEY TERMS & SKILLS

KEY TERMS

align (p. 2-3)
attributes (p. 2-5)
delete (p. 2-4)
enhance (p. 2-1)
font (p. 2-5)
format (p. 2-1)
Insert mode (p. 2-4)
justify (p. 2-13)

Overtype mode (p. 2-4)
paste (p. 2-8)
Redo (p. 2-13)
replace (p. 2-4)
spelling checker (p. 2-14)
Undo (p. 2-13)

SKILLS

Add text to text boxes (p. 2-22)
Align text (p. 2-13)
Copy and move text (p. 2-9)
Copy text format (p. 2-11)
Create and use AutoCorrect (p. 2-18)
Create text boxes (p. 2-21)
Display and use the Office Clipboard (p. 2-8)
Enhance and format text (p. 2-5)
Find and replace text (p. 2-16)
Insert, delete, and replace text (p. 2-4)
Navigate text (p. 2-3)
Spelling checker used in files (p. 2-15)
Use Undo and Redo (p. 2-13)

STUDY QUESTIONS

MULTIPLE CHOICE

1. Moving from character to character, paragraph to paragraph, screen to screen, or page to page is called
a. scrolling.
b. skipping.
c. navigating.
d. keystroking.

2. You can change the appearance of text by changing the font, size, and
a. art.
b. attributes.
c. paragraph.
d. selection.

3. To move up one screen, the key that is used in all applications is
a. PrtScr .
b. ↑ .
c. Ctrl + Home .
d. Page Up .

4. To move to the end of a file, press
a. End .
b. Ctrl + End .
c. PageDown .
d. none of the above

5. Which application contains numerous objects but enables text formatting in only one type of object?
   a. Word
   b. Excel
   c. Access
   d. PowerPoint

6. All of the following are text attributes, *except*
   a. font face.
   b. superscript.
   c. emboss.
   d. hidden.

7. To remove text to the left of the insertion point, press
   a. Del.
   b. Bksp.
   c. Shift + ←.
   d. Insert.

8. The feature that holds multiple snippets of information in Office XP is
   a. the Clipboard.
   b. AutoCorrect.
   c. the Office Clipboard.
   d. the shortcut menu.

9. To remove selected text from its current location, click
   a. Cut ✂ .
   b. Copy ▤ .
   c. Paste ▤ .
   d. Italic *I* .

10. To reverse the last action, click
   a. Cut ✂ .
   b. Undo ↩ .
   c. Redo ↪ .
   d. Format Painter ✍ .

SHORT ANSWER

1. What must you do before you can apply, enhance, or change the text font of existing text?
2. List three ways to delete text.
3. Which buttons can you use to reverse the last action or selected actions?
4. List the four basic alignments that can be applied to text in Office XP applications.
5. Identify the three-step process required to copy text formats using the Format Painter.
6. What are the keyboard shortcuts for Cut, Copy, and Paste?
7. Describe the difference between right alignment and justified alignment.
8. How do you turn off the grammar checker after starting the spelling checker?
9. How does formatting text contained in text boxes differ from formatting text contained in files?
10. What menu do you access to create an AutoCorrect entry from selected text?

FILL IN THE BLANK

1. You can use the keyboard or the _____ to move within a file.
2. _____ mode enables you to replace existing text as you type new text in Word.
3. Double-click the _____ button to copy a text format to multiple places.

4. Misspelled words are located and corrected using _____.
5. After clicking the Format Painter button, the mouse pointer appears to carry a _____.
6. The _____ _____ is automatically activated when you start the spelling checker.
7. _____ can be used to store frequently used, long phrases so that you can type an abbreviation and automatically enter the expanded text.
8. The _____ feature helps you move swiftly to a particular word or phrase in an Office XP file.
9. To be able to move text to specific positions in files, place the text in a _____ _____.
10. The Office Clipboard can hold _____ pieces of information.

DISCUSSION

1. Discuss several different ways of enhancing and formatting text.
2. Discuss the advantages of placing text in text boxes rather than within document margins, within spreadsheet cells, or in other locations.
3. Identify the different ways that the Office Clipboard can be used and how the Office Clipboard is accessed.

GUIDED EXERCISES

1 FORMATTING TEXT AND CREATING TEXT BOXES

Figure 2-36 contains two text boxes that appear side by side on the document page.

Figure 2-36

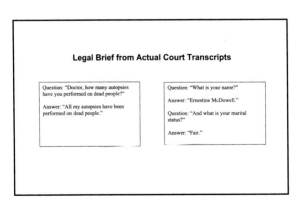

To ensure that the text boxes are the same size, you can create the first text box and then copy it before adding text to the text boxes. To create the text boxes, follow these steps.

1 Launch Word, if necessary, and create a new blank document.

2 Change the Zoom setting to **Page Width**.

3 Create the title:
- Type the title text Legal Brief from Actual Court Transcripts.
- Center the title.
- Format the title text using an Arial 18-point type.

4 Display the Drawing toolbar and create a new text box on the left side of the document, ensuring that the text box does not extend beyond the approximate center point on the page.

5 Press Shift and click the text box border to select it.

6 Copy the first text box:
- Click the **Copy** 📋 button.
- Click the white area on screen to clear the existing text box.

 Troubleshooting If the text box remains selected, the new text box will appear within the existing text box when you paste.

- Click the **Paste** 📋 button to paste a second text box on the screen.
- Drag the copy of the text box so that it appears to the right of the first text box and align the text boxes as precisely as possible.

7 Click inside the text box on the left and type the following text:

Question: "Doctor, how many autopsies have you performed on dead people?"

Answer: "All my autopsies have been performed on dead people."

8 Click inside the text box on the right and type the following text:

Question: "What is your name?"
Answer: "Ernestine McDowell."

Question: "And what is your marital status?"
Answer: "Fair."

9 Save the document using the file name *Legal Briefs*, print a copy of the document, and then close the file.

2 CREATING AN AUTOCORRECT ENTRY

One of the most effective uses of AutoCorrect is to expand your name by simply typing your initials. Follow these instructions to create an AutoCorrect entry that enters your name.

1 Launch Word, if necessary, and create a new blank document.

2 Type *Your Name* at the top of the document and then select *Your Name*.

3 Choose **Tools | AutoCorrect Options** and type *Your Initials* in the **Replace** field; click OK.

4 Press Enter and then type *Your Initials* followed by the Spacebar to test your AutoCorrect entry.

5 Close the file without saving it.

WEB TIP

Government Web addresses generally have a .gov extension. Search for Government Web sites to locate the official site for the Interagency Fire Center.

ON YOUR OWN

The difficulty of these case studies varies:

 are the least difficult; *are more difficult; and* *are the most difficult.*

1 FORMATTING TEXT

 Open the file Fire Center. Format text contained in the file as follows:

- Title: 18 point Arial, Small Caps, centered
- Bulleted list: 14 point Arial

Replace the text Your Name at the bottom of the file by typing *Your Name* and then right align the text. Check the spelling in the file. Save the file using the file name Your Initials Fire Center.

2 ADDING A TEXT BOX TO AN EXISTING FILE

Open the file *Fire Center* (Substitute *Your Initials Fire Center* if you completed On Your Own Exercise 1) and add the following text to a new text box below the bulleted list:

Visit the National Interagency Fire Center Online.

Center the text, change the font size to 17 points, and format the text using Arial font. Then print a copy of the file and save changes to the file using the file name *Your Initials Fire Center*.

3 CREATING A FUN NOTICE

Create the notice shown in Figure 2-37 using a font and font size similar to the font shown in the figure. Save the file using the file name *Phantom Ghost*, print a copy of the document, and then close the document.

Figure 2-37

Good . . . Evening!

If you do not wish a curse on this house,
you must make two treats
and deliver them to two houses
in the neighborhood.
You have only two days.
Post the picture of the Phantom Ghost on
your door 'til Halloween.
This will ward off any other phantoms
that may visit!

Copy this letter and the Phantom Ghost
twice and give it with treats
to two homes that do not have
a Phantom Ghost posted.

Share the Spirit!
Have a Happy Halloween!

FROM THE FILES

You Will Need

✔ e-Selections Online Graphics.doc
✔ e-Selections Logo.jpg
✔ Stars.wmf
✔ Phantom Ghosties.doc

P R O J E C T 3

Common Graphics Elements

Adding art to Office XP files dresses them up and makes them more inviting. Each Office XP application offers such a wide variety of methods for adding art to your files that it's sometimes difficult to decide which feature to use. You can add *clip art* images, *scanned images*, picture files, *WordArt*, and manual drawings to files in all Office XP applications. Each art type has a complete set of tools for editing and manipulating the art object. As a result, this project is designed to get you started on your artistic journey—you can explore the features that you will need to use the most on your own.

OBJECTIVES

After completing this project, you will be able to:

- Insert and edit clip art

- Display the Clip Organizer

- Insert graphic images

- Create and format WordArt

- Create and manipulate drawings

e-selections Running Case

With the advent of e-Selections.com, managers plan to start publishing information from different Office applications on the Web site. The graphics design specialist assigned to e-Selections.com has asked you to explore some of the graphics capabilities available in Office XP applications so that these capabilities can be reported to those who are in charge of the different e-Selections.com divisions. You will begin your explorations using Word.

P R O J E C T   3

Common Graphics Elements

The Challenge

As you explore the Internet and specific Web pages, you will notice that graphics have been used extensively to create Web page designs. As you begin working with Office XP applications, you will be expected to know how to add graphics and drawings to the files you create using the different applications.

The Solution

Office XP applications share many of the same graphics and art elements. As a result, introducing the basic concepts of adding art images and drawing provides a base on which to build additional skills as you move through the different applications. Because you are already more familiar with Word than any of the other Office XP applications, you will continue to use Word as you develop your artistic talents.

 Troubleshooting Be sure to review the setup section of Common Elements Project 2 for screen features and other settings that affect this project.

Working with Clip Art

All Office XP applications share a common *Clip Organizer* that contains a variety of different images that you can add to files. The first time you access the Clip Organizer, the Office XP application takes a few moments to build the gallery and then presents *thumbnails*—very small copies—of the images.

Inserting Clip Art Images

Clip art images appear at the insertion point when you add them to most Office XP files. After you get the image in the file, you can position and size the image so that it appears in the file where you want it.

Task 1:
To Insert Clip Art Images

1 Launch Word, if necessary, and create a new blank document.

2 Choose **Insert | Picture | Clip Art** to open the Insert Clip Art task pane.

Figure 3-1

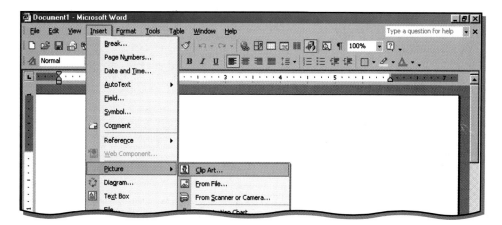

3 Type People in the **Search text** box and click **Search**.

Troubleshooting
Depending on the clip art that is installed on your computer, the graphics you see may be different from those displayed here.

Figure 3-2

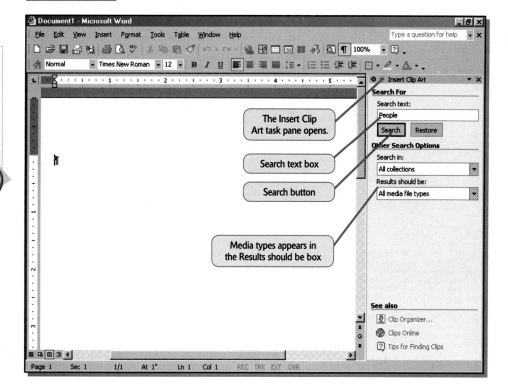

Tip   If Office XP has been installed more than one time on your computer, it is possible that you will see two sets of the same clip art images. If a previous version of Microsoft Office has been upgraded to Office XP, some image duplication may occur.

4 Point to one of the thumbnail images.

Figure 3-3

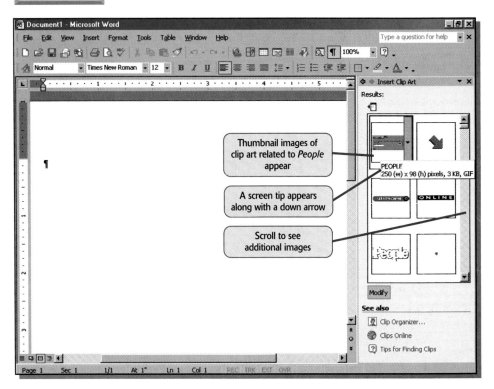

Troubleshooting
Screen tips may require several seconds to appear when you point to an image. Be careful to hold the mouse pointer still to see the screen tip.

Thumbnail images of clip art related to *People* appear

A screen tip appears along with a down arrow

Scroll to see additional images

5 Scroll to locate the image of the golfer similar to the image shown in Figure 3-4.

Figure 3-4

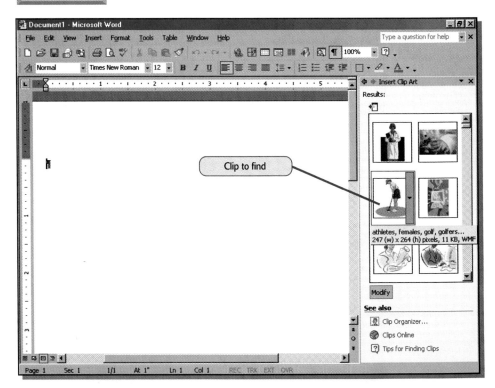

Tip The down arrow appears on the right side of the image to which you are pointing. Other images will not display a down arrow.

Clip to find

Click the thumbnail image in the task pane and save your file using the name *Your Initials Golfing.*

 Close the task pane.

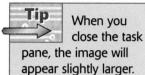 When you close the task pane, the image will appear slightly larger.

Troubleshooting
Clip art image size and position may appear distorted in Normal view. To view the images in better format, choose **View | Print Layout.**

Figure 3-5

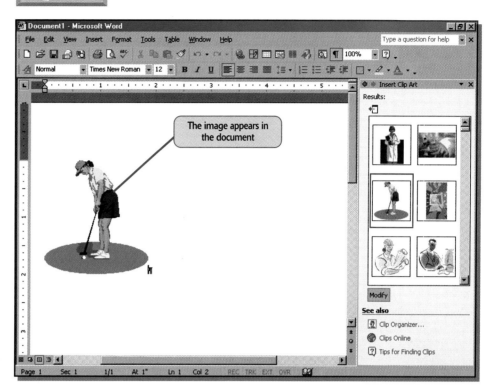

The image appears in the document

WEB TIP

The Internet is a great source for locating clip art to add to your files. You can search for sites containing clip art and download clips. In addition, Microsoft has set up a special site from which users can download new clips. Access the Microsoft Design Gallery Live from the task pane by clicking the Clips Online link or display the Clip Organizer and click the Clips Online toolbar button.

 Before you can move or size a clip art image that appears on a document, you must select it. The easiest way to select an image is to click it.

Moving and Sizing Clip Art Images

After you insert a clip art image into a file, you can size the image so that it fits the space you want it to occupy and move the image to position it more precisely. However, before you can move most clip art images, you have to change the image layout settings.

Task 2:
To Move and Size Clip Art Images

1 Launch Word and open the *Your Initials Golfing.doc* document, if necessary.

2 Click the golfer image and then position the insertion point on the black square in the lower right corner of the image.

Troubleshooting
If the rulers are hidden, choose **View | Ruler** to display them.

Figure 3-6

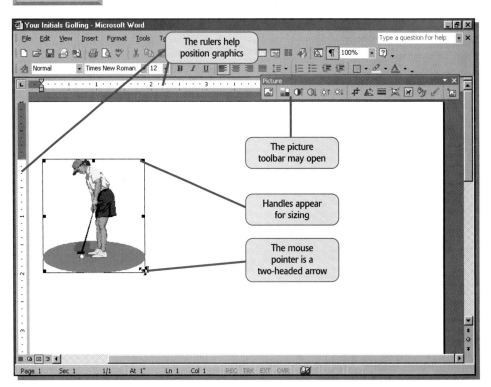

The rulers help position graphics

The picture toolbar may open

Handles appear for sizing

The mouse pointer is a two-headed arrow

3 Drag the corner handle until the right edge of the graphic appears at about the 4" mark on the horizontal ruler and to about the 4 1/2" mark on the vertical ruler.

4 Point to the center of the selected image and right-click. The shortcut menu appears.

5 Select **Format Picture**. The Format Object dialog box appears.

Figure 3-7

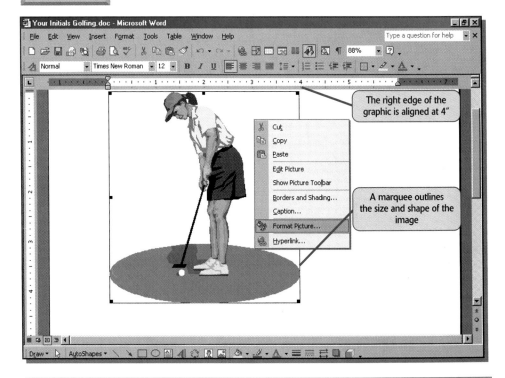

The right edge of the graphic is aligned at 4"

A marquee outlines the size and shape of the image

Cut
Copy
Paste
Edit Picture
Show Picture Toolbar
Borders and Shading...
Caption...
Format Picture...
Hyperlink...

Tip Options available in the Format Object dialog box vary depending on the type of object that is active. In addition, the page of the dialog box that appears is controlled, to some extent, by the type of object selected.

6 Click the **Layout** tab.

7 Select **Square** and then click **Advanced** to display the Advanced Layout dialog box.

Tip The default layout places clip art images and other pictures in line with text. In this case, it lines up the image at the left margin because text in the document is left-aligned by default.

Figure 3-8

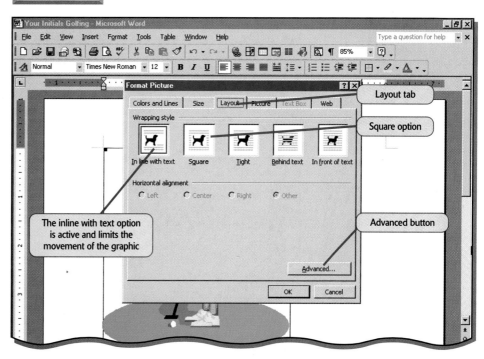

8 Clear the **Move object with text** option and click **OK** twice.

Tip Word normally attaches clip art you add to files to the text in the paragraph closest to the image. In this document, the picture is attached to the empty paragraph marker that appears on each new blank document you create. Because the paragraph is left-aligned, the clip art image appears left-aligned. Clearing the Move object with text option removes the invisible connection between the clip art image and the paragraph so that you can position the image anywhere on the page.

Figure 3-9

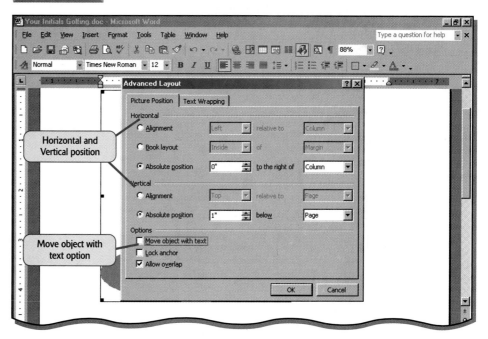

9 Point to the center of the image and click.

Tip Most clip art images can be rotated freely to position them at just the angle you want to display. To rotate an image, position the mouse pointer on the green circle that appears above the image. When you see a circular black arrow as the mouse pointer, drag the green circle to rotate the image.

Figure 3-10

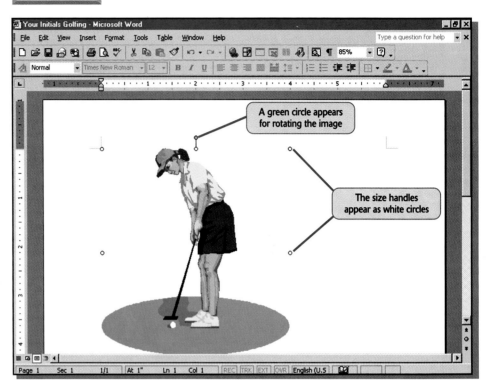

A green circle appears for rotating the image

The size handles appear as white circles

10 Drag the picture to a different location on the page.

11 Save changes to the file.

Troubleshooting
Be sure to position the mouse pointer in the middle of the figure you want to move rather than on a sizing handle. Dragging a size handle changes the figure size but leaves the left edge of the figure in its original position.

Figure 3-11

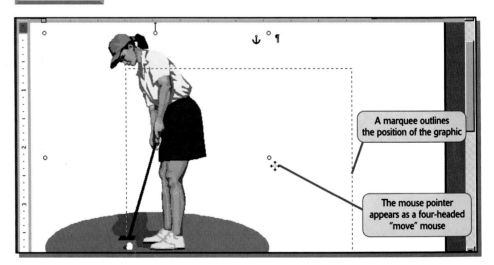

A marquee outlines the position of the graphic

The mouse pointer appears as a four-headed "move" mouse

Manipulating Clip Art Images

The white handles that appear on clip art images can be used to size the image, just as the black squares were used to adjust the image layout. After the image layout is adjusted so that you can move the graphic, the Rotate tool enables you to change the angle of the graphic. Clip art images can also be ungrouped so that different parts of the image can be edited, regrouped, flipped, and rotated.

Task 3:
To Ungroup Clip Art Images

1 Launch Word and open the *Your Initials Golfing.doc* document, if necessary.

2 Select the clip art image and click the **Drawing** button on the Standard toolbar.

Tip The Drawing button on the Standard toolbar opens the Drawing toolbar. The Drawing toolbar appears anchored at the bottom of the Word window by default. However, you can float or reposition the toolbar just as you can other toolbars.

3 Click the **Draw** **Draw ▼** button on the Drawing toolbar to display the Draw menu.

4 Click **Ungroup** to break the image into individual pieces.

Figure 3-12

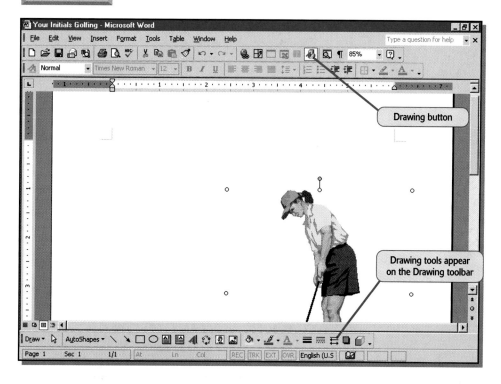

Figure 3-13

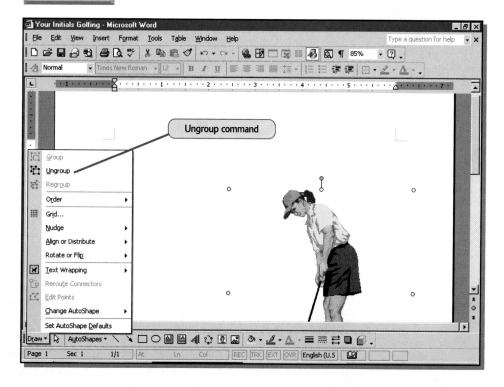

Tip

Each clip art image is compiled of numerous lines and shapes grouped together so that you can move and size the whole image. To change the color of a piece of the image, you must first ungroup it. When you ungroup a clip art image, handles appear on all the individual pieces that make up the image. In some cases, an image is made up of smaller groups images that can also be ungrouped.

5 Click **Yes** to convert the image to an Office object.

Figure 3-14

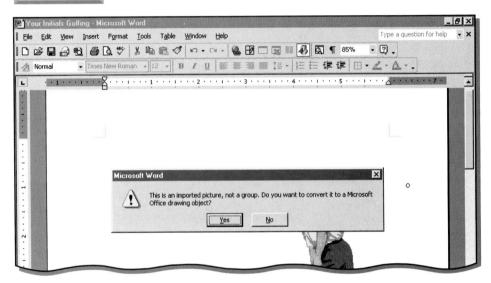

Tip Right-click on the Canvas edge and select **Show Drawing Canvas Toolbar**, if necessary, to display the *Drawing Canvas* toolbar.

6 Save changes to your work.

Figure 3-15

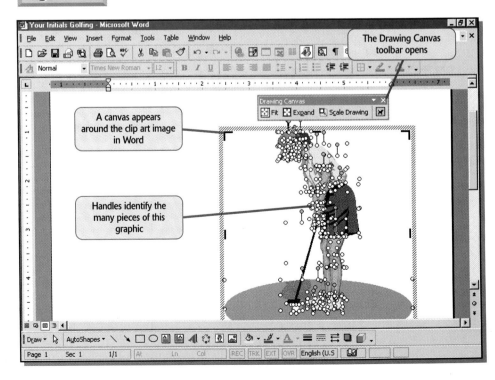

Task 4:
To Edit Clip Art Images

1 Click a white area away from the selected pieces, but inside the canvas border. All selection handles disappear.

2 Click the golfer's shorts to select the individual piece of the graphic.

3 Click the **Fill Color** down arrow on the Drawing toolbar and select the **Red** fill color. The shorts change color.

4 Click the **Expand** button on the Drawing Canvas toolbar two or three times to move the canvas border away from all parts of the graphic.

5 Position the mouse pointer below and to the right of the putting green, and then drag a marquee around all pieces of the clip art image.

6 Choose **Draw | Group** on the Drawing toolbar. The clip art image is reformed to a single object.

Figure 3-16

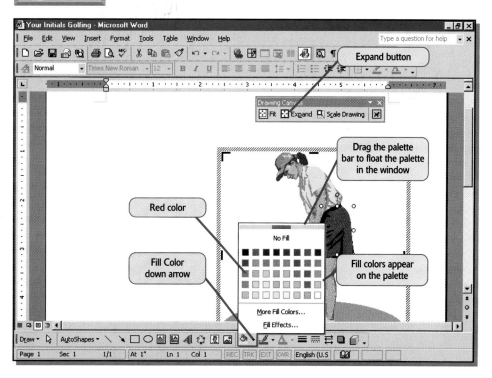

Figure 3-17

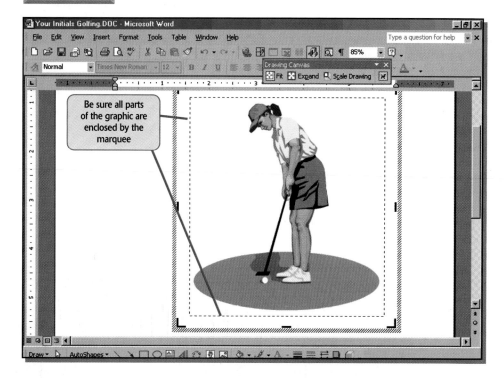

 Troubleshooting The Drawing Canvas is a feature unique to Word. As you work with clip art in other applications, you will not see the Drawing Canvas.

7 Choose **Draw | Rotate or Flip | Flip Horizontal**. The golfer faces the opposite direction.

8 Save changes to your work and close the file.

Tip Design specialists often recommend that clip art and pictures added to documents be positioned so that they face toward the middle of the page. Flipping a clip art image is a great way to make the image conform to good design recommendations.

Figure 3-18

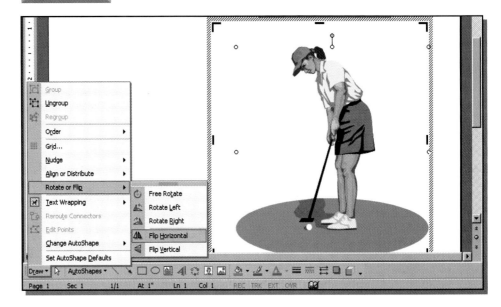

Displaying the Clip Organizer

In the previous tasks, you have worked with clip art that you inserted from the task pane. The Clip Organizer displays a list of folders containing the clip art that is available on your computer as well as other media clips, such as movies, sounds, and so forth. Images are grouped by type and placed in appropriate folders. Opening the folder related to the topic you are addressing displays thumbnails of the clip art that is available in the folder. Until you add images to the Favorites folder and download graphics from other sources, many of the folders are empty. The images displayed when you searched for banner clips are part of a set of standard clip art images that come with Office XP. These images are grouped by type into numerous folders in the Office Collection.

 CHECK POINT

Do you recall how you displayed clips in the task pane that relate to a specific topic? You typed the topic in the search box and then clicked Search.

Task 5:
To Display and Use the Clip Organizer

1 Launch Word, if necessary, and create a new blank document.

2 Choose **Insert | Picture | Clip Art**. The task pane opens.

3 Click the **Clip Organizer** link at the bottom of the task pane.

> ### Troubleshooting
> If this is the first time the Clip Organizer has been started on your machine, a Microsoft Clip Organizer message may appear. Check the **Don't show this message again** option and click **OK**. The system will build the Clip Organizer for you.

4 Click the **Expansion** 🔲 button beside the **Office Collections** folder to display collection subfolders.

Figure 3-19

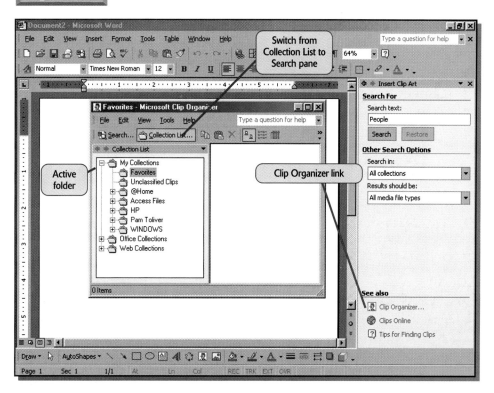

Figure 3-20

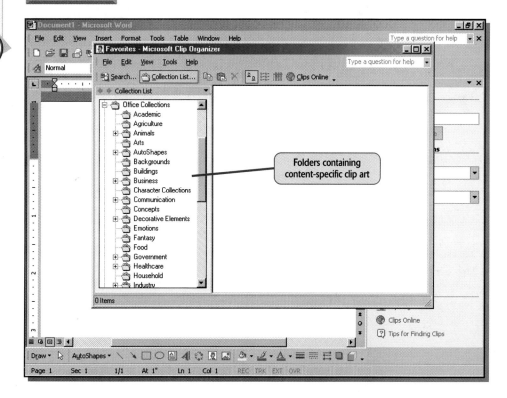

5 Select **Buildings** to open the folder and display thumbnail images contained in the folder.

6 Close the Clip Organizer and close the task pane.

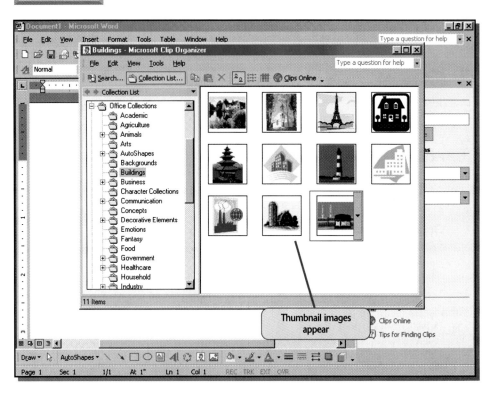

Figure 3-21

Thumbnail images appear

WEB TIP

As you locate clips on the Internet, you can download the clips and store them in the My Collections folders found in the Clip Organizer. You can also create new collection folders in My Collections. Simply select the My Collections folder, choose **File | New Collection,** type the name of the new collection folder, and click OK.

Inserting Graphic Images

 Tip Graphic images are easy to identify by their extensions. Look for files with extensions such as .jpg, .bmp, .tif, .wmf, and .pcx.

As you continue to work with Office XP applications, you will begin to acquire images from a variety of sources—from the Internet, from scanned images from friends and relatives, and from graphics collections that you purchase. As you accumulate these images, you will often want to insert them into Office XP files. The procedure for inserting graphic images basically uses the same techniques you used to insert clip art images.

Task 6:
To Insert Graphic Files

1 Open the *e-Selections Online Graphics.doc* file.

2 Position the insertion point at the top of the document and choose **Insert | Picture | From File** to open the Insert Picture dialog box.

3 Open the disk and folder containing the *e-Selections Logo.jpg*

4 Select **e-Selections Logo** and then click **Insert** to place the figure in the document.

5 Change the layout of the graphic so that you can reposition it freely on screen and then size and position the graphic so that it appears in the upper left corner outside the margin area, as shown in Figure 3-23.

6 Save changes to the file and print a copy of the document.

Tip While most clip art images can be ungrouped and edited, pictures you insert into files usually require a graphics editing program to edit.

Figure 3-22

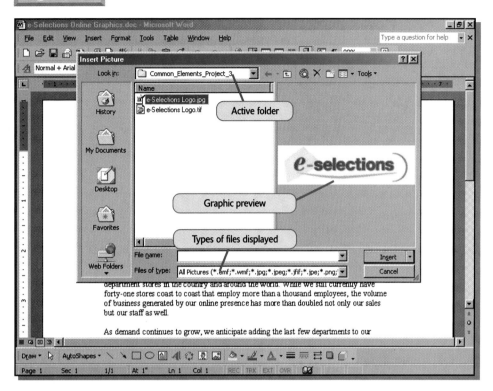

Figure 3-23

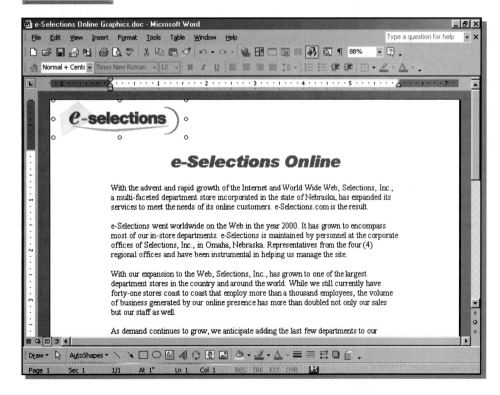

CHECK POINT

Have you received pictures of your relatives attached to an e-mail message? Have you been impressed by photos that appear in newsletters? Perhaps you've even seen family photos on personal Web pages. If you have, you may have wondered how your family and friends converted their pictures to electronic files that can be sent with messages and posted on the Web.

Microsoft Office contains features that enable you to scan photographs and save them as graphics. Then it's simply a matter of inserting the files in e-mail messages or positioning the file in newsletter documents. You will, of course, need a scanner or a *digital camera* and you will also need to know the basics of how to use this equipment. Once you've got the equipment under control, you can get graphics directly from a scanner or camera using Microsoft Office XP applications. From any Microsoft Office Application, choose **Insert | Picture | From Scanner or Camera** and follow the screen prompts to capture the picture. Then use the skills you've learned in this project to manipulate the graphic.

Creating and Formatting WordArt

Task 7:
To Create WordArt

WordArt is a feature that enables you to dress up your files by creating graphic text—shaping text on curves and flows. WordArt is easy to create and can be positioned in a file to fit the size and shape you need. You can use WordArt to create a letterhead for your e-Selections stationery.

1 Launch Word, if necessary, display the Drawing toolbar, if necessary, and open a copy of *e-Selections Online Graphics.doc.*

Figure 3-24

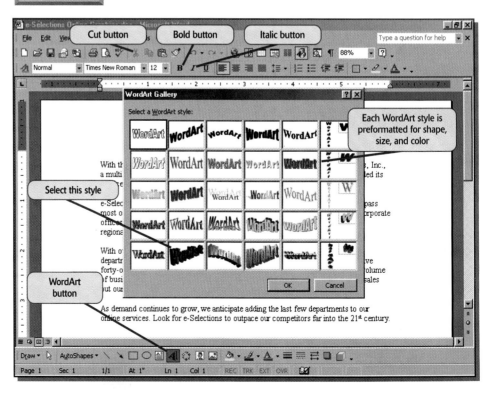

2 Delete the logo graphics, select the title text, and then click the **Cut** ✂ button to place the text on the clipboard.

3 Click the **Bold B** and **Italic** *I* buttons to turn them off, if necessary.

4 Click the **Insert WordArt** 🖋 button on the Drawing toolbar to open the WordArt Gallery.

5 Double-click the WordArt style identified in Figure 3-24.

6 Press Ctrl + V to insert the title text and then click **OK**.

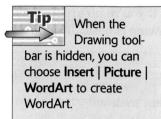

Tip When the Drawing toolbar is hidden, you can choose **Insert | Picture | WordArt** to create WordArt.

Figure 3-25

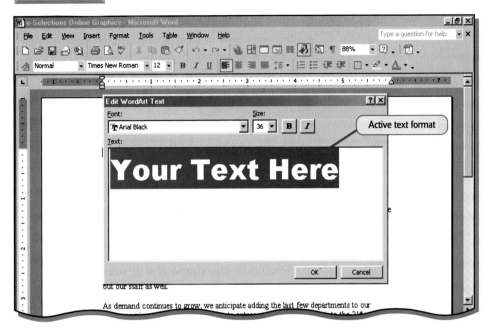

7 Save the document using the file name *Your Initials WordArt* and then close all open files.

WEB TIP

If you've purchased a book, a CD, a movie, or a video game lately, you know how quickly costs associated with these purchases can add up. Search the Web for online companies that act as resellers of these popular media items. You'll find that you can save more than half the cost by buying previously owned items!

Figure 3-26

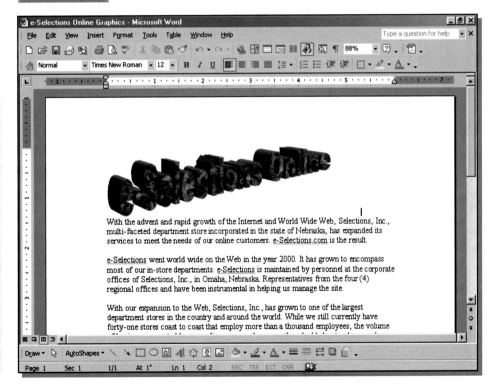

5 Click **OK** and then select the vertical oval on the left.

6 Display the **Fill Effects** dialog box and set the options listed in Step 4, changing the Shading Styles to **Diagonal Down**; then click **OK**.

7 Click the **Line Color** ✎ ▾ drop-down list arrow and select **No Line**.

8 Save the file using the file name *Your Initials Floating Circles*.

> **Tip** Removing the line from drawn objects makes them appear to blend in with other drawn objects or with file background colors.

Task 11:

To Change a Drawn Shape

1 Launch Word and open the *Your Initials Floating Circles.doc* document, if necessary.

2 Select the oval on the right to select it.

Figure 3-38

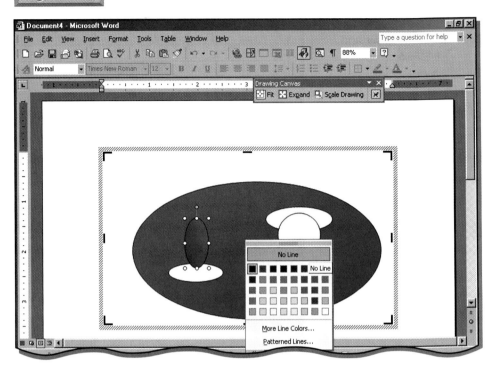

Changing Shapes

After a shape is created and formatted, you can change the shape just as you change the line and fill colors. The format you apply to drawn shapes can create special effects.

Figure 3-39

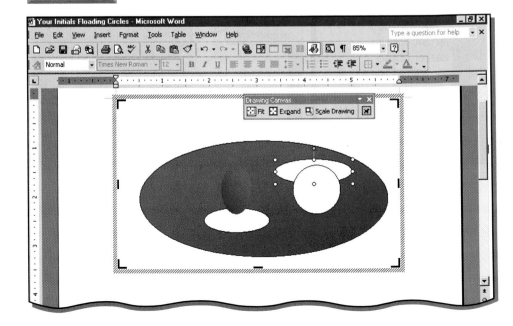

6 Press Ctrl + V to insert the title text and then click **OK**.

Figure 3-25

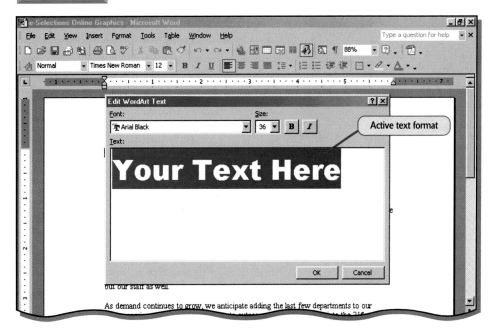

Tip When the Drawing toolbar is hidden, you can choose **Insert | Picture | WordArt** to create WordArt.

7 Save the document using the file name *Your Initials WordArt* and then close all open files.

Figure 3-26

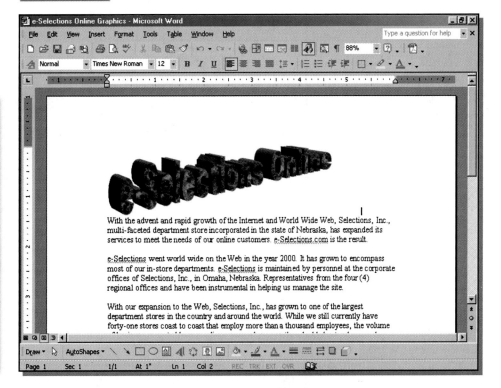

WEB TIP

If you've purchased a book, a CD, a movie, or a video game lately, you know how quickly costs associated with these purchases can add up. Search the Web for online companies that act as resellers of these popular media items. You'll find that you can save more than half the cost by buying previously owned items!

Creating and Manipulating Drawings

When you want to add shapes, lines, text boxes, and arrows to your Office XP files, you will find a sophisticated set of drawing tools that enable you to enhance files with original freehand creations. Even if you're no artist, you'll find the tools on the Drawing toolbar easy to use. Drawing is basically a three-step process:

1 Select the tool that represents the shape you want to draw.

2 Position the pointer where you want to start the drawing.

3 Click and drag the pointer to the shape ending point.

Then, while the shape is still selected, you can move, size, and edit the shape as needed.

Creating Basic Shapes and AutoShapes

Buttons for the shapes that are drawn most frequently appear on the Drawing toolbar. Other shapes are found grouped by type on the *AutoShapes* menu found on the Drawing toolbar.

Task 8:

To Create Shapes

1 Launch Word, if necessary, and create a new blank document.

2 Display the Drawing toolbar, if necessary, and click the **Rectangle** button.

Figure 3-27

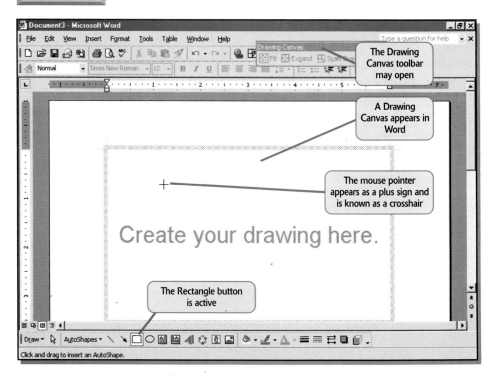

3 Position the *crosshair* mouse pointer on the left side of the Drawing Canvas and then click and drag the crosshair diagonally to form a rectangle.

Tip You can set different colors for shape fills and border. In addition, you can change the line size to add weight to shape borders. Experiment with drawing tools to create different types of custom effects.

Figure 3-28

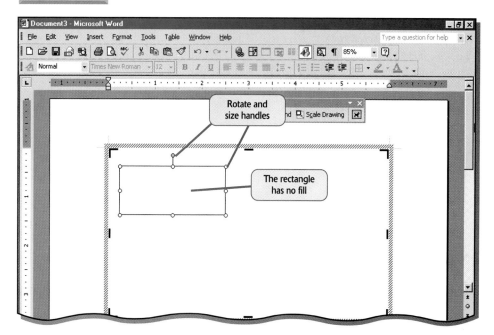

4 Click the **Fill Color** button to fill the rectangle with the default fill color.

5 Click the **AutoShapes** menu on the Drawing toolbar.

6 Select **Basic Shapes** to open the Basic Shapes palette and select the **Lightning Bolt** shape.

Tip Point to each shape on the Basic Shapes palette to identify the different shapes available. Screen tips help locate specific shapes.

Figure 3-29

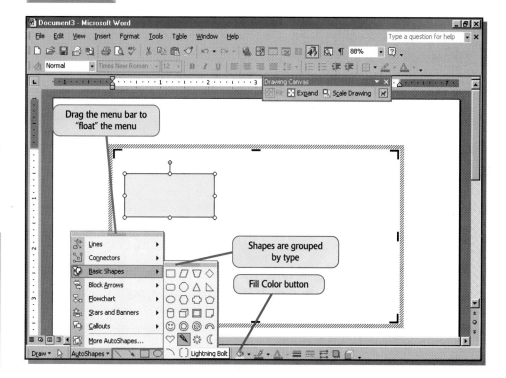

7 Repeat the procedures outlined in Steps 3 and 4 to create a lightning bolt shape to the right of the rectangle and fill it with color.

Figure 3-30

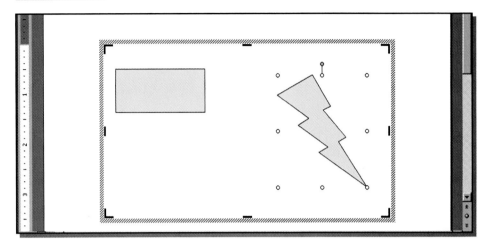

 CHECK POINT

As you become more comfortable with the drawing tools available in Microsoft Office Applications, you'll find yourself wanting to be more precise in drawing shapes. Here are some tips to get you started and help you position and size both clip art and drawn objects:

- Press and hold the Ctrl key as you size objects to size the object from the center point out.

- Press and hold the Shift key while you draw lines to make them straight and while you draw shapes to make them symmetrical—rectangles become squares, ovals become circles, and triangles are equilateral.

- Press and hold the Alt key to release the "snap to" feature so that you can move a boundary or size a shape more precisely.

Formatting Shapes

You can use many of the same techniques that you used to format clip art to format drawn objects. You can size, flip, rotate, and change the color of drawn objects just as you can edit and manipulate clip art.

Setting Wrap Text Options. Text can be added to most drawn objects. After adding text, you will often need to change the text wrap option so that text appears properly on the drawn object.

Task 9:
To Set Text Wrap Options

1 Right-click the **lightning bolt** and select **Add Text**. The insertion point appears within the lightning bolt.

Figure 3-31

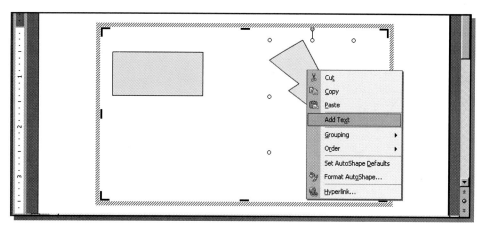

2 Type **Lightning Strikes Again!**

Figure 3-32

Troubleshooting
Text may be hidden as you type. Don't worry— we're about to fix it.

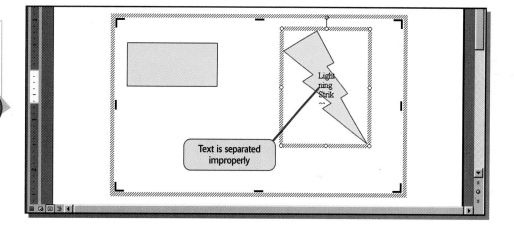

3 Right-click a blank area of the lightning bolt and select **Format AutoShape** to open the Format AutoShape dialog box.

4 Click the **Text Box** tab, select the **Resize AutoShape to fit text** option, and then click **OK**. The lightning bolt changes size to accommodate the text.

Figure 3-33

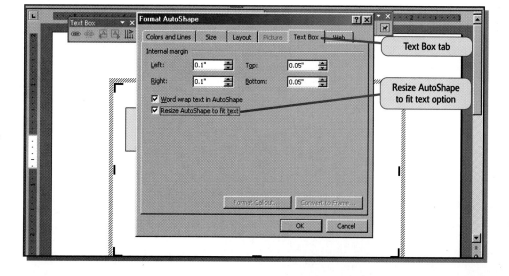

5 Manually drag handles to size the lightning bolt so that the text is within the bolt boundaries.

6 Close the document without saving the changes.

Figure 3-34

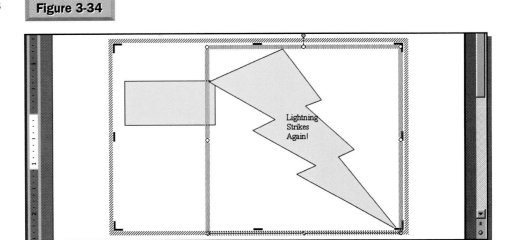

Changing the Fill and Line Color. Fill and line color can be changed to format drawn objects. In addition, special fill effects can be used to create special visual effects.

Task 10:
To Create Special Effects Using Fill and Line Color

1 Create a new blank document in Word.

2 Double-click the **Oval** ◯ button on the Drawing toolbar and create the drawing shown in Figure 3-35.

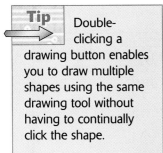

Tip Double-clicking a drawing button enables you to draw multiple shapes using the same drawing tool without having to continually click the shape.

Figure 3-35

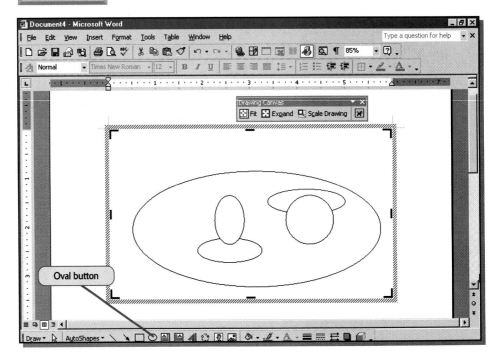

Oval button

3 Press Esc, select the largest oval in the Drawing Canvas, click the **Fill Color** down arrow, and select **Fill Effects** to open the Fill Effects dialog box.

Tip The Fill Effects dialog box contains tabbed pages that display a number of different fill effect options. Explore these effects as time permits.

Figure 3-36

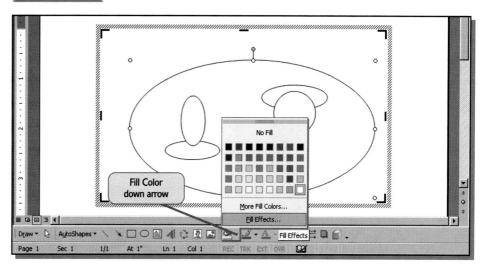

4 Click the **Gradient** tab and set the following options:
- Two colors
- Color 1: Light Blue
- Color 2: Dark Blue
- Shading Styles: Diagonal up

Troubleshooting
After you select a shading style, the Variants palette displays different shading angles. The active variant appears with a darker border that is sometimes easy to miss.

Figure 3-37

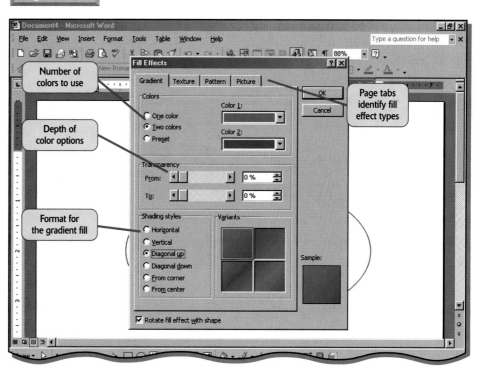

5 Click **OK** and then select the vertical oval on the left.

6 Display the **Fill Effects** dialog box and set the options listed in Step 4, changing the Shading Styles to **Diagonal Down**; then click **OK**.

7 Click the **Line Color** drop-down list arrow and select **No Line**.

8 Save the file using the file name *Your Initials Floating Circles*.

> **Tip** Removing the line from drawn objects makes them appear to blend in with other drawn objects or with file background colors.

Task 11:
To Change a Drawn Shape

1 Launch Word and open the *Your Initials Floating Circles.doc* document, if necessary.

2 Select the oval on the right to select it.

Figure 3-38

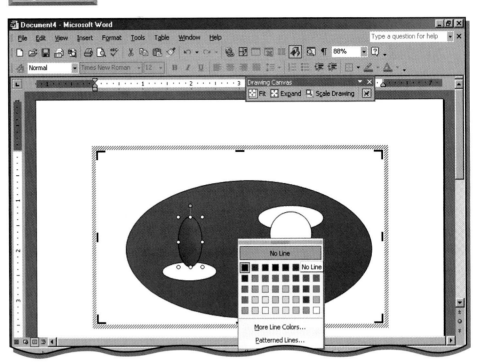

Changing Shapes

After a shape is created and formatted, you can change the shape just as you change the line and fill colors. The format you apply to drawn shapes can create special effects.

Figure 3-39

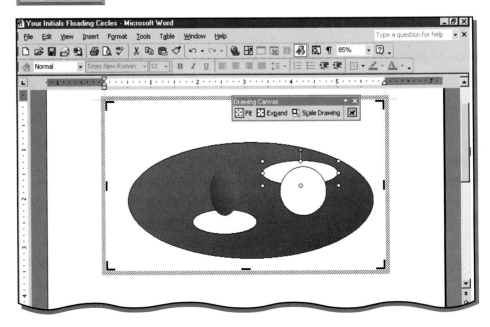

3 Choose **Draw | Change AutoShape | Basic Shapes**.

4 Select the **Change Shape to Rectangle** shape on the Basic Shapes palette.

Tip Notice that the screen tip that appears when you point to different shapes on the palette includes the "Change Shape to" text to let you know that you are changing an existing shape to a different shape. When no drawn shape is selected, the screen tip simply identifies the shape.

Figure 3-40

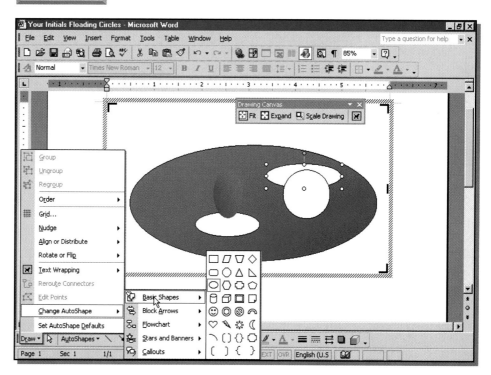

5 Save and close the document and exit Word.

Troubleshooting You will work with this diagram in the exercises at the end of Project 3, so be sure to save it.

Figure 3-41

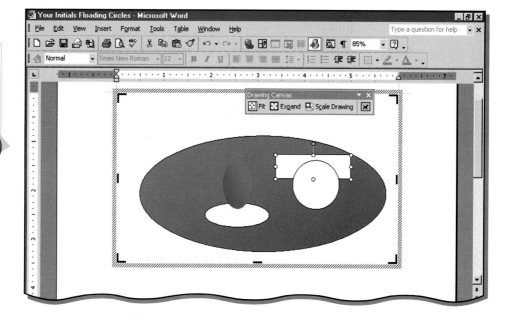

SUMMARY AND EXERCISES

SUMMARY

- Clip art images, scanned images, WordArt, and manual drawings enable you to dress up files in all Office XP applications.
- The Clip Organizer contains graphics on a number of topics and enables you to search by topic for related images.
- Clip art images added to Office XP files can be flipped, rotated, ungrouped, edited, and regrouped.
- Graphics scanned into computers or input from digital cameras as well as files of graphics received from other sources or downloaded from the Internet can be inserted in Office XP files.
- WordArt enables you to graphically format text to enhance Office XP files.
- The sophisticated set of drawing tools on the Drawing toolbar enables you to create original freehand art.
- When a shape or object is inserted, you can move, size, and edit the selected item.
- AutoShapes are grouped by type on the AutoShapes menu of the Drawing toolbar.
- Text can be added to most drawn shapes as well as to clip art and graphic items inserted into files.
- The shape chosen for a particular drawing can be changed to different shapes without deleting the original shape and redrawing it.
- Fill and line color can be changed for drawn shapes as well as for pieces of ungrouped clip art objects.

KEY TERMS & SKILLS

KEY TERMS

AutoShapes (p. 3-18)	fill (p. 3-11)
clip art (p. 3-1)	gradient (p. 3-23)
Clip Organizer (p. 3-2)	scanned images (p. 3-1)
crosshair (p. 3-19)	thumbnails (p. 3-2)
digital camera (p. 3-16)	WordArt (p. 3-1)
Drawing Canvas (p. 3-10)	

SKILLS　　Change a drawn shape (p. 3-24)
Create special effects using fill and line
　　color (p. 3-22)
Create WordArt (p. 3-16)
Display and use the Clip Organizer
　　(p. 3-132)
Draw shapes (p. 3-18)
Edit clip art images (p. 3-11)

Insert clip art images (p. 3-2)
Insert graphics from scanners and
　　digital cameras (p. 3-14)
Move and size clip art images
　　(p. 3-5)
Set text wrap options (p. 3-21)
Ungroup clip art images (p. 3-9)

STUDY QUESTIONS

MULTIPLE CHOICE

1. The dialog box that displays clip art images is the
   a. Format Object.
   b. Clip Organizer.
   c. Drawing Palette.
   d. Edit Picture.

2. When you search for clip art images that are related to a particular topic, possible images that meet your needs appear in the
   a. task pane.
   b. active file.
   c. status bar.
   d. toolbars.

3. All of the following are different types of graphic images *except*
   a. .tif.
   b. .pcx.
   c. .jpg.
   d. .xfx.

4. The button on the Standard toolbar that displays the Drawing toolbar is
   a. Tables and Borders 🔲.
   b. Insert Hyperlink 🌐.
   c. Drawing 🎨.
   d. Insert Chart 📊.

5. Before you can move most clip art images, you must change which settings?
   a. Picture Layout
   b. Graphic Format
   c. Image Size
   d. Object Format

6. To create a letterhead that arches over the top of a page, you would choose which feature?
   a. Headers
   b. Clip Art
   c. TextFont
   d. WordArt

7. Clearing which option restores free placement of a graphic?
   a. enable overlapping
   b. lock anchor
   c. move object with text
   d. none of the above

8. The toolbar that contains tools for drawing free shapes is the
   a. Standard toolbar.
   b. Picture toolbar.
   c. Drawing toolbar.
   d. Web toolbar.

9. The Change AutoShape command is found on what menu?
   a. Format
   b. Insert
   c. AutoShapes
   d. Draw

10. To view all text added to drawn shapes, it is sometimes necessary to set the
    a. wrap text options.
    b. shape format.
    c. fill color.
    d. line color.

SHORT ANSWER

1. What are the first three steps of adding a clip art picture to a file?
2. What commands do you use to fill a drawn object with two different colors and where are the commands located?
3. Which feature would you use to draw lines, arrows, and boxes?
4. What steps would you follow to insert a graphic from the Internet?
5. Where is the AutoShapes menu located?
6. How are shapes organized on the AutoShapes menu?
7. What are the very small copies of images in the Clip Gallery called?
8. How do you add text to drawn objects?
9. What is the difference between flipping an object and rotating it?
10. What are some additional sources for graphics that you can add to files?

FILL IN THE BLANK

1. _____ is a feature that enables you to dress up files by creating graphic text.
2. Office XP applications share a common _____ that contains a variety of different images you can add to your files.
3. _____ appear on selected images, which enable you to resize or drag the object.
4. Clip art images are stored in collection _____ that sort images by type.
5. Before you can change the color of a piece of a clip art image, you must first _____ it.
6. The Drawing Canvas for drawing shapes appears only in the _____ application.
7. Color added to the center of drawn objects is called _____.
8. Small copies of clip art images are called _____.
9. Commands for adding graphics to Office XP files appear on the _____ menu.
10. Graphics can be captured as electronic files from printed pictures using a _____.

DISCUSSION

1. Describe the steps you would follow to move and resize a clip art image.
2. How do the procedures for adding clip art differ from the procedures for adding other graphics to Office XP files?
3. When would you use the Clip Organizer instead of the task pane for adding items to Office XP files?
4. Explain the procedures you would follow to put a clip art image back together.

GUIDED EXERCISES

1 FLOATING OBJECTS

The ovals and rectangles you added to the *Your Initials Floating Circles.doc* document are not yet complete. The finished graphic is pictured in Figure 3-42.

Figure 3-42

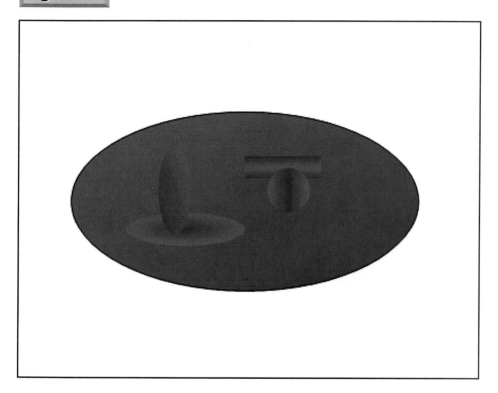

You can complete this task before moving on to other tasks. Follow these instructions:

1 Launch Word and open *Your Initials Floating Circles.doc*, if necessary.

2 Display the Drawing toolbar, if necessary.

3 Select one of the unfilled ovals.

4 Click the **Fill Color** ⬧ ▾ button on the Drawing toolbar and select **Fill Effects**.

5 Set the following options on the Gradient page of the Fill Effects dialog box:
  - Colors: Two colors
  - Color 1 Light Blue
  - Color 2 Dark Blue

Create the graphic for the flyer by following these steps:

1 Launch Word, if necessary, and create a new blank document.

2 Create the square in the center of the building blocks and set the following options:

- Change the fill color to green.
- Click the **Line Style** ≣ button on the Drawing toolbar and select **3 pt**.

3 Choose **AutoShapes | Basic Shapes | Isosceles Triangle**, draw and position the triangle as shown in Figure 38, and set the following format:

- Change the fill color to blue.
- Change the line style to 3 pt.

4 Draw the ellipse, position it as shown, and set the following format:

- Change the fill color to yellow.
- Change the line style to 3 pt.

5 Right-click each of the drawn objects separately, type the text shown, and format the text as follows:

- Center the text in all shapes.
- Change the size of text in the first line to 28 pts.
- Italicize text on the second line.

6 Adjust the size of the objects to accommodate the text.

7 Save your file using the file name *Your Initials Building Blocks* and print a copy of the file.

ON YOUR OWN

The difficulty of these case studies varies: *are the least difficult;* *are more difficult; and* *are the most difficult.*

1 ADDING A TEXT BOX

Open the file *Phantom Ghosties.doc*. Insert a text box below the existing text on the second page and type **Phantom Ghost** in the text box. Center the text box and arrange the text so that it appears on one line. Size and format the text in the text box using the same font and size as text in the document but change the text color to black and fill the text box with orange background. Save changes to the file and print a copy of the document.

2 LOCATING LICENSE AGREEMENTS FOR CLIP ART USAGE

Search the Internet for clip art. Visit numerous sites and locate at least two different license agreements for downloading the clip art collections that you find. Print copies of the license agreements.

3 CREATING A FUN NOTICE GRAPHIC

Open the file *Phantom Ghosties.doc*. Access Clips Online to locate a clip of a ghost. Insert the clip art of a ghost below the text box. Format the graphic so that it is centered on the page and size the graphic so that it covers a large portion of the page. Save changes to the file and print a copy of the file.

4 FINDING CLIP ART ONLINE, INSERTING CLIP ART, AND ADDING TEXT

 Search the Microsoft Design Gallery Live site for clip art graphics of apples. Download the apple you like best. Then create a new blank document in Word and add the clip art image of the apple to the document. Size the graphic so that it encompasses most of the page and position the apple in the center of the page. Then add the following text to a text box in the center of the apple:

An apple or two for lunch on Monday is an excellent antidote to a weekend of overeating. Apples travel well, come in their own packaging, and keep for a long time. What could be simpler?

Center the text in the text box and size and format the text as desired. Then change the fill color of the text box to the color of the apple. Save your file using the file name *Your Initials An Apple a Day* and print a copy of the file.

5 CREATING STATIONERY USING WORDART

Create personal stationery that contains each of the following features:

- WordArt containing your name.
- A text box containing your address and phone number—formatted using a unique font.
- A graphic that represents your personality.

Size and arrange the features attractively on the page in such a way that there is room to type letters on the stationery. Save the document using the file name *Your Initials Personal Stationery*.

6 CREATING FAMILIAR LOGOS

Many logos are quite popular and easily recognized by the general population. However, how easy are these logos to duplicate? Locate at least three logos that appear relatively simple in their construction and try to recreate these logos altogether on the same page of a document. Then download a copy of the logo from the Internet and insert the graphic logo beside your reconstructed logo. Save the file using the file name *Your Initials Logos* and print a copy of the file.

You Will Need

✔ **Time Tracking.doc**
✔ **Promo Proposal.doc**
✔ **Demographic Report by Matthew.doc**
✔ **IdentifyingTools.doc**
✔ **IdentifyingCommands.doc**

FROM THE FILES

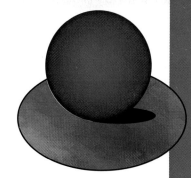

Introducing Word 2002

W ord is the key program in the Microsoft Office suite—and with good reason. Almost every person, business, or organization that uses a computer uses a word processing program. Word processing programs create all the traditional documents, such as reports, memos, letters, envelopes, and labels. In Word, you will find a large array of features for creating simple as well as complex documents. These features are easy to learn and easy to use, so you'll be creating great-looking documents in no time.

e-selections) Running Case

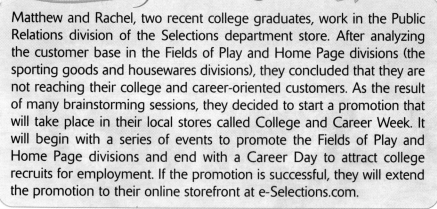

Matthew and Rachel, two recent college graduates, work in the Public Relations division of the Selections department store. After analyzing the customer base in the Fields of Play and Home Page divisions (the sporting goods and housewares divisions), they concluded that they are not reaching their college and career-oriented customers. As the result of many brainstorming sessions, they decided to start a promotion that will take place in their local stores called College and Career Week. It will begin with a series of events to promote the Fields of Play and Home Page divisions and end with a Career Day to attract college recruits for employment. If the promotion is successful, they will extend the promotion to their online storefront at e-Selections.com.

OBJECTIVES

After completing this project, you will be able to:

* *Launch Word*

* *Identify window elements*

* *Identify indicators and icons in the status bar*

* *Set Word defaults*

* *Open multiple documents*

* *Change the view*

* *Check spelling and grammar*

* *Preview a document*

* *Print a document*

* *E-mail a document*

* *Close a document and exit Word*

Introducing Word 2002

The Challenge

Matthew and Rachel have drafted a preliminary proposal to send to the vice president of sales and the vice president of operations to see if they are interested in the idea. It will be your job as the administrative assistant to proofread the proposal and print the final document that will go to the VPs.

The Solution

You will use various views of the document while you are proofreading, and you will use the Spelling and Grammar tool to correct any spelling or grammar errors. Before printing the document, you will use the Print Preview to make sure the formatting looks good. After printing the final document, you will e-mail a copy of the document to Matthew and Rachel.

Figure 0-1

Memorandum

To:	Deborah Ritch and John Vicenti
CC:	Anne Hanson
From:	Matthew Brainard and Rachel Crawford
Date:	3/15/01
Re:	Proposed promotional campaign

Conclusive research data indicate that we could be doing more to attract purchases from the college and career age group (from 19 to 23 years of age), particularly in the Fields and Home Page departments. By comparison, the percentage of buyers in this group is as much as 10-20% lower in these two departments than in all other departments in the store.

Rachel Crawford and I propose that the five stores in our home state host a College and Career Week with special events and sales aimed at this group. Special events would include appearances by celebrities, seminars, and sales.

If a significant increase in sales occurs, we recommend rolling out the promotion to all stores across the country. Although some of the events that we propose can take place only at the local stores, we recommend a corresponding promotion on our Web site.

If you are interested in this promotion, Rachel and I are prepared to supply you with a detailed proposal.

Thank you for your consideration.

Figure 0-1 shows how the finished proposal looks after editing.

Launching Word

There are several ways to launch Word. In the next task, you will use one of the most common methods. For other methods, see Common Elements Project 1.

Task 1:
To Launch Word

1 Click the Start button and point to **Programs**.

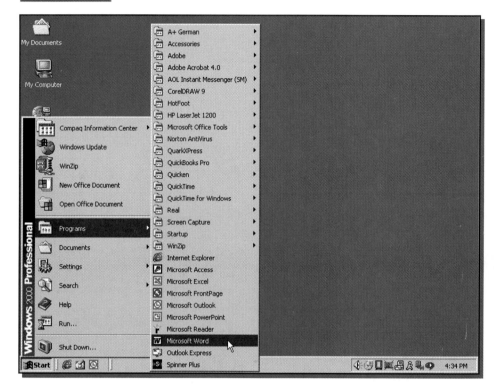

Figure 0-2

2 Select **Microsoft Word**. The Word window opens and Document1 appears in the document window.

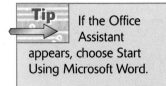

Tip If the Office Assistant appears, choose Start Using Microsoft Word.

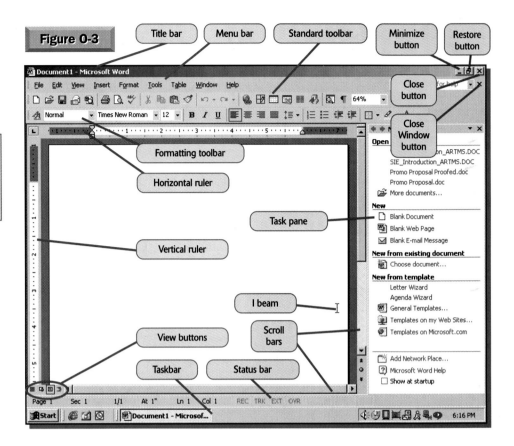

Figure 0-3

Troubleshooting Because some screen elements can be hidden and the Word window can be customized in different ways, your screen may not look exactly like the one in Figure 0-3. For example, the two default toolbars, *Standard* and *Formatting*, may occupy only one line below the menu bar, or the task pane may be displayed. (See Resetting Menus and Toolbars in Common Elements Project 1.)

Identifying Window Elements

The Word window has many of the common elements of a typical window, such as a title bar, menu bar, and scroll bars. It also has many elements that are unique to Word. Table 0-1 describes the elements that are unique to Word.

Table 0-1	Elements of the Word Window
Element	**Description**
I-beam	The *I-beam* is the name of the mouse cursor. To position the insertion point in text, you must click the I-beam. In Word, the *Click and Type* feature also uses the I-beam to position the insertion point in blank areas of the document. When the I-beam moves through a blank area of the document, an icon connected to the I-beam displays the alignment that will be applied to text if you use Click and Type in that area. You will learn more about the Click and Type feature in Project 1.
Insertion point	The *insertion point* is a vertical blinking line that marks the typing position.
View buttons	The View buttons, located on the left side of the horizontal scroll bar, change the view of the document. They are, from left to right, *Normal View*, *Web Layout View*, *Print Layout View*, and *Outline View*.
Rulers	Word has two rulers—a horizontal ruler below the toolbars and a *vertical ruler* at the left edge of the screen. The term *ruler* always applies to the horizontal ruler. It displays the settings for the margins, tabs, and indents, and it can be used to make these settings as well. The vertical ruler appears only in the Print Layout view and only if the option to display it is selected. It displays the top and bottom margins.
Browse buttons	The *Browse buttons,* located at the bottom of the vertical scroll bar, include the following default buttons (from top to bottom): Previous Page, Select Browse Object, and Next Page. The Select Browse Object button displays a palette of objects, such as graphics and tables, that you can use to browse through a document. If you select the Graphics object, the names of the Previous/Next Page buttons change to Previous/Next Graphic. Clicking the Next Graphic button moves the insertion point forward in the document to the next graphic.

Tip To display or hide the Vertical ruler in the Print Layout view, choose **Tools | Options**. Click the **View** tab, if necessary, and select or clear the check for the **Vertical ruler** (Print view only) option. Then click **OK**.

Identifying Indicators and Icons in the Status Bar

The status bar is a screen element found in every Microsoft Office XP application. What appears in the status bar is unique to each application. The information that appears in the status bar in Word is different from the information that appears in the status bar in Excel. Figure 0-4 shows a typical status bar in a Word document. Notice that some of the elements on the status bar (REC, TRK, EXT, and OVR) are dim, which indicates that the features are not currently active. These elements are *status indicators*. The REC indicator is active when a macro is being recorded, the TRK indicator is active when the Track Changes feature is on, the EXT indicator is active when Extend Selection mode is on, and the OVR indicator is active when Overtype mode is on.

Tip Double-clicking an indicator turns the feature on or off.

2 Click the AutoCorrect tab. Set the options to match those shown in Figure 0-6.

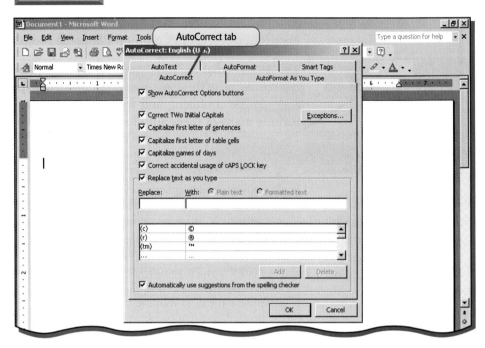

3 Click the **AutoFormat As You Type** tab and set the options to match those shown in Figure 0-7.

Troubleshooting

It is important that settings on your computer match those shown in Figure 0-7. Be sure to clear the checkmarks from options on AutoFormat As You Type that appear unchecked.

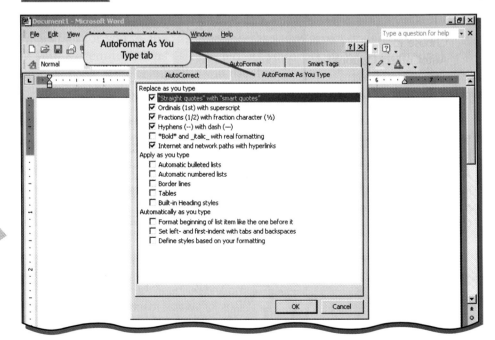

4 Click the **AutoText** tab and clear the **Show AutoComplete suggestions** check box, if necessary.

Tip The Show AutoComplete suggestions option, when active, displays a suggested word or phrase when you type the first four letters of certain items—dates, months, days of the week, etc. When a suggestion appears on screen, you can press `Enter` to complete the typing of the suggestion. The continual appearance of these suggestions can become annoying and can also lead to unexpected text entry when you press `Enter` without realizing that the suggestion is active. Turning off the option prevents suggestions from appearing onscreen.

5 Click the **Smart Tags** tab and select all options.

6 Click **OK**.

Figure 0-8

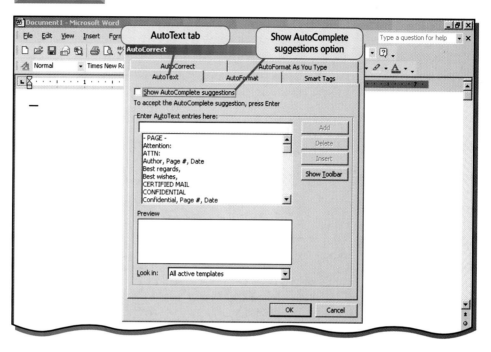

Figure 0-9

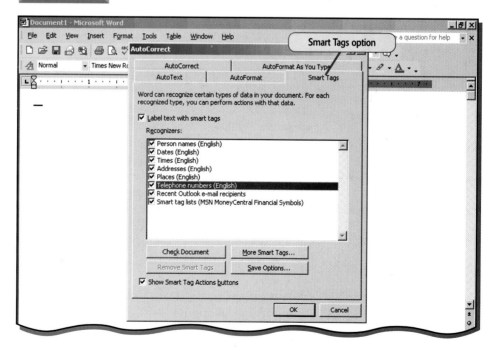

Tip Buttons that appear at the bottom of the Smart Tags page enable you to check the document for Smart Tags, access additional Smart Tags on the Microsoft Web site, set Smart Tag options, and remove Smart Tags. These settings are usually controlled by information technology specialists and may be unavailable on your computer.

Setting Additional Options

Options set in other Office XP applications affect the way Word appears when you launch it. As a result, the features displayed in the Word window on your computer may be different from those shown here. Table 0-1 shows the settings that are used throughout Word. Please change your settings to reflect those in the table. As you progress through the tasks in this section, you will display and hide additional screen elements as needed.

Table 0-1 Word Settings	
Feature	**Setting**
Office Shortcut bar	Close the Office Shortcut bar
Office Assistant	Hide the Office Assistant
Toolbars	Close all toolbars except the Standard, Formatting, and Drawing toolbars. Choose **Tools | Customize | Options** and check the **Show Standard and Formatting toolbars on two rows option**.
Menus	Choose **Tools | Customize| Options** and select the **Always show full menus option**.
Task pane	Choose View | Task Pane to display the task pane.

Opening Multiple Documents

In all Office programs, you can open multiple files. Each file opens in its own window, called a *document window*, and each window appears as a button on the taskbar. Of course, you can work in only one document window at a time, and the document window that you are working in is the *active window*. Clicking the document window button on the taskbar is the easiest way to select the window you want to work in, but you can select a document from the Window menu as well.

> **Tip**   In every Word document window, the names of the other Word documents that are open appear at the bottom of the Window menu. Clicking a document name in the Window menu makes that window active.

When a document is open in Word, the Word window looks like the one in the background of Figure 0-16. Notice that there are two buttons in the upper right corner that look the same. One is in the application title bar and one is in the menu bar. The button in the application title bar is the *Close button* and it exits Word. The button on the menu bar is the *Close Window button* and it closes the document.

Task 3:
To Open Multiple Documents and Switch Between Them

1 Click the Open button on the Standard toolbar.

2 Navigate to your data directory and click the document named *Time Tracking.doc*.

Figure 0-10

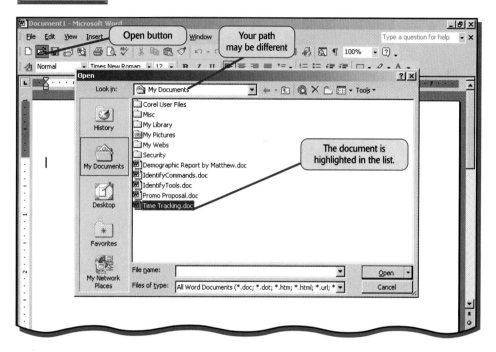

Tip   Depending on how your system is set up, you may not see the extensions on file names.

3 Click **Open**. The document opens and is displayed on the screen.

Troubleshooting
Because screen settings may vary and monitors are different sizes, the document may appear differently on your computer.

Figure 0-11

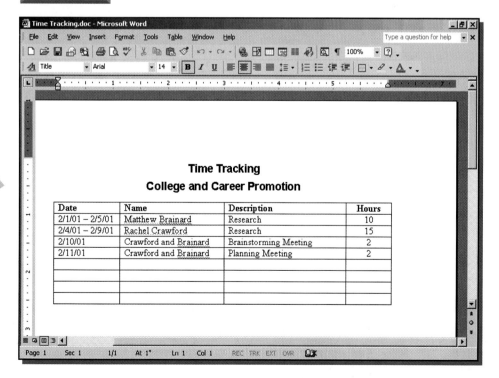

4 Click the Open button again. The Open dialog box opens again.

> **Tip**
> The folder you opened last appears automatically when you click the Open button again.

Figure O-12

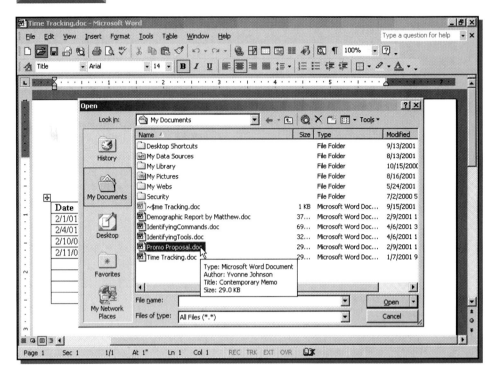

5 Double-click the document named *Promo Proposal.doc*. The document opens and is displayed on the screen. The other document is still open but is not visible on the screen.

6 Click the button in the taskbar for the Time Tracking document to display the Time Tracking document.

7 Click the button in the taskbar for the Promo Proposal document to display the Promo Proposal document.

> **Other Ways**
> To switch to another window:
> • Press Alt + Tab.

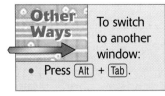

Figure O-13

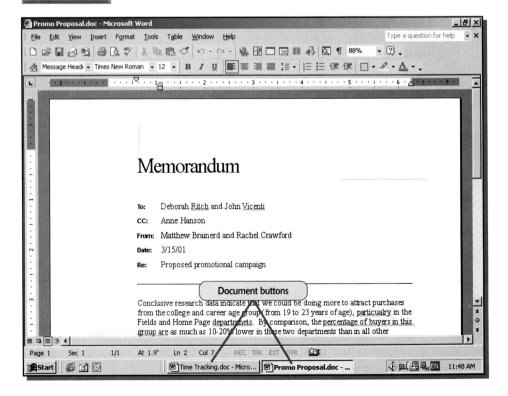

Changing the View

Word has four views for working with documents—Normal, Web Layout, Print Layout, and Outline. Each view has features that are useful in different situations. Table 0-2 describes the views and when to use them. Notice that the description of Normal view explains that this view shows more text on the screen. This is the view that you will use in the next task when you are proofreading.

Table 0-2	Using Views
View	**Description**
Normal	Does not display unused white space on the page, including the margin space, headers and footers, or floating graphics. It does display inline graphics and drawing objects. Use this view when you need to see the maximum possible amount of text on the screen.
Web Layout	Wraps all text to fit the width of the window. Use this view when you are viewing a document on screen or on the Web.
Print Layout	Displays margins and unused white space on the page, all graphics, and headers and footers, as well as a visual page break between pages. Use this view when you want to see how the page will look when it prints.
Outline	Displays the text of a document in outline form. Use this view for viewing and rearranging the structure of documents that contain headings and subheadings.

Each of the four standard views can be further enhanced with the Zoom feature. The Zoom feature zooms in to display a closer view of a page in a document or zooms out to display more of the page. Word can zoom from 500% to 10% as well as show multiple pages.

Task 4:
To Change the View and the Zoom

1 Choose **View | Normal** to switch to Normal view.

Tip Normal view displays document text between the margins and separates pages with a dashed line.

Figure 0-14

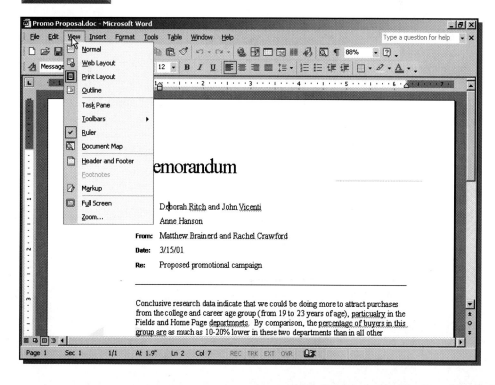

2 Click the Print Layout View ▤ button on the left side of the horizontal scroll bar to change to the Print Layout view.

3 Click the down arrow in the Zoom control to display the Zoom drop-down list.

Tip Print Layout view displays documents with breaks between pages and shows document pages as they will print.

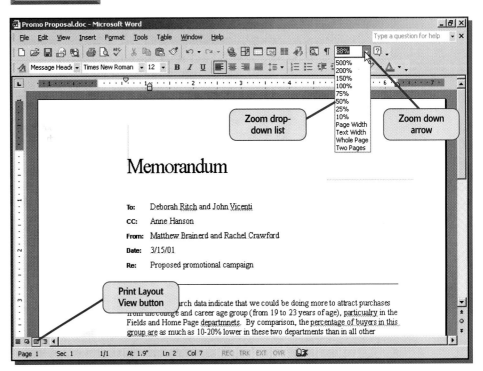

Figure O-15

4 Click 75% in the Zoom drop-down list to change the magnification of the document to 75%.

Troubleshooting The portion of the document you see on your screen may be different because of screen size and resolution.

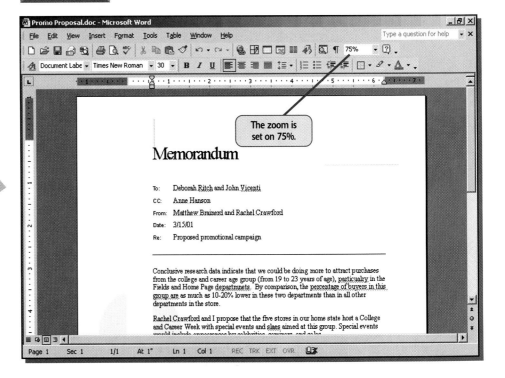

Figure O-16

5 Change the Zoom to Page Width.

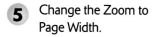

Tip 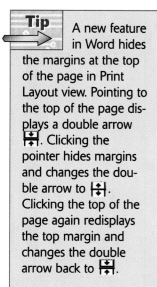 A new feature in Word hides the margins at the top of the page in Print Layout view. Pointing to the top of the page displays a double arrow. Clicking the pointer hides margins and changes the double arrow to. Clicking the top of the page again redisplays the top margin and changes the double arrow back to.

Figure 0-17

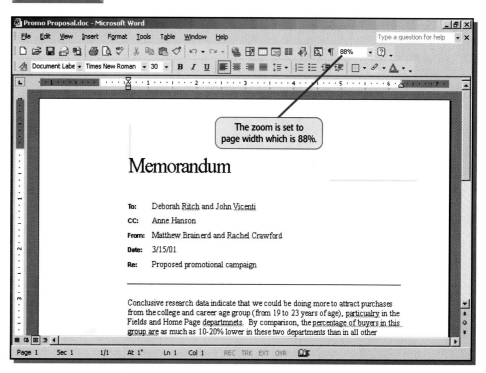

The zoom is set to page width which is 88%.

Checking Spelling and Grammar

Word checks the spelling in the document by comparing the words in the document to the words in its dictionary and the user dictionary. The *Grammar Checker* looks for incorrect spacing and punctuation, incorrect verb tense, disagreement between the subject and the verb, sentence fragments, incorrect use of *that* and *which*, passive voice, and so on.

Tip If the *Spelling and Grammar Status* icon in the status bar has an *X* on it, Word has found a spelling or grammar error in the document.

Sometimes the Grammar Checker questions things that are correct or suggests changes that would be incorrect. The Grammar Checker is not infallible. So, be careful. You may have to ignore some of Word's suggestions. The Spell checker also is not infallible. It highlights words that are correctly spelled if they are not in the default dictionary.

Tip  You can customize the Grammar Checker by selecting the *writing style* and specific rules you want the Grammar Checker to use. Choose **Tools | Options | Spelling and Grammar**. To select a writing style, click the **Writing style** down arrow and select **Grammar Only** or **Grammar & Style**. To select specific rules, click **Settings**, select the options you want, and click **OK**. Close the Options dialog box by clicking **OK**.

Task 5:

To Check Spelling and Grammar in a Document

1 Press [Ctrl] + [Home] to go to the top of the document, if necessary, and click the Spelling and Grammar 🔤 button. The Spelling and Grammar dialog box opens and finds the first word that is not in its dictionary.

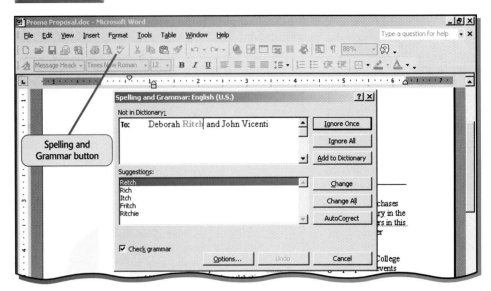

Figure 0-18

2 Click **Ignore All** to skip all occurrences of the word. The Spell Checker displays the next word that is not in the dictionary or the next grammatical problem.

3 Click **Ignore All** to skip all occurrences of this word too. The Spell checker goes to the next spelling error or grammatical problem.

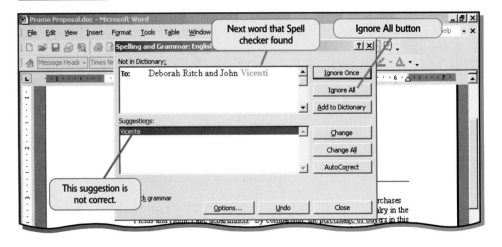

Figure 0-19

4 Click Change to accept the selected suggestion. Word goes to the next spelling error or grammatical problem.

5 Continue checking the spelling and grammar until Word displays the message that the check is completed.

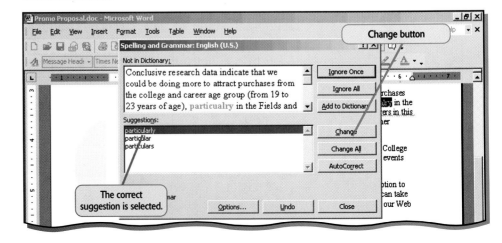

Figure 0-20

6 Click OK.

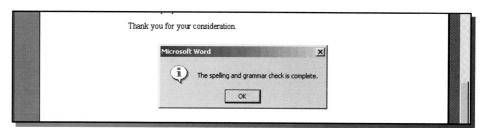

Previewing a Document

Previewing a document is one of the procedures that you will perform frequently when working on a document. Although the Print Layout view displays the document as it will look when printed, you may prefer to use the *Print Preview* feature, which allows you to see the complete page or as many as 50 pages on the computer screen at the same time. In Print Preview, you also can edit, print, and use all the menu options that are available to you in other views, except some of the options on the Window menu.

> **Tip**
> Always preview a document before printing, so you can catch and correct as many errors as possible. This will eliminate printing multiple copies before the final copy is printed. You will save paper and help the environment at the same time.

In the next task, you will use the new Smart Tag feature that is associated with the text that is underlined with a dotted line. Just for practice, you will remove one of the tags.

Task 6:
To Preview the Document

1 Click the Print Preview button to open the Print Preview window.

Figure O-22

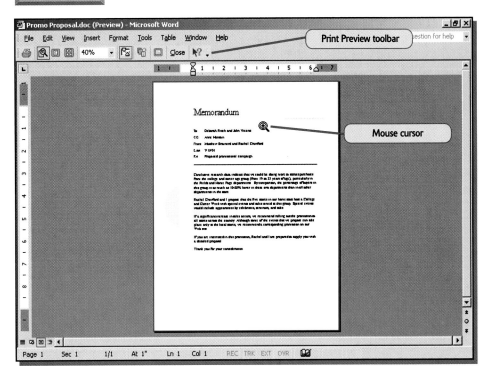

Figure O-22

2 Click the heading information at the top of the memo. The Zoom changes to 100%, and the pointer appears as a magnifying glass with a minus sign in its center.

> **Tip** Clicking the pointer when it looks like a magnifying glass with a minus sign in it returns the Zoom to the default setting.

3 Click the Magnifier button on the Print Preview toolbar. The Magnifier button toggles between the zoom mode and the editing mode. The mouse pointer looks like a magnifying glass in zoom mode and an I-beam in editing mode.

Figure O-23

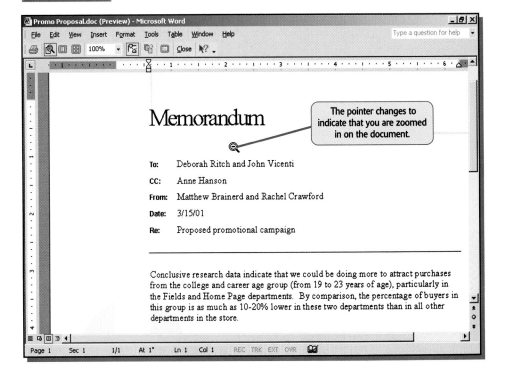

4 Click before the *e* in *Brainerd*. A Smart Tag button is displayed.

5 Point to the Smart Tag button until a down arrow appears and click the arrow.

6 Select **Remove this Smart Tag**.

> **Tip** If Smart Tag labels and buttons are enabled, a Smart Tag label and button are displayed (in any view) when you point to a name, address, date, time, or place.

Figure 0-24

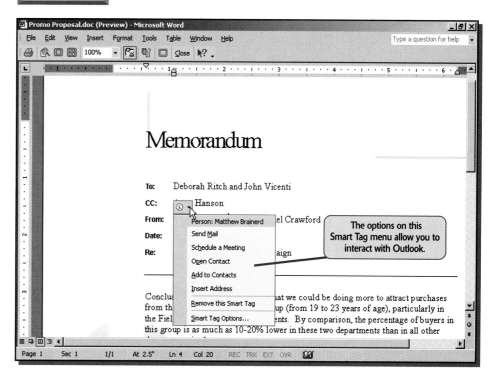

7 With the insertion point before the *e* in *Brainerd*, press Delete. Type **a** to correct the spelling.

8 Click the Close Close button in the Print Preview toolbar.

> **Troubleshooting** Be sure to click the Close button on the Print Preview toolbar rather than the document close button.

> **Tip** As you become more familiar with Word, you may want to explore additional options available on the Print Preview toolbar and menus.

Figure 0-25

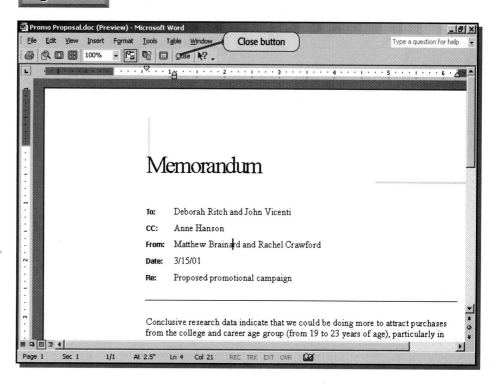

Printing a Document

It seems that no matter how thoroughly you proofread a document on the screen, you always miss something that jumps out at you when you print it. So before printing the final copy, it's very likely that you will have to print at least one copy of a document for proofreading purposes. The Print dialog box in Word contains the same options available in almost any Windows program, but it also contains some options that are unique to Word. Table 0-3 explains these options.

Task 7:

To Print a Document

1 Choose **File** | **Print** from the menu bar.

2 Verify that the correct printer is selected.

3 Click OK. The file prints.

Figure 0-26

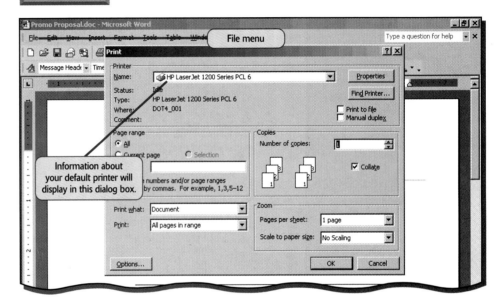

Table 0-3	Additional Print Options in Word
Option	**Description**
Print what	In addition to the option to print the document, contains options for printing the properties of the document, the document showing markup, a list of markups, a list of styles used in the document, a list of AutoText entries in the template used by the document as well as the entries in the default template, and a list of keys assigned to functions.
Pages per sheet	Prints more than one page on a sheet of paper. Unless you have specified a custom paper size, however, the text is reduced to fit on the page. For example, if the paper size for the document is 8 1/2-by-11-inch, and you print multiple pages on an 8 1/2-by-11-inch sheet of paper, the text will be reduced to fit all the pages on the sheet. On the other hand, if you specify a custom paper size of 5 1/2-by-8 1/2-inch in the Page Setup dialog box, you can print two pages on an 8 1/2 by-11-inch sheet of paper, and the text will not be reduced.
Scale to paper size	Increases or decreases the font used in the document so that each page of the document will fit on a different size paper than the one specified in the Page Setup dialog box. For example, if you create a document to print on 8 1/2-by-11-inch paper, you can use this option to make the text of each page fit on A4-size paper (a smaller-size paper used extensively in Europe).
Manual duplex	Prints the document on both sides of the paper by printing the odd pages and prompting the user to insert the printed pages back into the printer input source.

Tip

To print noncontiguous pages, enter the page numbers separated by commas in the Pages text box in the Print dialog box. To print a range of pages, enter the page numbers separated by a hyphen. To print both noncontiguous pages and a range of pages, separate the noncontiguous pages from the ranges with commas—for example 1,3,6-10,12.

E-Mailing Documents

Using Outlook, Word can send a copy of a file as an e-mail message. In the next task, you will e-mail yourself a copy of the file that you are working on just to see how it works.

Task 8:

To E-Mail a Document

1 Choose **File | Send To | Mail Recipient**.

Troubleshooting

If you use an e-mail program other than Outlook, follow the direction of your instructor to complete this task.

Figure 0-27

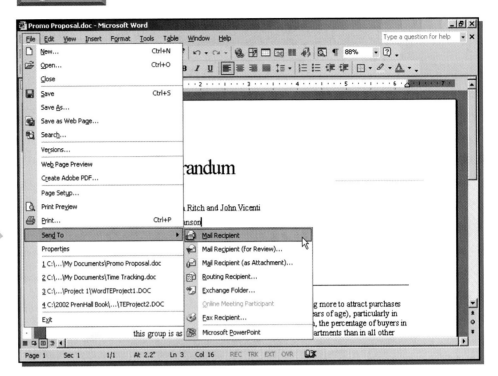

2 Type your own e-mail address for **To**.

Figure 0-28

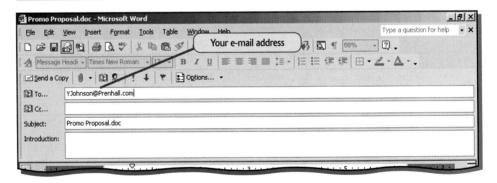

3 Select the text for **Subject**, and type Test.

Figure 0-29

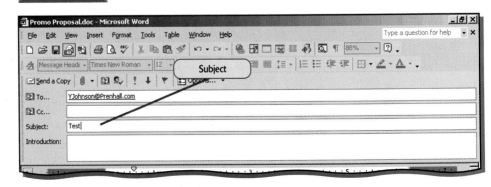

4 Type **This** is a test for **Introduction**.

5 Click the Send a Copy [🖃 Send a Copy] button. If the Spell Checker option in Outlook is on, the Spell Checker starts.

6 Respond appropriately to the prompts.

Figure 0-30

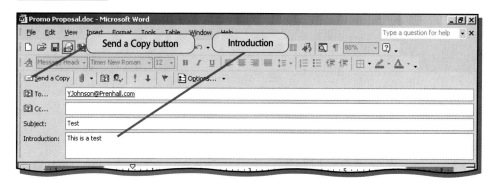

Closing a Document and Exiting Word

When you are finished with a document, you should close it to free memory in the computer. Likewise, when you are finished with Word, you should exit the program.

> **Tip** If you make changes in the document without saving the document, Word asks whether you want to save the document before closing it.

Task 11:
To Close a Document and Exit Word

1 Choose **File | Save As** to open the Save As dialog box.

Figure 0-31

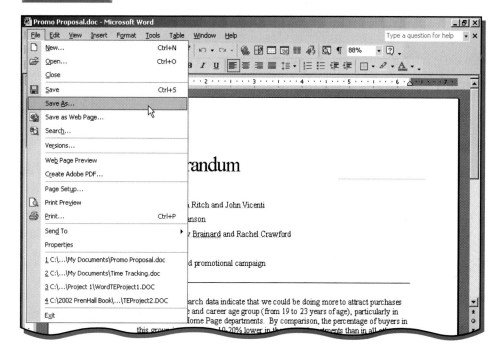

2 Specify the location where you are saving your files in the **Save in** text box.

3 Type Promo Proposal Proofed for the **File** name.

4 Click **Save**.

Figure 0-32

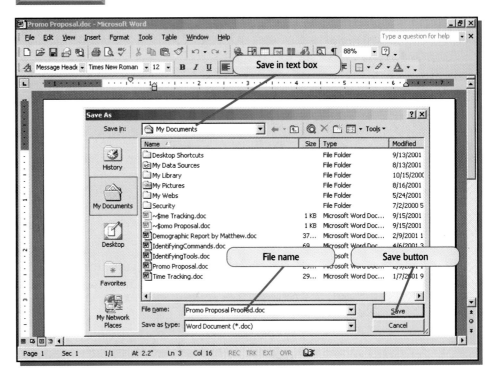

Tip Instead of closing all open files individually, you can simply click Word's Close button, and Word will close all files automatically. If a file has been edited since the last save, Word will ask if you want to save it before closing it.

5 Click the Close Window **X** button (in the menu bar). The document closes, and the Time Tracking document window is displayed.

Figure 0-33

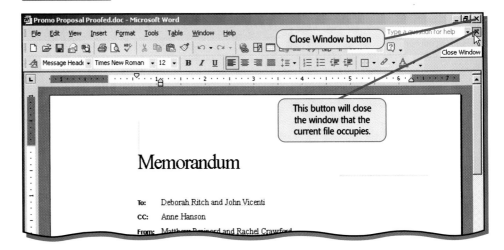

6 Click the Close Window **X** button in the menu bar. The Time Tracking document closes.

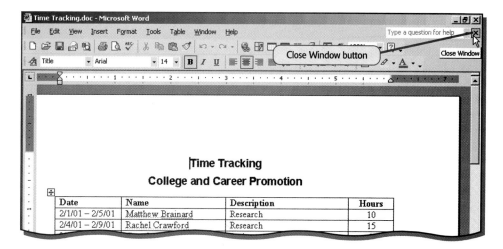

Figure 0-34

7 Click the Close **X** button in the application title bar. Word closes.

Figure 0-35

SUMMARY AND EXERCISES

SUMMARY

- Word has tools for creating traditional documents.
- You can launch Word from the Programs menu.
- Word creates Document1 when it is launched.
- The Word window has common window elements as well as its own unique elements.
- The status bar contains status indicators that provide environment information.
- The Options dialog box and the AutoCorrect dialog box contain options for setting up the Word environment.
- Word opens separate windows for each document and displays a button in the taskbar for each window.

- Word has four views: Normal, Web Layout, Print Layout, and Outline.
- The Zoom feature changes the magnification of the document on the screen.
- The Spelling and Grammar tool checks a document for spelling and grammar errors.
- Print Preview displays the complete page or as many as 50 pages on the screen at the same time.
- Word contains unique print options, such as Scale to paper size.
- You can send a copy of a file as an e-mail message.
- When you are finished with a document, you should close it, and when you are finished with Word, you should exit the program.

KEY TERMS & SKILLS

KEY TERMS

active window (p. 10)
Browse buttons (p. 5)
Click and Type (p. 5)
Close button (p. 10)
Close Window button
  (p. 10)
document window
  (p. 10)
Formatting toolbar
  (p. 10)

Grammar Checker
  (p. 15)
I-beam (p. 5)
insertion point (p. 5)
Normal view (p. 13)
Outline view (p. 13)
Print Layout view
  (p. 13)
Print Preview (p. 17)
ruler (p. 5)

Spelling and Grammar
  (p. 15)
Standard toolbar
  (p. 4)
status indicator (p. 5)
vertical ruler (p. 5)
Web Layout view
  (p. 5)
writing style (p. 15)

SKILLS

Change the view (p. 13)
Check spelling and grammar (p. 15)
Close a document (p. 23)
E-mail a document (p. 22)
Exit Word (p. 23)
Launch Word (p. 3)

Open a document (p. 10)
Preview a document (p. 17)
Print a document (p. 20)
Set Word defaults (p. 6)
Switch to another document (p. 11)
Zoom (p. 13)

STUDY QUESTIONS

MULTIPLE CHOICE

1. Which of the following is a false statement?
   a. The insertion point blinks.
   b. The insertion point marks the typing position.
   c. The insertion point is a vertical line.
   d. The insertion point can change shapes.

2. The names of the Previous Page and Next Page buttons change
   a. if you switch to the Normal view.
   b. when you select a different browse object.
   c. to Previous Screen and Next Screen if the document does not contain page breaks.
   d. when you choose **Insert | Page Numbers**.

3. The Select Browse Object button
   a. displays the Find dialog box.
   b. is located in the status bar.
   c. displays a palette of buttons.
   d. is located in the Standard toolbar.

4. If REC is dimmed in the status bar, it means that
   a. the macro recorder is on.
   b. the macro recorder is not on.
   c. the document is displayed in Normal view.
   d. the document is displayed in Print Layout view.

5. The I-beam
   a. displays the alignment that will be used for Click and Type.
   b. is another name for the insertion point.
   c. is a blinking vertical line that marks the typing position.
   d. is moved by the Up, Down, Left, and Right keys.

6. Print Preview mode
   a. can show only one page at a time.
   b. can zoom to different magnifications.
   c. can display as many as 52 pages at once.
   d. appears automatically before you print a document.

7. Which of the following statements concerning Print Preview mode is false?
   a. Not all options on the Window menu are available.
   b. You cannot edit the document.
   c. You can print the document.
   d. You can view multiple pages at the same time.

8. An X on the Spelling and Grammar Status icon indicates that
   a. the option is not active.
   b. there is a spelling error in the document.
   c. there is a grammar error in the document.
   d. there is either a spelling or grammar error in the document.

9. To print noncontiguous pages, enter the page numbers
   a. separated by hyphens.
   b. separated by commas.
   c. separated by spaces.
   d. one at a time.

10. The Scale to paper size print option
   a. increases or decreases the size of the paper on which a document will print so that the complete document will print in a specified number of pages.
   b. changes the orientation of the printed page so that a complete page will fit on the specified paper size.
   c. was eliminated in this version of Word because usability studies indicated that it was not commonly used.
   d. increases or decreases the font used in the document so that each page will fit on a different size of paper other than the one specified in the Page Setup dialog box.

SHORT ANSWER

1. List the two default toolbars.
2. What is the name of the document that Word creates automatically when it is launched?
3. How do you activate a dimmed indicator on the status bar?
4. What does the vertical ruler display?
5. Where are the View buttons located?
6. Can you edit a document in the Print Preview mode?

7. What print option allows you to print on both sides of the paper?
8. How do you switch from one document to another when you have several documents open at the same time?
9. How do you magnify the document in Print Preview?
10. How does Print Preview mode help the environment and save money too?

FILL IN THE BLANK

1. The _____ displays the settings for the margins, tabs, and indents.
2. The OVR indicator in the status bar stands for _____.
3. The vertical ruler appears only in _____ view.
4. The Spelling and Grammar Status icon appears in the _____ bar.
5. The feature that allows you to type in blank areas of a document is _____.
6. In Print Preview, the pointer looks like a(n) _____.
7. Use the _____ feature to enlarge or reduce the size of the text on the screen.
8. To e-mail a document, choose **File |** _____ **| Mail Recipient**.
9. The Writing style option that is selected influences how the _____ Checker works.
10. The _____ Layout view wraps all text to fit the width of the window.

DISCUSSION

1. Discuss scenarios in which you would use the Normal, Web Layout, Print Layout, and Outline views.
2. Explain the different indicators in the status bar.
3. Discuss the strengths and weaknesses of Word's Grammar Checker.
4. Discuss the features of Print Preview.
5. Discuss the additional print options that Word offers that are unique to Word.

GUIDED EXERCISES

1   ADDING WORDS TO THE USER DICTIONARY

Although it is possible to open the user dictionary and add words directly to the dictionary, one simple way to enter words in the user dictionary is to create a list of the words you want to enter and then run a spelling check on the words. Many of the brand name products sold at e-Selection stores are not in the dictionary. Follow these steps to add these words to the custom dictionary:

1 Start Word and use the new document or create a new document by clicking the New Document button if necessary.

2 Type the following:
FliteRite Skis
Sasson Suits

Suitables
Florsheim
Giorgio Sant Angelo
Samsonite

3 Check the spelling and click **Add to dictionary** for each word.

4 Close the document without saving when finished.

2 USING PRINT PREVIEW TO REVIEW AND EDIT A DOCUMENT

Matthew intends to present the report shown in Figure 0-36 to the vice president of marketing, so you want to be certain that it looks professional and is well written. You will use Print Preview mode to review the document and to make a few edits.

Figure 0-36

Demographic Report on Our Target Market:
The College and Career Group

The group that we are targeting with the College and Career Week promotion is referred to as "Generation Y" or the "Echo Boom", and it includes 70 million people. Reaching this group with advertising for the promotion may prove to be challenging. According to Nancy Shepherdson in her article entitled *Life's Beach 101* published in the May 2000 issue of *American Demographics*, this group has "seen as many as 20,000 commercials every year since they were old enough to sit up."

According to Shepherdson, we can make the following statements about this group:

1. As a group, they are unaware of the clout they wield in the job market.
2. Soon-to-graduate college seniors underestimate their worth and overestimate the difficulty they will have finding a job.
3. Generation Y was the first generation to grow up with the Internet, and they will define how we integrate the Internet into everyday life.
4. This group responds best to integrated marketing that doesn't strike you as advertising.
5. They are more likely to respond to anything that makes their lives easier.
6. Some recent college grads may be wealthier than previous generations were at the same age.
7. This group has more savvy than previous generations, and they are starting to make big decisions earlier than ever.
8. They aren't as inclined to respond to celebrity endorsements or to idolize established market leaders, but they do exhibit strong brand loyalty after they have selected a brand.
9. They respond to practicality and individual expression.
10. The Echo Boom is diverse in taste and culture.
11. This group sees through "hype" fairly quickly.
12. They prefer buying experiences that are customized for them.
13. They are much more likely to become interested in products through word of mouth or "buzz" than any traditional media outlet.

The article by Shepherdson cites an interesting case that illustrates point 13 above. The findings of a 1999 survey of 500 college students conducted by Strategic Mindshare, a Miami-based research firm, concluded that students preferred to learn about Web sites from friends. The case involved an e-promotion by Ikea, the Swedish home-furnishings retailer which offered $75 off purchases if customers sent Internet postcards to their friends announcing a store opening. Within two weeks, the promotion generated 37,000 referrals.

One thing we should include in our promotion is multiple opportunities for customers to participate in activities, not just to buy things that are on sale. Shepherdson's article points out that

...the store concept most preferred by today's college student is one in which "the five senses are engaged," where there are "experimentation and hang-out areas" (à la Barnes & Noble and Borders Books) and places to "engage in activity and buy products." This generation enjoys the cross between retailing and

activity-based businesses such as gyms, copy centers, and sporting venues.

nk about this promotion in the stores and on the Web site, the following advice should ered from Shepherdson:

Currently, most marketers see e-commerce as a way to target a specific group, or simply as an extension of their existing sales operations. But as e-commerce matures, marketers will need to do more than just enable consumers to buy online. Eventually, they'll need to make online buying/returning/asking for help as seamless as it is in a store.

y, the article included the following table that relates the average starting salary for ads by job title:

Job Category	February 2000	February 1999
Computers & Information Science	$44,722	$41,316
Engineering	$43,740	$44,594
Education	$38,898	$40,328
Sales & Marketing	$35,746	$33,223
Business & Management	$35,452	$34,254
Accounting & Finance	$35,104	$34,173
Public Affairs & Social Services	$29,535	$28,372
Communications/Media	$28,446	$27,892
Source: JobTrak.com		

1 Open *Demographic Report by Matthew.doc*.

2 Click the **Print Preview** button.

3 Click the Multiple Pages ⊞ button and click the 1 x 2 pages icon.

4 Click the One Page ▣ button.

5 Click the mouse pointer at the top of the first page.

6 Click the Magnifier ▨ button on the Print Preview toolbar.

7 Type a comma after *Echo Boom* in the first sentence.

8 Click the Magnifier ▨ button on the Print Preview toolbar again.

9 Click the Close button on the Print Preview toolbar.

10 Save the file as *Demographics Edited* and close the file.

3 CHECKING GRAMMAR IN A FORMAL REPORT

Because the demographic report by Matthew is too casual in tone to present to the vice president of marketing, you will change the writing style used to check the grammar in the document to a more formal style and make appropriate changes.

1 Open *Demographic Report by Matthew.doc*.

2 Choose **Tools | Options** and click the **Spelling & Grammar** tab, if necessary. Select **Grammar Only** for the **Writing style**, if necessary, and select **Check grammar as you type**, if necessary. Click **OK**.

3 Scroll through the document and observe any occurrences of wavy, green lines. These indicate possible grammar errors.

4 Choose **Tools | Options** again. Select **Grammar & Style** for the **Writing style** and click **OK**. Select Grammar & Style for the Writing style on the Spelling & Grammar tab and click OK. As you continue to work with the document, you will see more grammatical markings.

5 Check the spelling and grammar in the document. When Word marks a word or phrase that is too informal, change it to the more formal suggestion, but don't change any of the words in the passages that are indented on the left and right. These are direct quotes. Rewrite at least one of the sentences that use passive voice.

6 Change the **Writing style** option back to **Grammar Only**.

7 Save the file as *Demographics Edited 2* and close the file.

4 E-MAILING YOUR WORK

E-mailing your completed assignments is a great way to turn in your work on time.

1 Open *Demographics Edited* or *Demographics Edited 2*.

2 Choose **File | Send To | Mail Recipient**.

3 Type the e-mail address of your instructor in the **To** field.

4 At the end of the text for the **Subject**, type Assignment Attached.

5 Click the Send a Copy ⊟ Send a Copy button.

6 Close the file.

ON YOUR OWN

The difficulty of these case studies varies: are the least difficult; are more difficult; and are the most difficult.

1 PRINTING A LIST OF STYLES

 Open *Demographic Report by Matthew.doc*. Print the list of styles used in the document by choosing the appropriate option from the Print what drop-down list in the Print dialog box. Close the file. (Hint: See Table 0-3.)

2 PRINTING MULTIPLE PAGES ON A SINGLE SHEET

Open *Demographic Report by Matthew.doc* and print two pages per sheet. Close the file.

3 IDENTIFYING WORD TOOLS AND SCREEN ELEMENTS

Open the document named *IdentifyingTools.doc*. This document contains graphics of Word tools and screen elements. Click below each graphic and type the name of the screen element represented by the graphic. Save the document and close it or complete the next exercise.

4 DEFINING WORD TOOLS AND SCREEN ELEMENTS

Open *IdentifyingTools.doc*, if necessary. Click below the name of each graphic and write a short description of the tool or screen element. Save the completed file as *Tools* and close the document.

5 IDENTIFYING COMMANDS IN WORD

Open the document named *IdentifyingCommands.doc*. This document contains graphics of dialog boxes that appear as the result of a command in Word. Below each graphic, type the steps to display the dialog box. Save and close the file or continue with the next exercise.

6 DEFINING COMMANDS IN WORD

Open *IdentifyingCommand.doc*, if necessary. Below the steps, type a description of the purpose of each dialog box and the important options in the dialog boxes. Save the completed file as *Commands* and close it.

P R O J E C T **1**

Creating Documents

I n this project you will create a new document and then use standard methods for entering and editing text. You will learn to create some basic correspondence documents, including a letter, an envelope, a fax cover sheet, and mailing labels.

OBJECTIVES

After completing this project, you will be able to:

- Create a new document
- Enter text
- Edit text
- Create an envelope
- Create a fax cover sheet from a template
- Use Click and Type
- Create labels
- View and edit comments

e-selections) **Running Case**

Matthew and Rachel have been given the green light on College and Career Week. Before they turn in a detailed proposal, they need to contact the agents for several celebrities to inquire about scheduling celebrity appearances and the cost of such appearances.

Writing Business Letters

To Naphururiya, king of Egypt, my brother, say: thus speaks
Burnaburiash, king of Karduniash, your brother. I am well.
To you, your land, your house, your wives, your children,
your Grandees, your horses, your chariots, many greetings!

This formal greeting reflects the proper salutation that a Babylonian king used when addressing a business letter to another ruler. A remarkable collection of nearly 400 diplomatic letters "written" on clay tablets found in 1887 at El Amarna, Egypt, revealed that many rulers in the Middle East kept up lively letter-writing communications with the pharaohs in the fifteenth century B.C.

Today a modern business letter also adheres to a formal protocol that requires the following basic parts: the heading (or preprinted letterhead), date line, inside address, salutation, body, complimentary closing, and a signature line. The body paragraphs are separated by a double space, and the letter should be personally signed with the letter writer's own "John Hancock." Depending on the nature of the letter, it may also have some or all of these elements: attention line, reference line, subject line, special mailing instructions (e.g., FedEX), on-arrival notation (e.g., CONFIDENTIAL), identification initials, an enclosure notation, and courtesy copy (also called carbon copy) notation.

The formats of business letters include full block, modified block, and modified semiblock. In a full block letter, all components of the letter (except perhaps the preprinted letterhead) are aligned flush with the left margin. In

...Law recognizes digital signatures as legally binding...

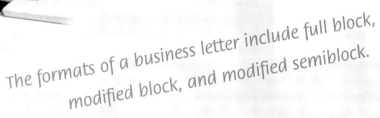

The formats of a business letter include full block, modified block, and modified semiblock.

a modified block letter, the following components are indented at the center of the page: the heading (unless preprinted letterhead is used), the date, the reference line, the complimentary close, and the signature line. A modified semiblock letter is exactly the same as the modified block format except the first line of every body paragraph is indented (usually half an inch or more).

Because many letters and other formal documents that require signatures are transmitted electronically via computer, the United States Congress passed the Electronic Signatures in Global and National Commerce Act. President Clinton signed the bill into law on June 30, 2000 in Constitution Hall in Philadelphia where John Hancock affixed his famous signature to the Declaration of Independence. Instead of using a quill pen to sign the law, he used a smart card encoded with a digital signature. The law mirrors and unifies the laws passed in most states and makes a digital signature as legally binding as a signature on paper.

Note:

A digital signature is not a graphic of a handwritten signature, but a method of identifying the sender of a message or the signer of a document by using a number that is encrypted with a public-private key. The encrypted number is actually the signature. Special software is required to digitize a signature.

Creating a Document

The Challenge

While Matthew is on vacation, Rachel will start the ball rolling and get the project organized. When necessary, she will stay in touch with Matthew by fax. She will begin by getting information about celebrity availability and price.

The Solution

As the administrative assistant, you will create a letter for Rachel to be sent to the agent for Christopher Pole, the star of the HGTV show *You Can Do It*, to inquire about his availability. You will use a file that already contains the letterhead and create the envelope using the Envelope and Labels tool. You will also take care of any faxing and create a set of labels for file folders to organize all the information in the project.

Figures 1-1 show the envelope and the first draft of the letter you will create, the fax cover sheet, and the file folder labels.

Figure 1-1

```
|..|||||..||.....|||.|.|.|.|
Talents, Inc.
Deborah Smythe
1500 Avenue of Americas
New York, NY 10019
```

e-selections

April 6, 2001

Talents, Inc.
Deborah Smythe
1500 Avenue of Americas
New York, NY 10019

Dear Ms. Smythe:

Our store, e-Selections, is planning a weeklong promotion aimed at the college and career market. We would like to schedule a few one-hour appearances by Christopher Pole during the promotion—tentatively scheduled for the second week of February. Is Mr. Pole available during this week? Please call me at your earliest convenience to discuss booking details.

Sincerely,

Rachel Crawford
Public Relations

cc: Matthew Brainard

Enclosure

Phone: 402-555-111
Fax: 402-555-1112   **Selections, Inc.**

Fax

To: Matthew Brainard   **From:** Rachel Crawford

Fax: 941-555-0001   **Pages:** 2 (including cover sheet)

Phone: 941-555-0000   **Date:** 4/6/01

Re: College Promotion   **CC:**

☐ Urgent   ☐ For Review   ☐ Please Comment   ☐ Please Reply   ☐ Please Recycle

● **Comments:** Matt, hope you are having a great vacation. Here is the first draft of the letter that I am sening to Christopher Pole's agent. Call me with your feedback when it's convenient.

Now try to relax and forget about work. You're supposed to be on vacation!

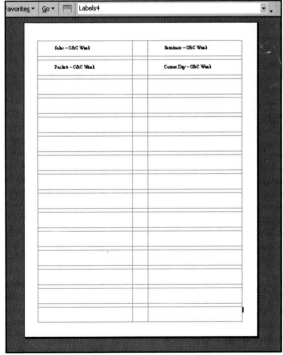

Creating a New Document

Word provides several methods for creating a new document. You can start with a new blank document or base a new document on an existing document. In the next task, you will learn to create a new document by opening a copy of an existing document.

Tip   You also can create a new document by opening an existing document and saving it with a different name. This is potentially dangerous, however, because you might make changes to the document and forget to use the Save As command.

Task 1:

To Create a Document from an Existing Document

1 Open Word and then choose **File | Open**. The Open dialog box opens.

Figure 1-2

2 Navigate to your data directory and click the document named *ColorLetterhead.doc*. Note that your screen will look different from Figure 1-3.

3 Click the **Open** down arrow.

4 Select **Open as Copy**. The file opens with Copy (1) in the title bar.

Figure 1-3

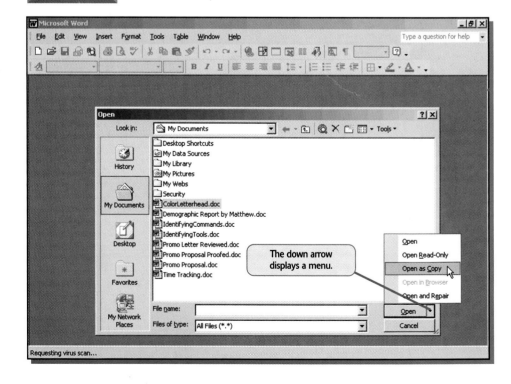

5 Choose **File | Save As**.

Figure 1-4

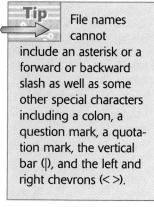

Tip You might want to create folders on your data disk for each project in this book. To create a folder, click the Create New Folder button in the **Save As** dialog box and specify the path and name of the folder.

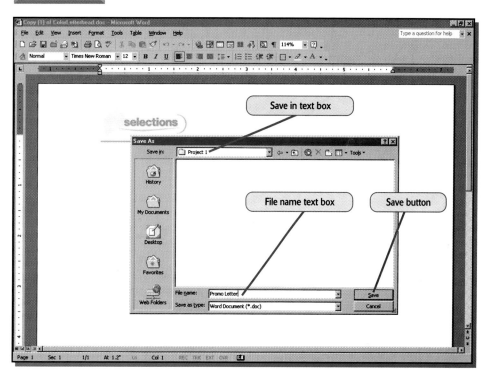

Save in text box

File name text box

Save button

6 Specify the drive and folder where you are keeping your work in the **Save in** text box.

7 Type **Promo Letter** in the **File name** textbox and click **Save. Notice that the new name appears in the title bar.**

8 Change the view to Normal.

Figure 1-5

Tip File names cannot include an asterisk or a forward or backward slash as well as some other special characters including a colon, a question mark, a quotation mark, the vertical bar (|), and the left and right chevrons (< >).

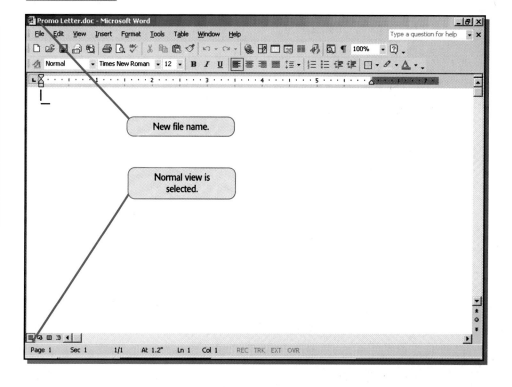

New file name.

Normal view is selected.

CHECK POINT

Why do the letterhead logo and the graphic line disappear when you change to Normal view? The letterhead logo and graphic line are located in the header, and headers do not display in Normal view.

Entering Text

Instead of typing the text of the letter all at once, you will type the letter in sections so that you can concentrate on individual features and commands. As you type, you will press the ⌷Enter⌷ key only to end short lines, end paragraphs, or create blank lines. As you type text continuously, Word will *wrap* the text to fit within the preset left and right margins.

Tip   Word presets the left and right margins to 1.25 inches and the top and bottom margins to 1 inch, but the letterhead file that you will be using has margins of 1 inch for all four margins.

Inserting the Date

Although it is easy to type the date in a letter, Word provides a command that inserts the date for you. The command can insert the date as text or as a date field. A *date field* automatically updates to the current date each time the file is opened.

In the next task you will insert the date field in the letter because you are not certain when you will actually send the letter; therefore, you are uncertain what date to type. When you open the letter to print and send it, the date field will change to the correct date.

Tip   Word provides other types of fields as well, such as fields that display the name of the file, the date the file is printed, the author's name, a cross-reference, and so forth.

Task 2:
To Insert a Date Field

1 Choose **Insert**. The Insert drop-down menu appears.

2 Choose **Date and Time**. The Date and Time dialog box appears.

Figure 1-6

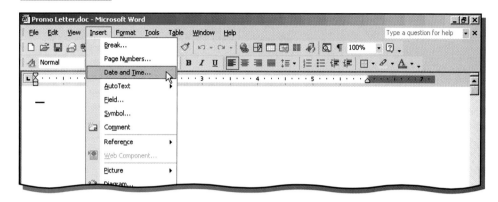

3 Select the third format in the **Available formats** list. (The third format spells out the month, followed by the date, and then a four digit year.)

Figure 1-7

Tip
If you want to use the same date format in all your documents, click **Default** and then click **Yes.**

4 Select **Update automatically** so that the date will change to the current date each time the file is opened. If you do not select this option, Word inserts the date as text.

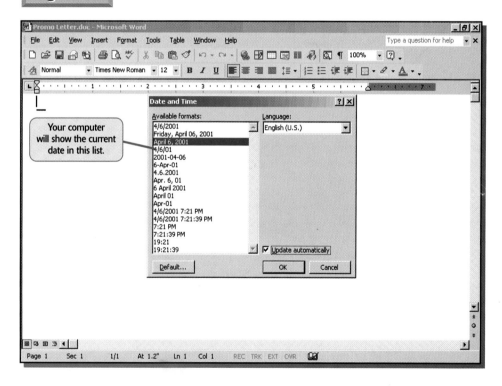

5 Click **OK**. The current date (if the date in the computer is accurate) appears in the document.

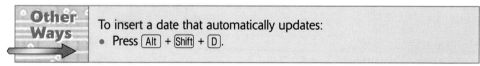

Other Ways
To insert a date that automatically updates:
- Press [Alt] + [Shift] + [D].

Tip
When you want to convert a date field to text, such as when you want to keep the same date in the file for future reference, click in the date and press [Ctrl]+[Shift]+[F9].

In the next task, you will type the inside address—an example of text that does not use word wrap but requires you to press Enter after each line. Additionally, you will use the Bksp key to erase text to the left of the insertion point.

Task 3:

To Type the First Part of the Letter

1 Press Enter four times after the date, type Talents, Inc., and press Enter.

2 Type Deborah Smith and press Bksp three times. Then type ythe. The Bksp key erased three characters so you could retype the correct spelling of Deborah's last name.

3 Press Enter, type 1500 Avenue of Americas, and press Enter. Type New York, NY 10019 and press Enter twice.

4 Type Dear Ms. Smythe: and press Enter twice. The Office Assistant opens.

5 Select **Just type the letter without help** in the Office Assistant bubble. The Office Assistant closes.

Tip If you never want the Office Assistant to help you write a letter, select **Don't show me this tip again.** Anytime the Office Assistant appears, you can hide it by choosing **Help | Hide the Assistant.**

Figure 1-8

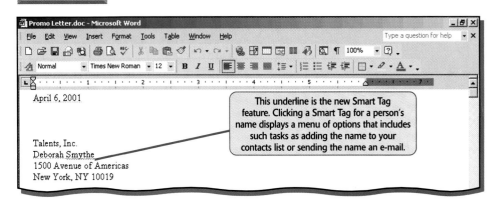

This underline is the new Smart Tag feature. Clicking a Smart Tag for a person's name displays a menu of options that includes such tasks as adding the name to your contacts list or sending the name an e-mail.

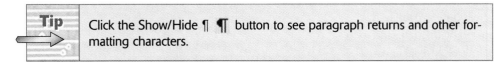

Tip Click the Show/Hide ¶ ¶ button to see paragraph returns and other formatting characters.

Figure 1-9

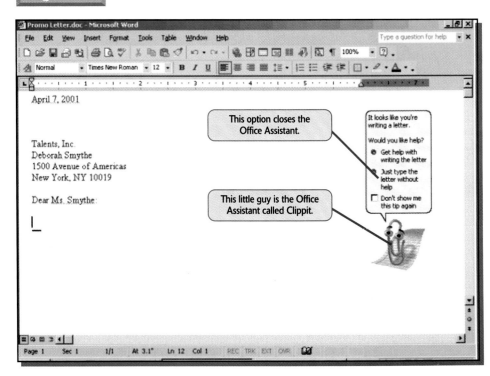

This option closes the Office Assistant.

This little guy is the Office Assistant called Clippit.

Troubleshooting If you find the Office Assistant annoying, you can turn it off. Just right-click the Office Assistant, choose **Options**, and clear the **Use the Office Assistant** check box.

6 Type the following and include a space at the end: Our store, Selections, Inc., is planning a week-long promotion aimed at

7 Type teh followed by a space and watch what happens. Word automatically corrects the typographical error *teh* because it is a default AutoCorrect entry.

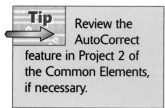

Tip Review the AutoCorrect feature in Project 2 of the Common Elements, if necessary.

Figure 1-10

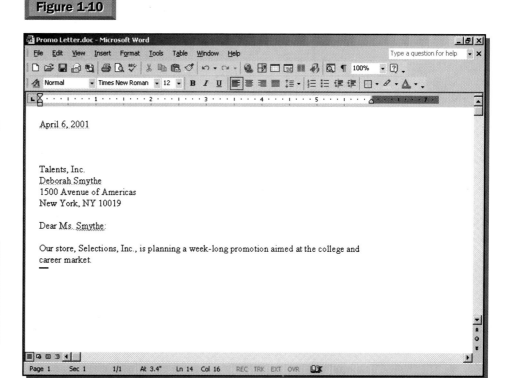

8 Type the following and type a space after the period: college and career market. Notice how the text wraps to the next line automatically.

9 Save the file.

Inserting Symbols and Special Characters

The keyboard has a limited number of alphanumeric and punctuation characters it can produce, but you can insert *symbols* and *special characters* by using the Symbol dialog box. The Symbol dialog box has two tabs, one for *Symbols* and one for *Special Characters*. The Symbols tab displays symbols (e.g., Greek letters, mathematical symbols, arrows, ornamental symbols, boxes, and other shapes and graphics) from the selected font; the Special Characters tab always displays the same list of special characters (e.g., dashes, spaces, hyphens, and other characters that you cannot enter from the keyboard).

Task 4:
To Insert a Special Character

1 Type We would like to schedule a few one-hour appearances by Christopher Pole during the promotion (don't space at the end) and choose **Insert | Symbol** to open the Symbol dialog box.

Figure 1-11

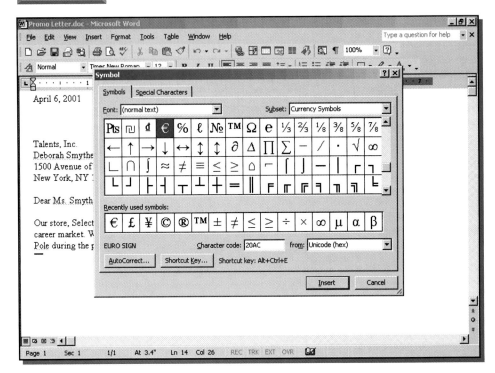

2 Click the **Special Characters** tab.

3 Click **Insert**. The em dash character is inserted in the document, but the dialog box remains open.

Figure 1-12

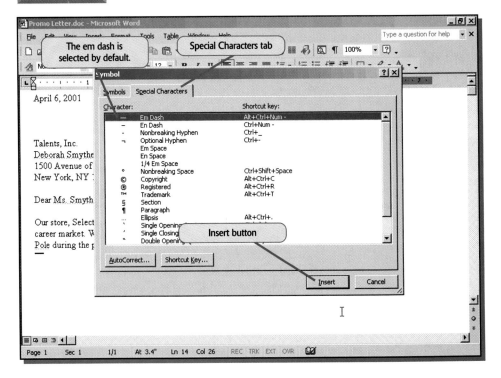

4 Click **Close**.

Troubleshooting
If you have a really long dash, you probably clicked **Insert** more than once. Just press Bksp to erase.

Figure 1-13

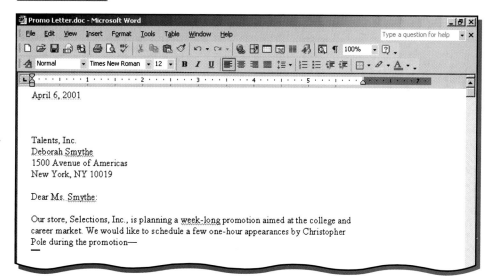

5 Type tentatively scheduled for the second week of February. Could you please inform me of Mr. Pole's availability and the cost for an appearance?

6 Press Enter twice and type Sincerely. Then press Enter four times and type the following:
Rachel Crawford
Public Relations

7 Press Enter twice and type cc. Word automatically capitalizes the first C.

Figure 1-14

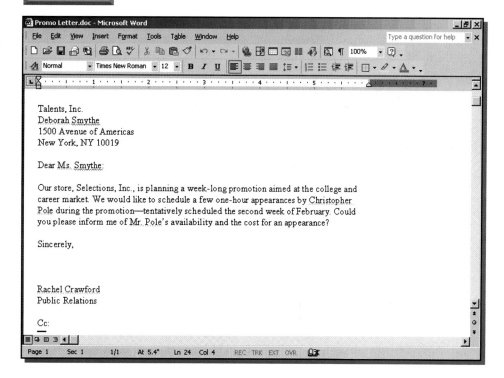

8 Point to the *Cc:* that you just typed until you see the AutoCorrect Options button.

9 Click the down arrow and select **Undo Automatic Capitalization** to change the capital C back to a lower case c.

Figure 1-15

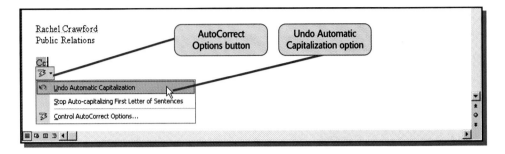

Troubleshooting If you set the defaults as instructed in the Introductory chapter, Word automatically capitalizes the first letter in *cc.* If Word did not capitalize *cc,* choose **Tools | AutoCorrect Options** and select **Capitalize first letter of sentences.** Click **OK** to close the AutoCorrect dialog box.

Figure 1-16

10 Type a space after the colon. Then type Matthew Brainard and press Enter.

Tip This letter fits on one page. If you had been typing a letter that would not fit on one page, Word would have inserted a page break for you automatically when the text exceeded what would fit on the page.

Figure 1-17

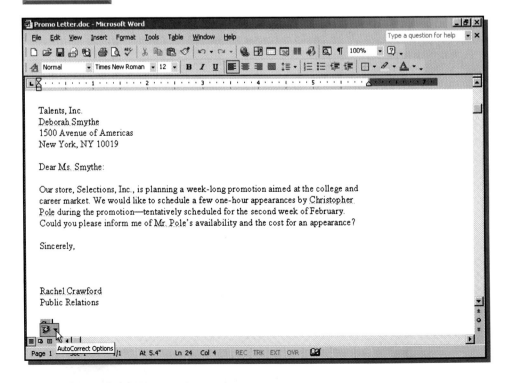

Creating and Using AutoText Entries

As the administrative assistant, you have a lot of letters to type for different people. It would be nice to be able to press a few keys and get the appropriate *signature block* (*Sincerely,* followed by four returns and the appropriate name) without having to type the same thing every time. The *AutoText feature* stores text, formatting, and even graphics and recalls them on command. Watch how it works in this task.

Task 5:
To Create and Use an AutoText Entry

1 Select the signature block text from Sincerely, on through to the department name. Be careful not to select the space after the letter *s* in the department name.

2 Press Alt + F3. The Create AutoText dialog box opens.

3 Type **sig block** to name the AutoText entry and click **OK**. The AutoText entry is saved and is now available for use in any document.

Figure 1-18

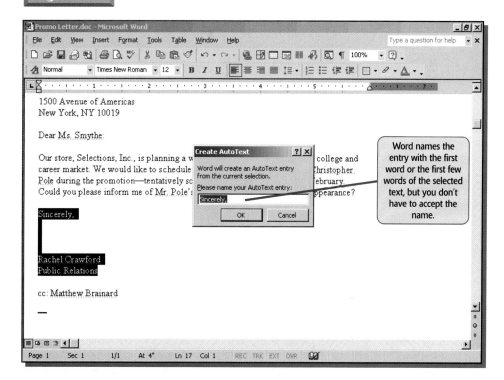

Word names the entry with the first word or the first few words of the selected text, but you don't have to accept the name.

Tip Think carefully about the name that you give an AutoText entry. You may want to name an entry with a short name or abbreviation. It is not a good idea to name an entry with a word that you use frequently. Also, AutoText entry names are not case-sensitive.

4 Press Delete. The signature block is deleted.

Figure 1-19

Our store, Selections, Inc., is planning a week-long promotion aimed at the college and career market. We would like to schedule a few one-hour appearances by Christopher Pole during the promotion—tentatively scheduled for the second week of February. Could you please inform me of Mr. Pole's availability and the cost for an appearance?

cc: Matthew Brainard

5 Type sig block (the name of the AutoText entry that you want to insert).

Figure 1-20

Our store, Selections, Inc., is planning a week-long promotion aimed at the college and career market. We would like to schedule a few one-hour appearances by Christopher Pole during the promotion—tentatively scheduled for the second week of February. Could you please inform me of Mr. Pole's availability and the cost for an appearance?

sig block

cc: Matthew Brainard

Name of the
AutoText entry

6 Press ⟨F3⟩ to insert the AutoText entry.

Figure 1-21

Our store, Selections, Inc., is planning a week-long promotion aimed at the college and career market. We would like to schedule a few one-hour appearances by Christopher Pole during the promotion—tentatively scheduled for the second week of February. Could you please inform me of Mr. Pole's availability and the cost for an appearance?

Sincerely

Rachel Crawford
Public Relations

cc: Matthew Brainard

7 Save the file.

Tip You can print a list of AutoText entries by selecting **AutoText entries** from the **Print what** drop-down list in the Print dialog box.

CHECK POINT

Remember what you learned in Project 2 of Common Elements about creating and using AutoCorrect entries? What is the main difference between an AutoCorrect entry and an AutoText entry? Word automatically corrects text with AutoCorrect, but you have to press ⟨F3⟩ to replace text with an AutoText entry.

Using AutoComplete

The *AutoComplete* feature completes text that you begin to type. When AutoComplete can complete the text for you, it displays a ScreenTip showing the word, phrase, or the beginning of the text that it will complete.

Setting the AutoComplete Option. If you want to use the AutoComplete feature, you must turn it on first. You will find the option that controls AutoComplete in the AutoCorrect dialog box on the AutoText tab.

Task 6:
To Turn on AutoComplete

1 Choose **Tools | AutoCorrect Options** to open the AutoCorrect dialog box.

Figure 1-22

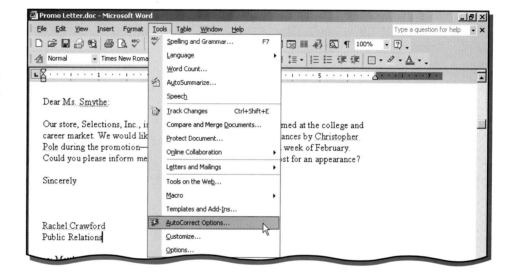

2 Click the **AutoText** tab.

3 Select **Show AutoComplete suggestions** to allow Word to display the AutoComplete Screen Tip.

4 Click **OK**. The dialog box closes.

Figure 1-23

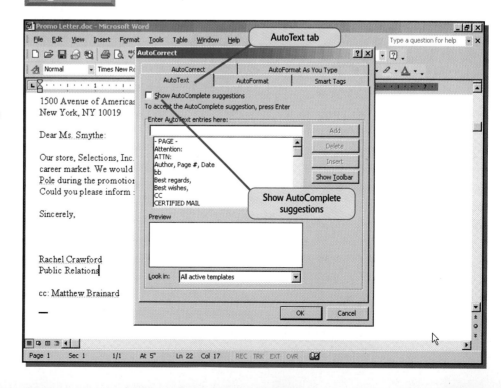

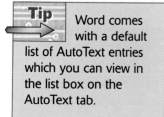

Tip Word comes with a default list of AutoText entries which you can view in the list box on the AutoText tab.

Using AutoComplete. Once AutoComplete is turned on, Word can complete the name of a day of the week, the name of a month, the current date, or an AutoText entry such as the one you created in the previous task.

Task 7:

To Complete an AutoText Entry with AutoComplete

1 Select the signature block, being careful not to select the space after the department name, and delete it.

2 Type **sig b** (just the beginning of the name of the AutoText entry).

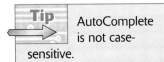 **Tip** AutoComplete is not case-sensitive.

Troubleshooting
If a ScreenTip does not display when you type the name of an AutoText entry, the name is probably not long enough. The name must be at least four characters.

Figure 1-24

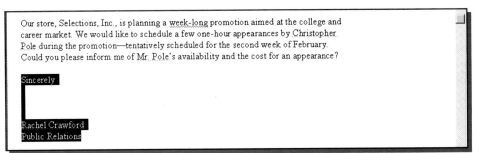

Our store, Selections, Inc., is planning a week-long promotion aimed at the college and career market. We would like to schedule a few one-hour appearances by Christopher Pole during the promotion—tentatively scheduled for the second week of February. Could you please inform me of Mr. Pole's availability and the cost for an appearance?

Sincerely

Rachel Crawford
Public Relations

Figure 1-25

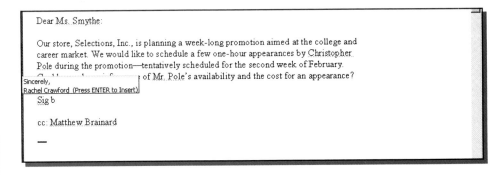

Dear Ms. Smythe:

Our store, Selections, Inc., is planning a week-long promotion aimed at the college and career market. We would like to schedule a few one-hour appearances by Christopher Pole during the promotion—tentatively scheduled for the second week of February. Could you please inform me of Mr. Pole's availability and the cost for an appearance?

Sincerely,
Rachel Crawford (Press ENTER to Insert)
Sig b

cc: Matthew Brainard

—

Tip If you don't want to use the AutoComplete tip, you can just keep typing when it appears and the tip will go away. For example, if you were typing the instruction, *Make sure the sig block is lined up with the left margin,* you would just keep typing because you don't actually want the signature block text to be inserted.

3 Press [Enter]. The signature block appears.

4 Save the file.

Our store, Selections, Inc., is planning a week-long promotion aimed at the college and career market. We would like to schedule a few one-hour appearances by Christopher Pole during the promotion—tentatively scheduled for the second week of February. Could you please inform me of Mr. Pole's availability and the cost for an appearance?

Sincerely

Rachel Crawford
Public Relations

cc: Matthew Brainard

Editing Text

You're almost finished with the letter now. To practice some basic editing and formatting skills, you will make a few changes to the document. Then you will check the spelling of the document and proof it on the screen.

Task 8:
Making Changes in the Document

1 At the end of the first body paragraph, select the word *inform* and type advise. Word replaces the text.

2 Click the Undo button. Word restores the original text.

3 Click the Redo button. Word changes the text back to *advise* again.

Figure 1-27

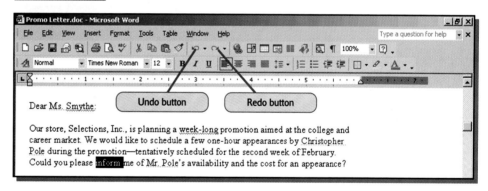

Dear Ms. Smythe:

Our store, Selections, Inc., is planning a week-long promotion aimed at the college and career market. We would like to schedule a few one-hour appearances by Christopher Pole during the promotion—tentatively scheduled for the second week of February. Could you please inform me of Mr. Pole's availability and the cost for an appearance?

Undo button   Redo button

Tip   Once you close a file, all the Undo actions are forgotten by Word. As long as the file is still open, however, you can undo in number of changes.

4 Click the insertion point before the words *tentatively scheduled* and press [Insert]. The OVR indicator is no longer dimmed in the status bar indicating that Word is now in Overtype mode.

5 Type currently.

Tip If you really prefer typing in the Overtype mode, you can make the mode the default by choosing **Tools | Options**, selecting the Edit tab, and choosing Overtype mode.

Figure 1-28

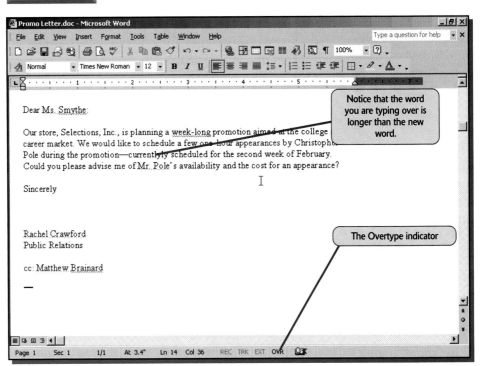

Notice that the word you are typing over is longer than the new word.

The Overtype indicator

6 Press [Delete] enough times to delete the remainder of the word *tentatively* and press [Insert] again. Insert mode is activated again.

Tip When deleting more than two or three characters, it is more efficient to select all the text and then press [Delete].

Figure 1-29

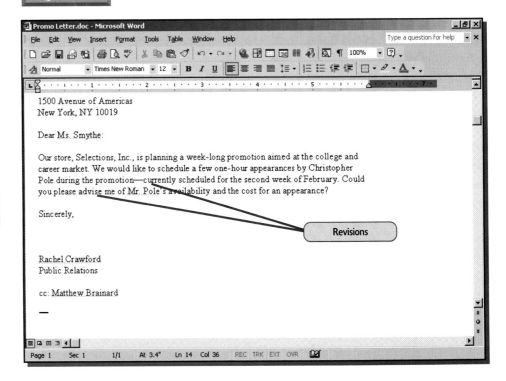

Revisions

7 Click the **Undo down arrow** to display the drop-down list.

Tip You will not see actions such as scrolling, moving the insertion point, or changing the view in the Undo list. These are not considered editing changes.

Figure 1-30

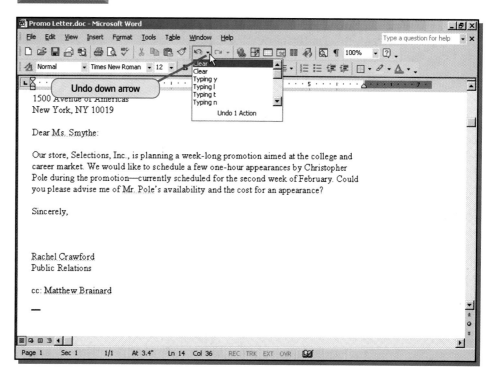

8 Scroll to **Typing "advise."** and select it. Word reverses all the actions you performed up to and including replacing the word *inform* with *advise*. Any actions you performed before that time remain.

Figure 1-31

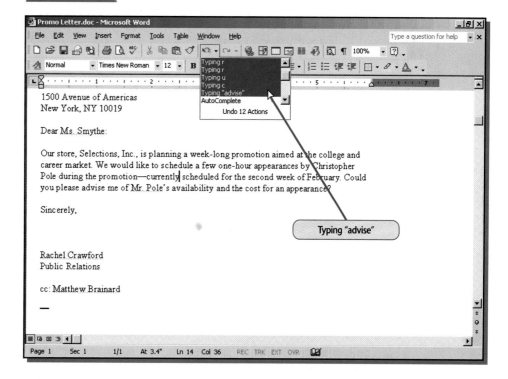

9 Look at the document in Print Preview and close the view.

10 Save the document.

Tip You can see more than one page at a time in the Print Preview by clicking the Multiple Pages button.

Figure 1-32

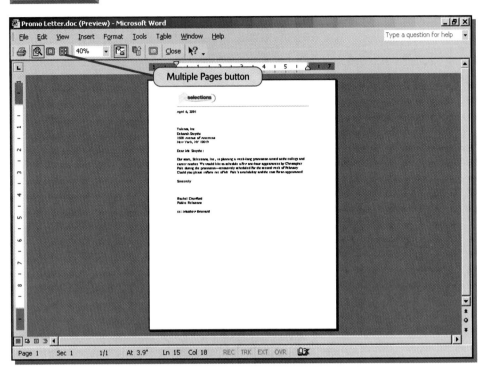

Multiple Pages button

Creating an Envelope

Now you need to create an envelope for the letter. To create the envelope, you will use the *Envelope and Labels tool*. This tool creates envelopes and labels using many standard sizes.

It is best to create the envelope while the letter is open so the Envelope and Label tool can use the address you have already typed in the letter for the address on the envelope. The Envelope and Label tool also inserts the return address automatically if you have previously specified a default return address.

Tip It is not necessary to specify a return address if you will be printing on a preprinted envelope—an envelope that already has the return address printed on it.

Word can even print a barcode on the envelope for you. The United States Post Office uses special scanning equipment to read barcodes for faster sorting of mail into zip code areas.

Tip If you use a barcode on an envelope, the barcode does not automatically update if you change the zipcode that you typed in the address.

Task 9:
To Create an Envelope

1 Choose **Tools | Letters and Mailings | Envelopes and Labels** to open the Envelopes and Labels dialog box.

Figure 1-33

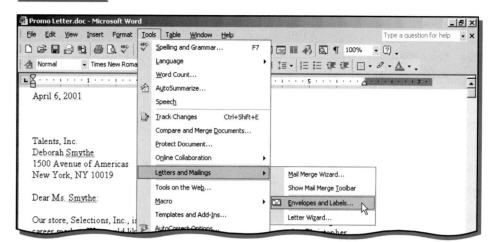

2 Click the Envelopes tab, if necessary.

3 Select **Omit**. This omits the return address if there is one.

> **Tip** If you type a return address, Word will ask you if you want to save it as the default return address.

Figure 1-34

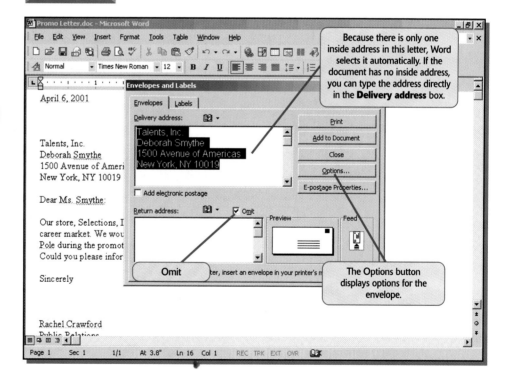

Because there is only one inside address in this letter, Word selects it automatically. If the document has no inside address, you can type the address directly in the **Delivery address** box.

The Options button displays options for the envelope.

WEB TIP

Check out e-postage services at Stamps.com. The software is free and it requires no special hardware or equipment licensing.

4 Click **Options** to open the Envelop Options dialog box.

5 Select **Size 10 (4 1/8 x 9 1/2 in)** for **Envelope size** and select **Deliver point barcode.**

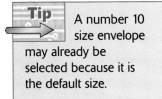

Tip A number 10 size envelope may already be selected because it is the default size.

Figure 1-35

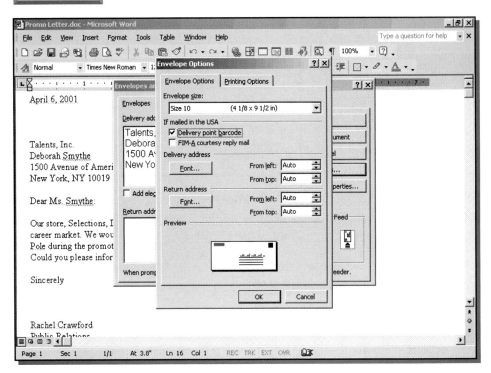

Figure 1-36

6 Click OK. The Envelopes and Labels dialog box is again visible.

7 Select **Omit**. This omits the return address if there is one.

8 Select **Add to Document.** Word adds the envelope at the beginning of the document as page 0. The letter remains as page 1. Word automatically inserts a section break between the envelope and the letter because they have different page layouts, as shown in Figure 1-37. You'll learn more about section breaks in Project 4.

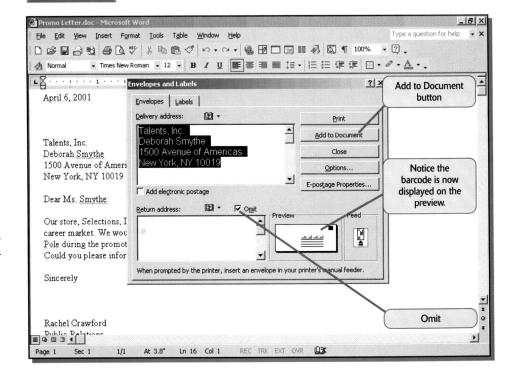

9 Click the Print Layout view ▤ button and scroll to see the page break, if necessary.

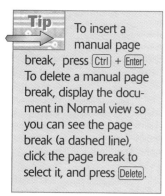

Tip To insert a manual page break, press Ctrl + Enter. To delete a manual page break, display the document in Normal view so you can see the page break (a dashed line), click the page break to select it, and press Delete.

10 Check the spelling and grammar.

11 Save and close the file.

Figure 1-37

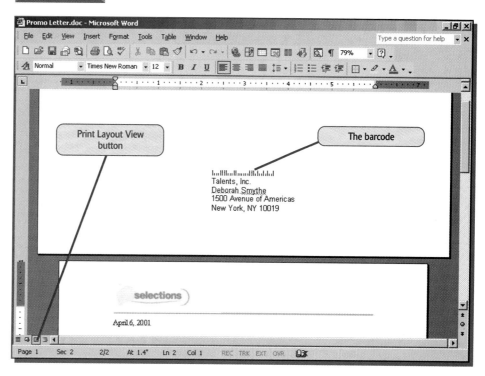

Print Layout View button

The barcode

Talents, Inc.
Deborah Smythe
1500 Avenue of Americas
New York, NY 10019

selections

April 6, 2001

Creating a Fax Cover Sheet from a Template

Before sending the letter, Rachel wants you to fax a copy of it to Matthew for her, and she has told you what to type on the cover page. To create the fax cover sheet, you will use a Word template. A *template* is a file with a professionally designed format that may include its own menus and toolbars, boilerplate text, text entry fields, specific fonts, colors, graphics, backgrounds, and so on. Word provides templates for creating legal documents, letters, faxes, memos, miscellaneous documents (invoices, résumés, newsletters, press releases, reports, and so on), and Web pages.

Tip If you have a fax modem that is configured properly, you can fax your documents directly from the computer.

Task 10:

To Create a Fax Cover Sheet from a Template

1 Choose **File | New** to open the New Document task pane.

Tip If the task pane other than the New Document task pane is already displayed, you can click the down arrow on the task pane's title bar and select New Document.

2 Click **General Templates** under **New from template** to open the Templates dialog box to the General tab.

3 Click the **Letters & Faxes** tab, if necessary.

Tip Word provides several different templates for letters and faxes in addition to a Fax Wizard and a Letter Wizard. If you select one of these Wizards, Word walks you through a series of dialog boxes that help you design the letter or fax.

Figure 1-38

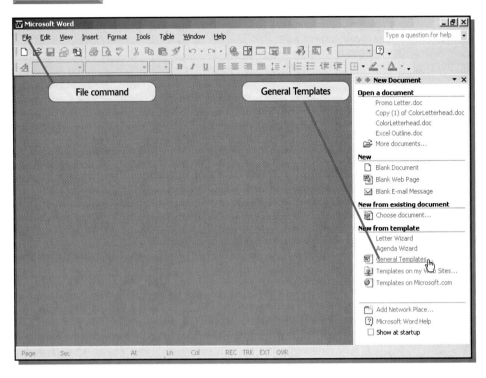

Figure 1-39

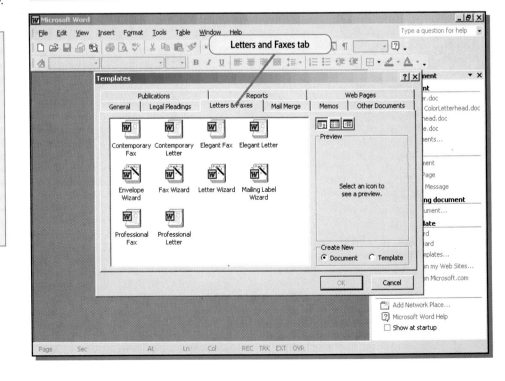

4 Select **Professional Fax**. A preview of the template appears in the Preview area.

5 Click **OK**. The task pane closes and the Professional Fax is displayed on screen.

Figure 1-40

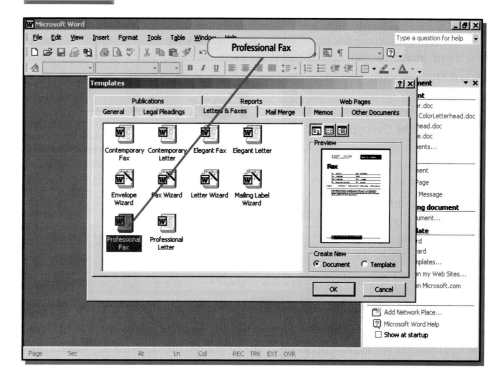

6 Click the instruction *Click here and type return address and phone and fax number* and then type Phone: 402-555-1111

Figure 1-41

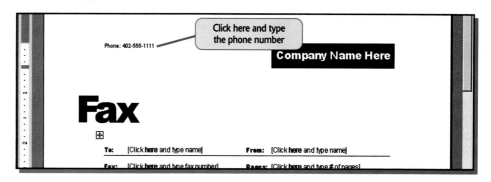

7 Press Enter and type Fax: 402-555-1112.

Figure 1-42

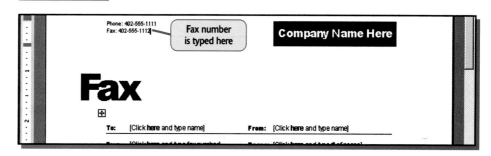

Task 11:

To Use Click and Type

1 Scroll to the bottom of the page and move the I-beam to the center of the document about an inch above the faint line at the bottom of the page.

2 Try to click in the area. The insertion point does not click on the line, but it does display the alignment that will be used in that area.

3 Move the insertion point, if necessary, until the center alignment appears on the I-beam. Then double-click and type **Now try to relax and forget about work. You're supposed to be on vacation!**

4 Save the file as *Fax*.

5 Keep this file open for the next task.

Figure 1-45

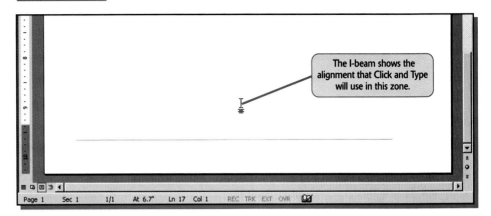

Figure 1-46

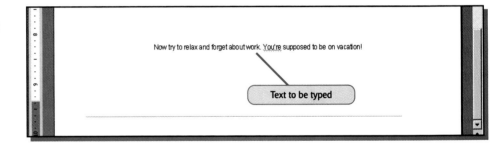

Creating Labels

Using the Envelopes and Labels feature in Word, the process of creating a label is almost as easy as creating an envelope. In this next task, you will create labels for the file folders you are using to organize the project.

Task 12:
To Create a Label

Figure 1-47

1 Choose **Tools | Letters and Mailings | Envelopes and Labels** to open the Envelopes and Labels dialog box.

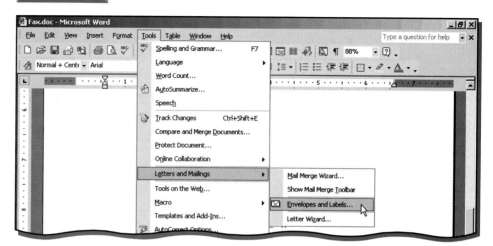

2 Click the **Labels** tab, if necessary.

Figure 1-48

3 Select **Options** to open the Label Options dialog box.

Tip Word remembers the last label that was created and assumes it is the label you want to create. The current label is shown in the preview area in the lower right corner of the Labels tab.

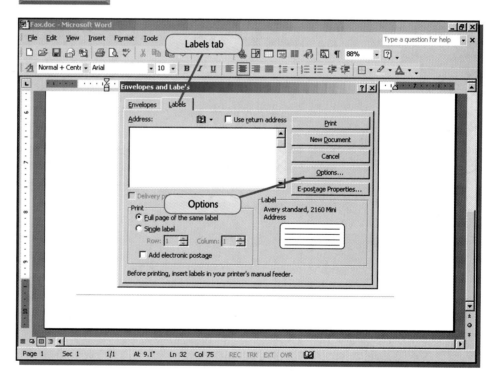

4 Select **5066–File Folder** from the **Product number** list and click **OK**.

Tip In the Label Options dialog box, Word lists brands of label products that can be purchased at most office supply stores. The product number in the dialog box corresponds to the product number of the particular brand of labels. Label information gives the label size and sheet size.

Figure 1-49

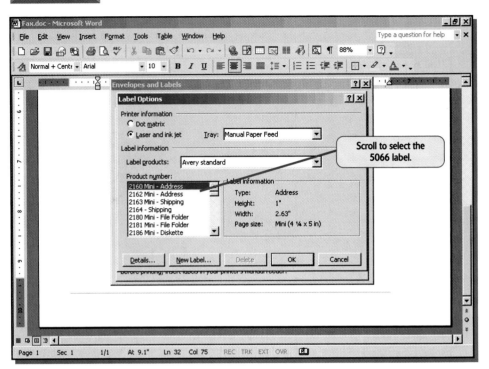

5 Select **New Document**.

Figure 1-50

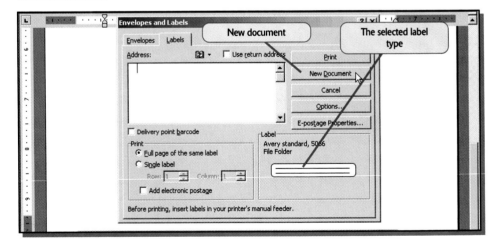

6 If your screen does not look like Figure 1-51, choose **Table | Show Gridlines** to display the table gridlines.

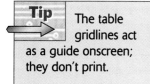

Tip The table gridlines act as a guide onscreen; they don't print.

Figure 1-51

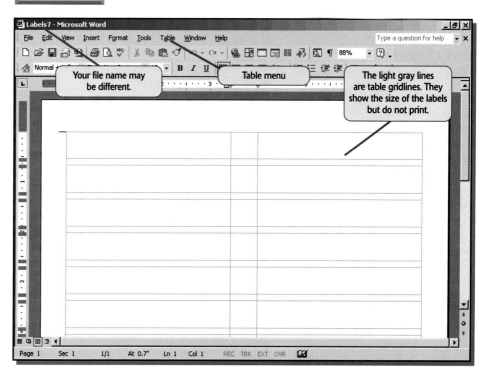

Your file name may be different.

Table menu

The light gray lines are table gridlines. They show the size of the labels but do not print.

CHECK POINT

Did you notice one significant difference between the options for creating labels and creating envelopes? On the Envelopes tab, there is an option to add the envelope to the current document. On the Labels tab, there is no such option. There is only an option to create a new document. So even though you were working in the Fax document and the labels were unrelated to the document, it was convenient to have a document open. If you had closed the Fax document, you would have had to create a new document or open another document. Then, you still would have had to create a new document for the labels.

7 Type Sales–C&C Week and press [Tab] twice. Type Seminars–C&C Week and press [Tab] four times. Type Packets–C&C Week and press [Tab] twice.

8 Type Career Day–C&C Week. Your document should look like the one in Figure 1-52

9 Save the file as C&C Labels and close the file. Close the *Fax.doc* file.

Figure 1-52

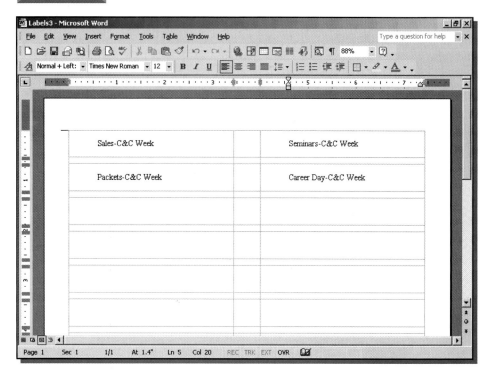

Viewing and Editing Comments

The *Comments* feature is a tool that you can use to annotate a document. The annotations appear in bubbles on the right side of the screen in the Web Layout or Print Layout views, but they do not print in the document unless you specifically choose to print them. Other views show a red I-beam at the insertion point where a comment has been inserted.

Tip To set options for comments, choose **Tools | Options** and click the Track Changes tab.

In addition to using comments to write notes to yourself, you can use comments as a way of collaborating with other people on a document. You might create a document and then pass it around to several people for their review. Instead of editing the document directly, the reviewers can insert their comments about how they think the document should be modified. Then you can view all the comments and decide how you want to modify the document based on the recommendations of the reviewers. As you make the revisions in the document, you can use the Reviewing toolbar to aid in deleting the comments when you no longer need them.

In the next task, you will review the comments made by your supervisor in the Promo Letter.

Task 13:
To View and Edit Comments

1 Open *Promo Letter Reviewed.doc* and scroll to the body of the letter

Figure 1-53

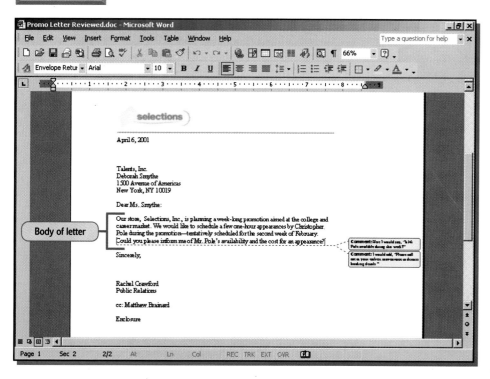

2 Point to one of the bubbles. The name of the commenter and the date appears in a pop-up box.

Figure 1-54

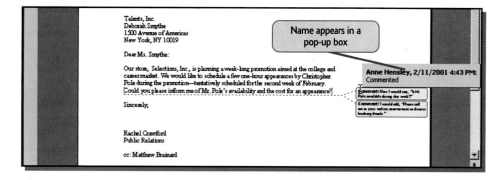

3 Display the Reviewing toolbar, if necessary.

4 Click the Next button in the Reviewing toolbar. The insertion point moves to the beginning of the text in the first comment bubble.

5 Select the text *Is Mr. Pole available during this week?*

Figure 1-55

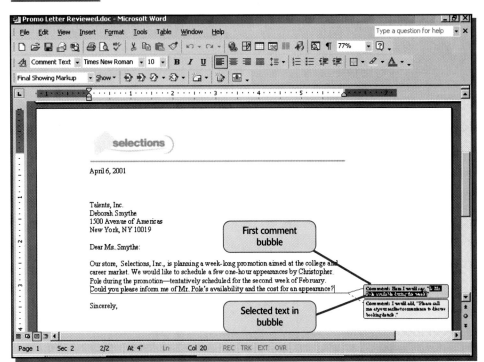

6 Click the Copy button in the Standard toolbar to copy the selected text.

7 Click the Reject Change/Delete Comment button. The comment is deleted and the insertion point is positioned before the text *Could you please inform me of Mr. Pole's availability and the cost for an appearance?*

Figure 1-56

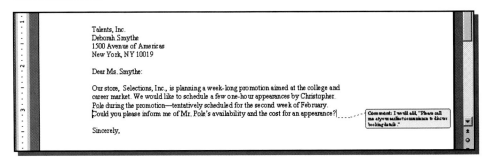

8 Press the left arrow button to move one space to the left and then click the Paste button. When you paste text, Word displays the Paste Options button.

Figure 1-57

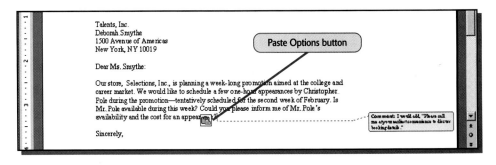

9 Click the Next ➡ button.

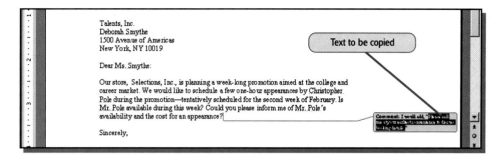

Figure 1-58

10 Select the text *Please call me at your earliest convenience to discuss booking details.* and click the Copy 🗎 button.

11 Click the Reject Change/Delete Comment 🔖 ▾ button to delete the text after copying it.

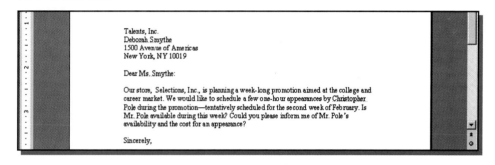

Figure 1-59

12 Click the Paste 🗎 button to paste the text. The Paste Options button is displayed at the end of the pasted text.

Tip The Paste Options button disappears as soon as you start to type again.

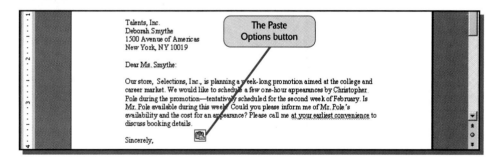

Figure 1-60

13 Delete the text *Could you please inform me of Mr. Pole's availability and the cost for an appearance?*

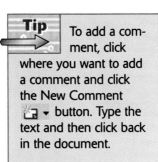

Tip
To add a comment, click where you want to add a comment and click the New Comment button. Type the text and then click back in the document.

14 Hide the Reviewing toolbar.

15 Save the file as *Promo Letter 2* and close the file.

Figure 1-61

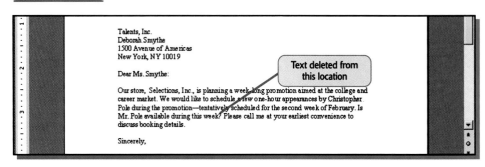

Figure 1-62

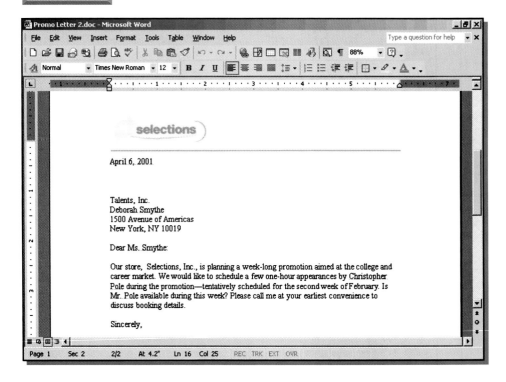

SUMMARY AND EXERCISES

SUMMARY

- You can create a new blank document or create a new document from an existing one.
- You can insert a date in various formats or insert a date field that automatically updates to the current date when the file is opened.
- You can insert special characters and symbols by using the Symbol dialog box.
- You can create Auto Text entries for frequently typed text.
- Word completes AutoText entries and some common words for you such as the names of the months and the names of the days.
- The Undo command reverses the last action and the Redo command restores an action that has been undone.
- The Envelopes and Labels feature creates envelopes and label layouts automatically.
- Word inserts page breaks automatically when a page fills up, but you can insert a page break manually.
- Word provides many templates for creating and formatting documents.
- Click and Type is a feature that allows you to type anywhere in a document.
- Comments annotate a document.
- The Reviewing toolbar aids in working with comments.

KEY TERMS & SKILLS

KEY TERMS

AutoComplete (p. 1-17)	date field (p. 1-8)	symbol (p. 1-11)
AutoText feature (p. 1-15)	Envelopes and Labels tool (p. 1-22)	template (p. 1-25) wrap (p. 1-8)
Click and Type (p. 1-29)	signature block (p. 1-15)	zones (p. 1-29)
comments (p. 1-34)	special characters (p. 1-11)	

SKILLS

AutoComplete (p. 1-17)	Enter text (p. 1-8)
Create an AutoText entry (p. 1-15)	Insert special characters (p. 1-11)
Create a document from a template (p. 1-6)	Insert symbols (p. 1-11)
Create an envelope (p. 1-22)	Redo an operation (p. 1-19)
Create a label (p. 1-31)	Undo an operation (p. 1-19)
Insert a date (p. 1-8)	Use an AutoText entry (p. 1-15)
Edit comments (p. 1-35)	Use Click and Type (p. 1-29)
	View comments (p. 1-35)

STUDY QUESTIONS

MULTIPLE CHOICE

1. A comment
   a. cannot be printed.
   b. displays the bubble on the screen in all view.
   c. can be deleted with a button in the Reviewing toolbar.
   d. displays in a bubble in either the left or right margin.

2. A date field
   a. displays the same date each time the document is opened.
   b. displays the current date each time the document is opened.
   c. displays the date the document was last printed.
   d. displays the date the document was created.

3. The AutoComplete feature
   a. displays an AutoText entry in a ScreenTip.
   b. displays a frequently used word or phrase that you can select from a drop-down list.
   c. replaces AutoText entries automatically after you type them.
   d. cannot be disabled.

4. Which of the following keystrokes should not be performed when typing a document?
   a. Press [Bksp] to erase the character to the left.
   b. Press [Enter] at the end of every line.
   c. Press [Enter] to create a blank line.
   d. Press [Enter] to end a short line.

5. When you add an envelope to a document, the envelope is inserted
   a. after the active page.
   b. before the active page.
   c. as the last page.
   d. at the beginning of the document.

6. The default envelope size is number
   a. 9.
   b. 10.
   c. 11.
   d. 12.

7. Word's options for labels include
   a. 10 standard size labels.
   b. only custom size labels.
   c. 10 standard size labels plus custom size labels.
   d. common brands of different size labels.

8. You accidentally pressed a key that caused something unexpected to happen to the format of the document. What is the best action to take to correct the problem if you are not sure what you did?
   a. Close the file without saving it.
   b. Click the Undo ↺ ▾ button.
   c. Click the Redo ↻ ▾ button.
   d. Choose **Tools | AutoCorrect.**

9. How do you access a document template?
   a. Click the New 🗋 button.
   b. Choose **File | Open.**
   c. Choose **Tools | Templates and Add-Ins.**
   d. Choose **File | New.**

10. Which of the following alignments is *not* used by Click and Type?
    a. left
    b. centered
    c. right
    d. justified

SHORT ANSWER

1. What is the difference in a date that is inserted as text and a date that is inserted as a date field?
2. How do you insert a character that cannot be entered from the keyboard, such as the copyright symbol?
3. How do you convert a date field to text?
4. What is a barcode and why would you use it?
5. If AutoComplete displays a phrase that you want to use, how do you use it?
6. What do you do if you do not want to use an AutoComplete phrase?
7. What determines the alignment that will be applied to text if you use Click and Type?
8. How do you position the I-beam when you want to use Click and Type?
9. What toolbar helps you work with comments?
10. Name the view(s) in which comments display onscreen.

FILL IN THE BLANK

1. To end a paragraph, press _____.
2. To insert a manual page break, press Ctrl + _____.
3. Word's default left and right margins are _____ inch(es).
4. Word's default top and bottom margins are _____ inch(es).
5. In Normal view a page break is a _____ line.
6. AutoComplete displays a(n) _____ when Word can automatically complete text for you.
7. You can insert © by using the _____ dialog box.
8. To insert a special character, choose **Insert** | _____.
9. To reverse an undo, click the _____ button.
10. To delete the character to the left of the insertion point, press _____.

FOR DISCUSSION

1. Discuss the pros and cons of inserting a date that automatically updates.
2. Describe the Click and Type feature.
3. Discuss the advantages of using a template to create documents.
4. Discuss the relationship between AutoComplete and AutoText.
5. Elaborate on the way comments may be used in a document.

GUIDED EXERCISES

1   CREATING ANOTHER LETTER

Now that Rachel has created one letter to a celebrity's agent, she can use the file to create additional letters to other agents. Figure 1-63 shows the letter envelope that you will create in this exercise.

Figure 1-63

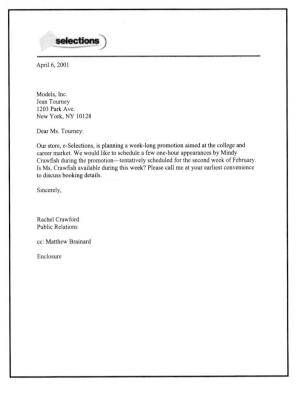

Models, Inc.
Jean Tourney
1203 Park Ave.
New York, NY 10128

1   Open a copy of *Promo Letter 2.doc.*

2   Change the address on the envelope and in the inside address to
Models, Inc.
Jean Tourney
1203 Park Ave.
New York City, NY 10128

3   Click in the bar code on the envelope and press Delete. (The bar-code does not update automatically when you change the zip code.)

4   Change the name in the salutation to Ms. Tourney.

5   Change all occurrences of the celebrity name Christopher Pole/Mr. Pole to *Mindy Crawfish* or *Ms. Crawfish.*

6   Save the file as *Crawfish Letter.*

7   Close the file.

2   **CREATING A MEMO**

So that Rachel and Matthew don't duplicate their efforts, Matthew is sending Rachel a memo as shown in Figure 1-64.

Figure 1-64

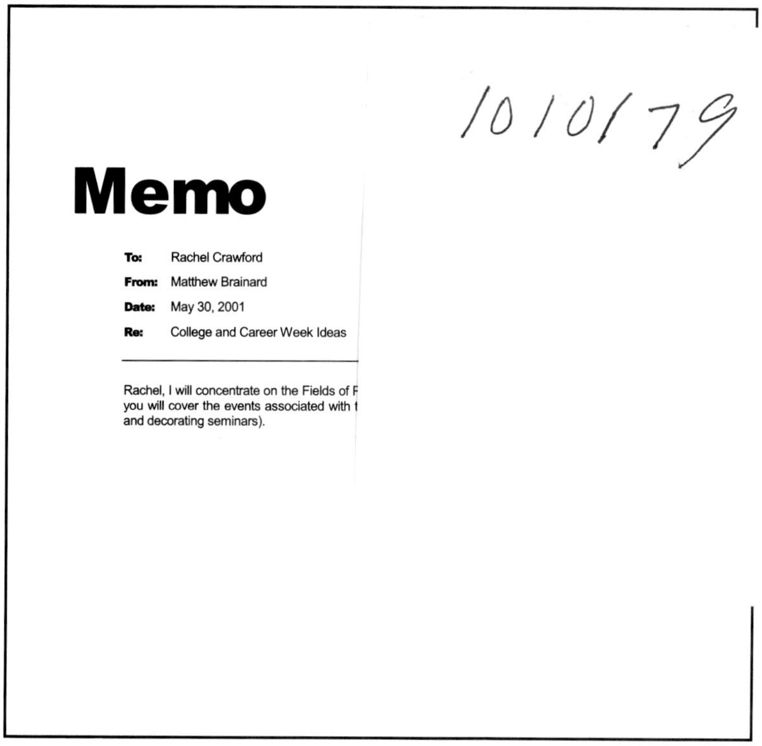

1010179

Memo

To: Rachel Crawford
From: Matthew Brainard
Date: May 30, 2001
Re: College and Career Week Ideas

Rachel, I will concentrate on the Fields of P
you will cover the events associated with t
and decorating seminars).

1 Create a new document using the General templates. Click the Memos tab, select the Professional Memo template, and click **OK**.

2 Select **Company Name Here** and type **Selections, Inc.**

3 Click the appropriate field codes and enter the following data:

To: Rachel Crawford
From: Matthew Brainard
Re: College and Career Week Ideas

4 Delete the entire line that contains CC: and the field beside it.

5 Select the text below the horizontal line and type the following:

Rachel, I will concentrate on the Fields of Play division, the drawing for the vacation, and Career Day if you will cover the events associated with the Home Page division (the fashion show and the cooking and decorating seminars).

6 Save the file as *Memo*.

7 Send the file to your instructor as an attachment.

8 Close the file.

3 ADDING COMMENTS

In *Promo Letter 2,* you incorporated the comments made by Anne Hensley, Rachel Crawford's supervisor. You have your own comments about the letter, so in the next exercise, you will add your comments to the document.

Figure 1-65

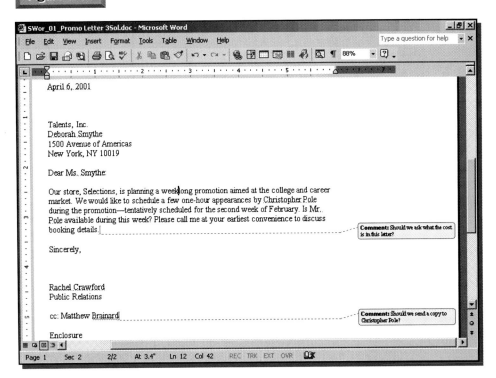

1 Open *Promo Letter 2.doc.*

2 Display the Reviewing toolbar, if necessary.

3 Click after the word *details.*

4 Click the New Comment [icon] ▾ button.

5 Type **Should we ask what the cost is in this letter?**

6 Click after the text *Matthew Brainard* and insert the comment **Should we send a copy to Christopher Pole?**

7 Save the file as *Promo Letter 3* and close the file.

4 CREATING MAILING LABELS

Rachel wants to form a volunteer advisory board made up of college students from colleges in the state. She intends to send a letter to the Dean of Students at each college asking for their cooperation and recommendations. You will create the mailing labels for the letters.

1 Create a new document.

2 Create a page of blank Avery 5160 address labels.

3 Search the Internet for the addresses of colleges and universities in Nebraska and type the addresses of at least five of those found.

4 Save the file as *College Labels* and close it.

The difficulty of these case studies varies:
are the least difficult; are more difficult; and are the most difficult.

---

1 WRITING A LETTER TO A FRIEND

Using the Letter Wizard, create a letter to a friend. (Choose **File | New**, click the General Templates hyperlink in the task bar, and click the **Letters & Faxes** tab. Double-click the Letter Wizard and select Send one letter. Click OK, if necessary, and then make selections or fill in information and click **Next** to continue. When finished, click **Finish**.) Add the proper spacing in the letter and then create and add an envelope to the document. Use Print Preview to view the letter and envelope. Save the file as *Letter1* and close it.

2 WRITING A LETTER TO ANOTHER FRIEND

Open a copy of the letter you created in the previous exercise. Choose **File | Save As**, type **Letter2**, choose a different **Save in** location if you want to, and click **Save**. Edit the letter so it uses the name of another friend in both the inside address of the letter and the envelope. Insert additional text and delete text as appropriate. Save and close the file.

3 CREATING YOUR OWN KEYBOARD SHORTCUT QUICK REFERENCE

Create a document that lists some of the shortcuts and tips that you need to remember. Include tips from this book, use Help to find a list of keyboard shortcuts, or peruse the drop-down menus for keyboard shortcuts. Save the file as Shortcuts.

4 CREATING AUTOTEXT ENTRIES

In this exercise, you will create your own AutoText entries. You should do this exercise on your own computer instead of on a lab computer if possible. Create a new document, enter text that you might use often, and create AutoText entries for them. Suggested entries include your name, your address, a signature block with your name, your e-mail address, and your phone number. Print the AutoText entries. (Hint: See the tip on page 16.)

5 CREATING YOUR OWN AUTOCORRECT ENTRIES

In this exercise, you will create your own AutoCorrect entries. You should do this exercise on your own computer instead of on a lab computer if possible. Think of all the typographical errors you frequently make or words that you misspell and then choose **Tools | AutoCorrect Options**. Scroll the list of default AutoCorrect entries and see if yours are included. For any of the words on your list that are not included, type the incorrect word in the **Replace** text box, type the correct word in the **With** text box, and Click **Add**. When you've added all your entries, click **OK**. Test your new entries by typing the incorrect word and pressing the **Spacebar**.

6 CREATING MAILING LABELS

Create a label document that has the mailing addresses of frequently used addresses. These might include addresses for your family and friends or billing addresses. Include duplicate labels for addresses that you might use more than others. Save the document as *Frequent Labels* and close it.

Photospread credits pages 1-2 & 1-3
©Photodisc; ©Pearson Education; ©Lorraine Castellano

P R O J E C T 2

Editing and Formatting a Document

Creating a document, typing, and navigating a document to proof the text are the first steps in completing a document. Making sure the content is complete, accurate, logically organized, and formatted are equally important tasks in the process of producing a complete document. In this project, you will polish a document by editing and formatting text and checking spelling and grammar.

OBJECTIVES

After completing this project, you will be able to:

- Insert a file

- Navigate through a document

- Use the mouse to navigate

- Use keystrokes to navigate

- Navigate by browsing for objects

- Use the Go To feature to navigate

- Use Find to navigate

- Copy and move text

- Find and replace text

- Format text

- Use writing and proofing tools

e-selections) Running Case

Rachel and Matthew have both created documents that contain their ideas for College and Career Week. As you will see, the two documents are quite different in appearance. Rachel's document doesn't have much formatting, while Matthew's has a lot of formatting and graphics. The two documents need to be combined into one cohesive report.

From the Caveman to Color Laser Printers with a Fiery RIP

Starting with the caveman, man has recorded the written word on a variety of materials using a variety of methods that were suited to the materials. Pressing letters into clay tablets and cutting letters into stone and wood, gave way to painting letters with a reed brush on papyrus. The shortage of papyrus in the second century led to the use of parchment (made of goatskin) and vellum (made of calfskin), both of which provided a smoother surface for writing with a more precise instrument—the goose quill pen. Enter Guttenburg's invention of the moveable-type printing press in 1448, N. L. Robert's invention of a paper-making machine in 1798, and Glidden S. Sholes' invention of the typewriter in 1867, and it was a quick trip to where we are today with computers and desktop printers available to the masses.

The proliferation of desktop computers demanded a corresponding proliferation of printing devices, starting with the daisy-wheel printer and the dot-matrix printer and eventually moving to the two most widely used printers today, the inkjet printer and the laser printer.

The daisy-wheel printer worked very much like the old ball-head typewriter. It had a plastic or metal wheel on which the shape of each character stood out in relief. A hammer pressed the wheel against an inked ribbon, which made an ink stain in the shape of the character on the paper. The dot-matrix printer used pins to strike against an inked ribbon. Each pin made a dot and the combination of dots formed the characters. An ink-jet printer sprays ink directly on a sheet of paper, and a laser printer uses the same technology as a copy machine.

Raster Image Processing (RIP)
for speed, art, and sharp text
with no jaggies or banding!

Depending on the type of laser printer, either the PC sends a bitmap image of the page directly to the printer's memory or the PC sends a description of the page to the printer and the printer creates the bitmap using its own processor. Inside the laser printer is a small rotating drum with a coating that allows it to hold an electrostatic charge. A laser beam scans the surface of the drum imparting points of positive charge onto the surface that represent the bitmap image in memory. The drum rotates attracting negatively-charged toner to its surface, which is then fused to the paper after the toner from the drum has been attracted to the paper.

Both the inkjet printer and the laser printer have popularized color printing, making it possible to actually print near-photographic quality pictures from scanned or digital-camera image files. Professional printers and design studios use more sophisticated inkjet and laser printers that are capable of higher resolution and larger formats than desktop printers. Often these printers are enhanced by a Raster Image Processor (RIP), one of the most popular of which is the Fiery system. A RIP makes printing faster, makes text look better (no jaggies), and eliminates banding.

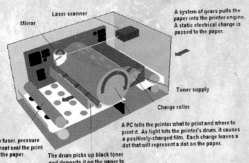

Laser scanner
Mirror

A system of gears pulls the paper into the printer engine. A static electrical charge is passed to the paper.

Toner supply

Charge roller

the fuser, pressure
d heat seal the print
to the paper.

The drum picks up black toner and deposits it on the paper to form either text or an image.

A PC tells the printer what to print and where to print it. As light hits the printer's drum, it causes a positively-charged film. Each charge leaves a dot that will represent a dot on the paper.

Editing and Formatting a Document

The Challenge

As the administrative assistant, it will be your job to combine the two documents from Rachel and Matthew and to arrange the text of the two documents in logical order. You will have to reconcile Rachel's and Matthew's different formatting and writing styles using Word's editing and formatting techniques. Then, before printing the documents, you will check the documents' spelling and grammar using the Spelling and Grammar icon in the status bar.

The Solution

You will begin by opening one of the documents and inserting the other document at the end using the Insert command. Then you will delete, rearrange, and format the text to create a professional-looking report. Figure 2-1 shows how you will combine the best features of both documents to produce the report.

Figure 2-1

College and Career Sales Promotion for Selections
The College and Career promotion is a week-long event with appearances by celebrities, seminars, sales, and various events.

Advertising
Local newspaper ads
Radio spots
Cable TV spots

Advisory Board
Form a volunteer advisory board made up of local college students and young career people – there would obviously have to be some perks for volunteering like discounts on merchandise. Get their recommendation for the promotion and enlist their help in promoting it.

Career Day
Promote the store's management training program.
Distribute information on the company, its benefits, etc.
Make a live multimedia presentation or run a continuous video in a kiosk area.
Take resumes and do interviews.
Have recruiting personnel on hand to answer questions.

Drawing
Hold a drawing for prizes such as ski equipment and/or a ski trip. Let Peek-a-boo draw out the winning names.
To enter the drawing, have customers write their names/addresses on the back of discount coupons that they redeem when they purchase something. No limit to the number of entries – the more sales the better!

Money-Saving Discount Coupons
Print coupons to be included in a packet.
Use a different format for each type of coupon. For example, coupons for 10% off in the Fields of Play department could look like tickets to a ball game.
Students must show their student IDs and register with their names and addresses to obtain the coupon packets.
Add names to our mailing list.

Sale in Fields of Play Department
Feature world-famous skier Peek-a-boo Streak and his new line of skis.
If possible, get Streak to make a personal appearance.

Sale in Net-Works Department
Try to get several popular musical personalities/groups to appear for autographs and media sales. We could invite celebrities such as Barf Crooks or Polly Darton for country and Industrial Nightmare or Steelica for rock.

Sale in Image Control Department
Have a fashion show. Clothes are modeled by members of the advisory board. Perhaps get someone like model Mindy Crawfish to host the show.

Sale in Home Page Department
Seminars aimed at college kids, such as a dorm room makeover seminar and a cooking in the dorm room seminar. Get celebrities for these events.

Giveaways
Give away the T-Shirts with the Selections logo.

Credit Card Applications
Set up booths throughout the store for applying for a Selections Credit Card.
Offer 10% off of the first credit card purchase.
Set up booths close to cash registers so sales clerks can refer buyers to the booth. (I've been in stores where the sales clerk tries to sign you up right at the register, but it's so annoying if you have to wait in line behind someone while they make an application!)

Inserting a File

You will begin with the report written by Matthew and insert the report written by Rachel at the end of the file. Inserting the file is a little easier than opening the file, selecting the text, copying and pasting the text, and then closing the file.

Task 1:
To Insert a File

1 Start Word and open *Ideas for College and Career Week.doc*.

Figure 2-2

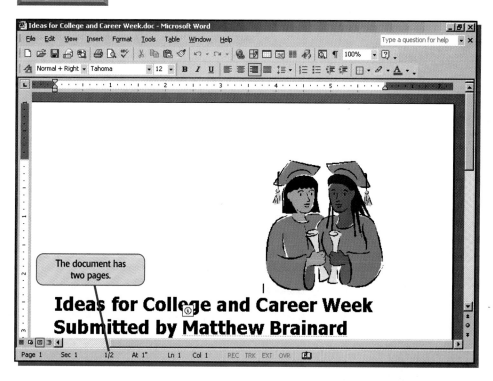

2 Press Ctrl + End. The insertion point moves to the end of the document.

3 Choose **Insert | File**. The Insert File dialog box opens to the same folder where the *Ideas for College and Career Week* document is stored.

Figure 2-3

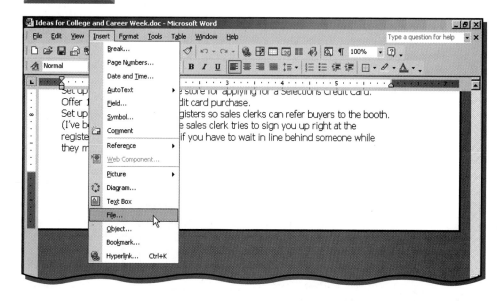

4 Scroll to *Ideas*.

Figure 2-4

> **Tip** Notice the down arrow on the Insert button that appears at the bottom of the Insert File window. You can insert a link to the file you are inserting by clicking the down arrow and selecting Insert as Link from the Insert list. By creating a link between the files, changes made to the original file can be updated in the document, to which it is linked.

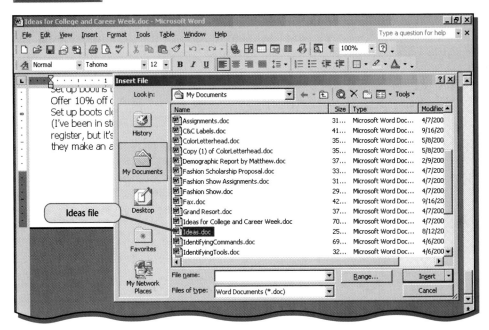

5 Double-click *Ideas.doc*.

Figure 2-5

> **Tip** Rachel's file is inserted and the insertion point is located at the end of the file. The document now has three pages. Check the status bar to confirm this.

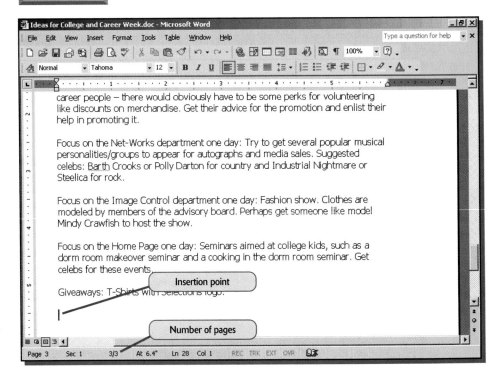

Navigating Through a Document

Being able to move around in a document quickly is key to editing efficiently. Word provides the following methods for navigating:

- Keystrokes
- Mouse techniques
- The Browse objects
- The Go To command
- The Find command

You will find that each method is best used in different situations.

Using the Mouse to Navigate

To move around in the document with the mouse, all you have to do is scroll with the vertical or horizontal scroll bar and then click the I-beam in the document. Use these methods to scroll with the mouse:

- Scroll up or down one line at a time by clicking the arrow buttons at the top or bottom of the vertical scroll bar.
- Scroll through large portions of the document by dragging the box in the vertical scroll bar.
- Move backward or forward one screen at a time by clicking in the vertical scroll bar above or below the vertical scroll bar's box.

It is important to remember that when using the scroll bars, the insertion point does not move. You must click the I-beam to actually move the insertion point to a location that is visible on the screen.

Tip Two additional navigation buttons at the bottom of the vertical scroll bar (See Figure 2-2) actually do move the insertion point.

Using Keystrokes to Navigate

Table 2-1 lists keystrokes you can use to move around in a document. When you use keystrokes to navigate, the insertion point actually moves. In the next task, you will use mouse and keyboard navigation techniques to look at the document so you can get an idea of how you need to edit and format the document.

Tip Word remembers the insertion point's last three positions. To return to a previous location, press Shift + F5.

Table 2-1 Navigation Keystrokes

To move to the:	Press:
End of the document	Ctrl + End
Beginning of the document	Ctrl + Home
Beginning of a line	Home
End of a line	End
Next word	Ctrl + →
Previous word	Ctrl + ←
Next paragraph	Ctrl + ↓
Previous paragraph	Ctrl + ↑
Top of the next page	Ctrl + PageDown
Top of the previous page	Ctrl + Page Up
Location of the insertion point when the document was last closed	Shift + F5
Position of the previous edit	Shift + F5

Task 2:
To Navigate in a Document

1 Press Ctrl + Home to move the insertion point to the top of the document and then scroll to the second page of the document.

2 Click the I-beam before the word *Promote* and then press End. The insertion point moves to the end of the line.

3 Press Home. The insertion point moves to the beginning of the line.

4 Press Ctrl + → three times. The insertion point moves forward three words.

Figure 2-6

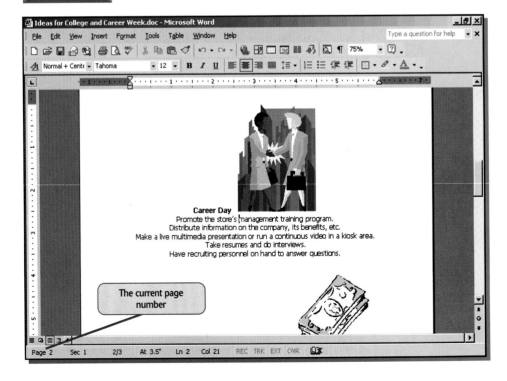

5 Press [Ctrl] + [↓] three times. The insertion point moves forward three paragraphs. Each paragraph is a single line in this case.

Figure 2-7

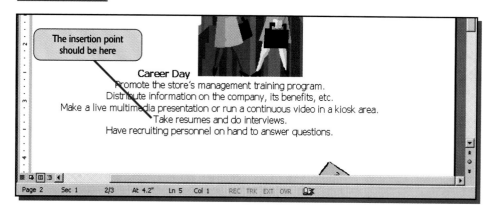

The insertion point should be here

Career Day
Promote the store's management training program.
Distribute information on the company, its benefits, etc.
Make a live multimedia presentation or run a continuous video in a kiosk area.
Take resumes and do interviews.
Have recruiting personnel on hand to answer questions.

Page 2   Sec 1   2/3   At 4.2"   Ln 5   Col 1   REC TRK EXT OVR

6 Click in the vertical scroll bar below the box repeatedly to advance to the end of the document one screen at a time.

7 Click the insertion point anywhere in the last paragraph.

Figure 2-8

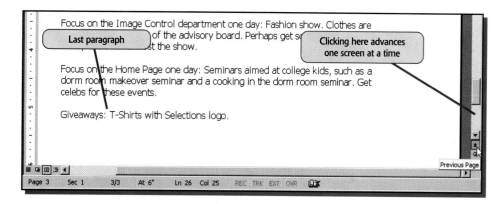

Focus on the Image Control department one day: Fashion show. Clothes are _____ of the advisory board. Perhaps get s__ __t the show.

Last paragraph

Clicking here advances one screen at a time

Focus on the Home Page one day: Seminars aimed at college kids, such as a dorm room makeover seminar and a cooking in the dorm room seminar. Get celebs for these events.

Giveaways: T-Shirts with Selections logo.

Previous Page

Page 3   Sec 1   3/3   At 6"   Ln 26   Col 25   REC TRK EXT OVR

Troubleshooting In Word, paragraphs are identified by the paragraph mark even if no text appears between the markers. If you have accidentally pressed [Enter] and added blank paragraphs to the document, advancing to the next paragraph on your computer will position the insertion point at a different location than the one shown here.

Tip Clicking the scroll bar above or below the scroll box on short documents of only one page will simply advance from the top of the page to the bottom of the page. Clicking the scroll bar does not move the insertion point.

8 Click the Previous Page button. The insertion point moves to the top of page 2. Notice that the insertion point is blinking before the first word on the page.

Tip Clicking the Previous Page or Next Page buttons also repositions the insertion point at the top of the page being displayed.

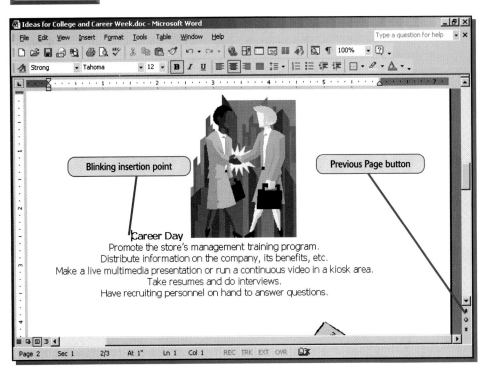

Figure 2-9

Blinking insertion point

Previous Page button

Career Day
Promote the store's management training program.
Distribute information on the company, its benefits, etc.
Make a live multimedia presentation or run a continuous video in a kiosk area.
Take resumes and do interviews.
Have recruiting personnel on hand to answer questions.

CHECK POINT

What's the major difference between using the navigation keystrokes and using the scroll bar? The navigation keystrokes actually move the insertion point, but the scroll bars do not.

Navigating by Browsing for Objects

The *Select Browse Object* button, located at the bottom of the vertical scroll bar, displays a palette of buttons from which you can select an object for browsing. The palette contains buttons that open the Go To tab and the Find tab in the Find and Replace dialog box and buttons that browse for fields, endnotes, footnotes, comments, sections, pages, edits, headings, graphics, and tables. In the next task, you will select the graphic button to help you find every graphic in the file.

In the next task, you will see how the Previous Page and Next Page buttons work and then browse the document for graphics so you can delete them.

CHECK POINT

One of the browse object buttons browses to fields. Do you remember what type of field you inserted in the letter in Project 1? You inserted the date field.

Tip

Each time you open Word, the Browse Object defaults to the page object and the browsing buttons are named Previous Page and Next Page.

Task 3:
To Browse for Objects

1 Press Ctrl + Home and then PageDown to position the insertion point just after the date, as shown in Figure 2-10.

Figure 2-10

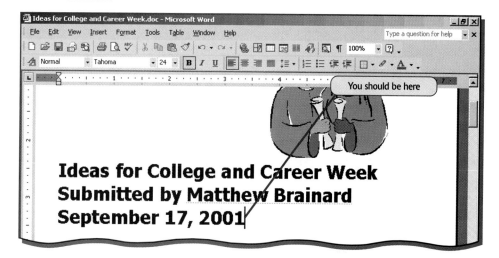

2 Click the Select Browse Object ⊙ button to open the Browse Object palette.

Figure 2-11

CHECK POINT

The navigation buttons above and below the Select Browse Object button move the insertion point backward or forward to the selected browse object. When the buttons are black, they move to the previous or next page. When the buttons are blue, then another object has been selected. The names of the Previous and Next buttons reflect the browse object that you select. For example, if you select the Table browse button in the palette, the navigation buttons will be named Previous Table and Next Table. So, if you forget the last browse object you selected, you can find out what it was by pointing to one of the navigation buttons to see the name of the button in a ScreenTip.

3 Click the Browse by Graphic 🖼 button.

Tip Four things happen: the palette closes, the insertion point moves to the next graphic, the arrows on the browse buttons change color from black to blue, and the names of the buttons change to Previous Graphic and Next Graphic.

4 Point to the Next Graphic ▼ button to see the ScreenTip.

Figure 2-12

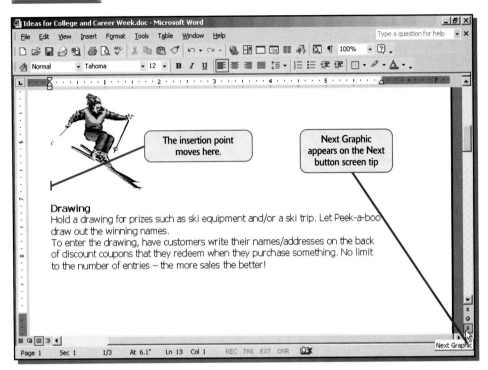

Tip After browsing by an object, you might want to reset the buttons manually to Previous Page and Next Page by choosing **Browse by Page**.

5 Click the Next Graphic button until the insertion point moves to the last graphic (the stack of bills).

6 Click the graphic to select it and then press Delete. The graphic is deleted.

7 Use the Previous Graphic button to go to the remaining graphics and delete them. There are three additional graphics to delete.

Figure 2-13

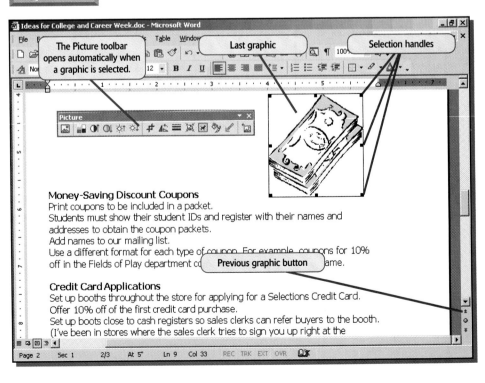

Using the Go To Feature to Navigate

The *Go To command* is used most often to go to a specific page number, but it also has options for going to footnotes, graphics, tables, and other items in a document. When you navigate with the Go To command, the insertion point moves to the desired page or to the specific item.

Task 4:

To Go to a Specific Page

1 Choose **Edit | Go To** to display the **Go To** tab of the Find and Replace dialog.

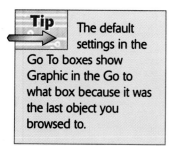

Tip The default settings in the Go To boxes show Graphic in the Go to what box because it was the last object you browsed to.

2 Scroll up, select **Page** from the **Go to what** list and type **2** for **Enter page number**.

3 Click **Go To**. The insertion point moves to the top of page 2.

Figure 2-14

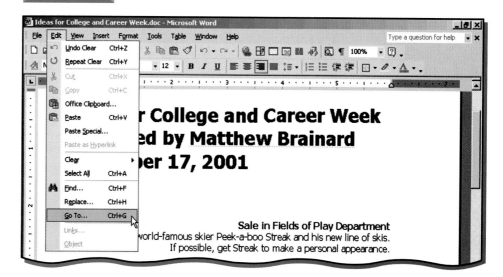

Figure 2-15

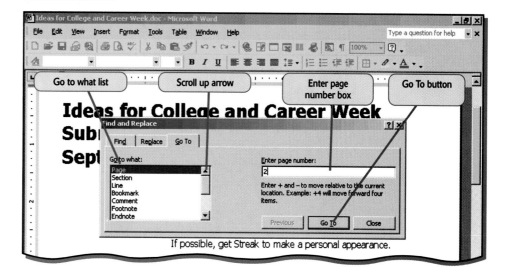

4 Click **Close**. The dialog box closes and the blue navigation buttons in the vertical scroll bar have changed to black.

5 Change the word *boots* in the first line on the page to *booths*.

Figure 2-16

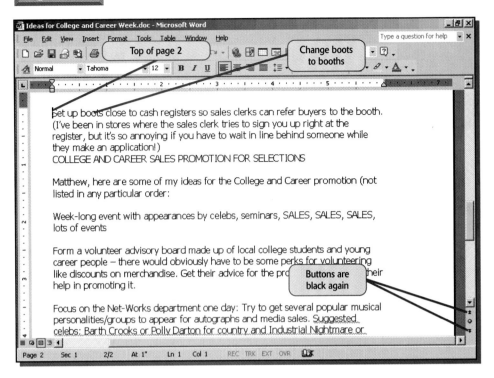

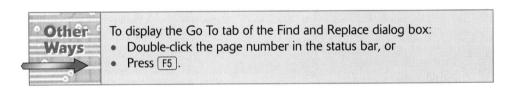

To display the Go To tab of the Find and Replace dialog box:
Other Ways
- Double-click the page number in the status bar, or
- Press F5.

Using Find to Navigate

When editing or formatting text in a document, the *Find command* is an essential navigation tool that you will use repeatedly. The command, which searches for specific text in the document, has an added bonus. It locates and also selects text so you can delete, copy, cut, or format text on the spot. If you need to select additional text, use the appropriate method as outlined in Table 2-2.

Table 2-2	Methods of Selecting Text	
To Select a	**With the mouse**	**With the keyboard**
Word	Double-click the word.	Position the insertion point at the beginning of the word and press [Shift] + [Ctrl] + [→].
Line	Click in the white area (called the selection bar) to the left of the line. The insertion point changes to an arrow when pointing in the selection bar.	Position the insertion point at the beginning of the line and press [Shift] + [End].
Sentence	Click anywhere in the sentence while pressing [Ctrl].	None
Paragraphs	Triple-click anywhere in the paragraph.	Position the insertion point at the beginning of the paragraph and press [Ctrl] + [Shift] + [↓].
Document (all text)	Triple-click in the selection bar.	Press [Ctrl] + [A].
Block of text	Drag the I-beam through the text.	Position the insertion point at the beginning of the block and then press and hold down [Shift] as you press any combination of arrow keys to move to the end of the block.
Vertical block of text	Drag the I-beam through the text while pressing [Alt].	Position the insertion point at the beginning of the block and press [Ctrl] + [Shift] + [F8]. Then use the arrow keys to extend the selection. Press [Esc] to turn this off.

Tip On the **Edit** tab of the Options dialog box, you can select the option **Use smart paragraph selection** to ensure that the paragraph symbol is always selected when you highlight the text of an entire paragraph.

In the next task, you will use the Find command to go to the locations in the document that require editing.

Task 5:
To Use the Find Command

1 Choose **Edit | Find**.

Troubleshooting
If your Find and Replace dialog box displays more options at the bottom of the dialog box, clear the checks for any options and click **Less**.

Figure 2-17

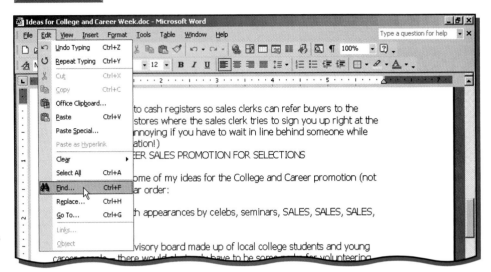

2 Type **Matthew** in the **Find what** text box to identify the text you want to find.

3 Click **Find Next**. Word moves to and selects the next occurrence of the word and the Find and Replace dialog box remains open.

Figure 2-18

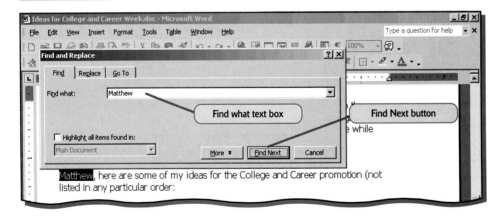

Tip If the Find dialog box covers the word, drag the dialog box to another location.

Tip Even though the Find dialog box is not open, Word remembers the last settings used in the Find dialog box.

4 Click **Cancel**. The dialog box closes.

Tip Notice that the two navigation buttons at the bottom of the vertical scroll bar are blue again.

Figure 2-19

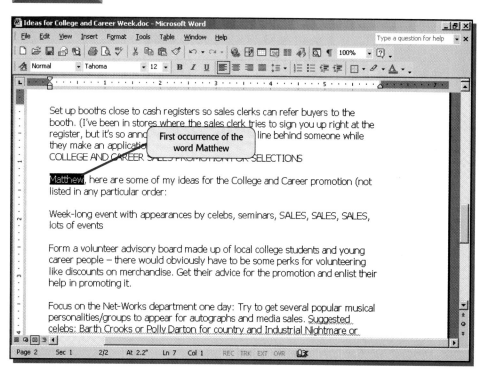

First occurrence of the word Matthew

5 Click the Next Find/ Go To button. Word searches to the end of the document and asks if you want to continue searching from the beginning.

Tip If you started searching for text from the beginning of the document, this message would not appear.

Figure 2-20

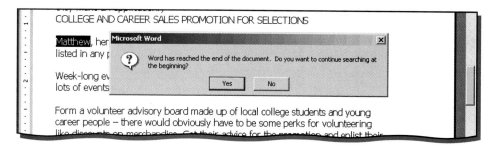

6 Click **Yes**. Word moves to and selects the next occurrence of the word.

Figure 2-21

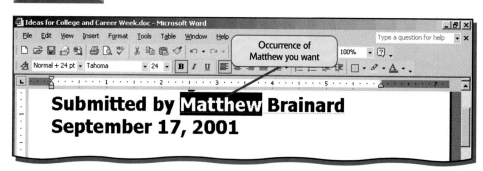

Occurrence of Matthew you want

7 Select the complete line and the following line by dragging the I-beam through the text.

8 Press Delete. The text is deleted.

Other Ways

To select complete lines of text:
- Click in the selection bar immediately to the left of the first sentence you want to select and drag down the margin area to the last sentence you want to select.

Figure 2-22

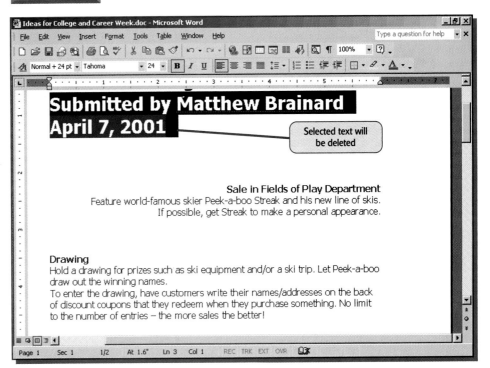

 Troubleshooting Be sure to select the space after the last character to include the paragraph marker. You want to delete it, too.

9 Use the Find command to locate the text *here are some of my ideas.*

10 Delete the entire line and the next one.

Figure 2-23

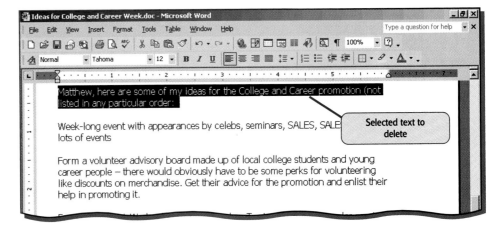

 Troubleshooting If you select and delete the wrong text, choose **Edit | Undo** to restore the deleted text and then try again.

11 Make the revisions shown in Figure 2-24: add the text that appears in red, don't change the font to red in your document, and delete the text that is marked out.

12 Save the document as *CC Ideas*.

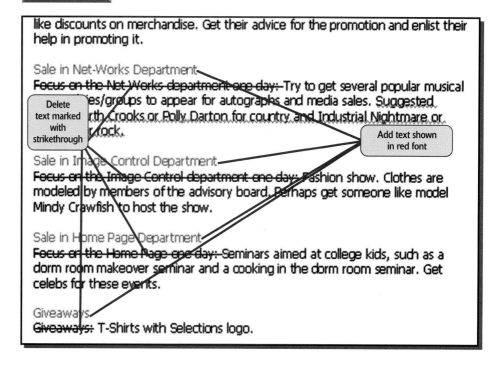

Figure 2-24

Copying and Moving Text

Word provides several different methods for copying and moving text (and other objects as well). You can use any of the following:

- Copy, Cut, and Paste buttons
- Copy, Cut, Paste, and Paste Special commands on the Edit menu
- Drag-and-drop method
- Office Clipboard

By default, all of these methods paste the text with the same formatting that it had when it was cut or copied. After the text is pasted, you can change the formatting easily by using the *Paste Options* button if the options are activated.

Tip The Paste Special command (on the Edit menu) provides options for changing the format of the text or object *before* it is pasted in its new location.

Using the Cut and Paste Buttons

The Cut and Paste buttons are handy tools for revising documents. With these tools, you can move text within the same document or cut text from one document and paste it into another.

Task 6:

To Move Text with Cut and Paste

1 Press Ctrl + F—the keyboard shortcut for the **Edit | Find** command. The Find and Replace dialog box opens to the **Find** tab.

2 Type format for **Find what** and click **More**.

3 Select **Find whole words only** and click **Find Next**. The word *format* is selected.

4 Click **Cancel**. The dialog box closes.

Figure 2-25

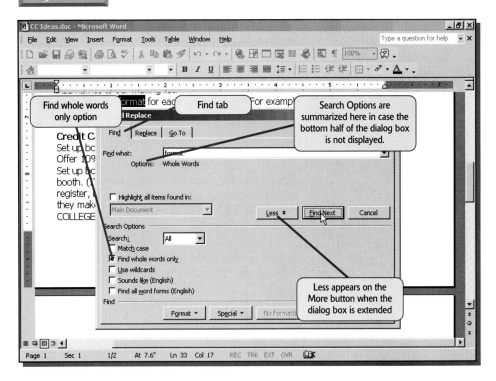

Tip

Selecting the Find whole words only option tells Word to locate the text only when it is preceded and followed by a space or end-of-sentence punctuation mark.

5 Select the entire paragraph that contains the word *format*.

6 Click the Cut button. The text is removed.

Troubleshooting

Be sure to select the paragraph symbol at the end of the paragraph.

Figure 2-26

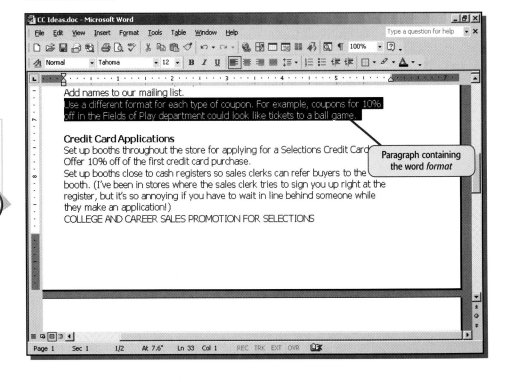

7 Scroll up, if necessary, and click the insertion point before the text that begins *Students must show their student IDs…*

Figure 2-27

8 Click the Paste button. The text is inserted and the Paste Options button appears. Figure 2-28 shows the button's menu, just in case you're curious. The option that you want, **Keep Source Formatting**, is selected by default.

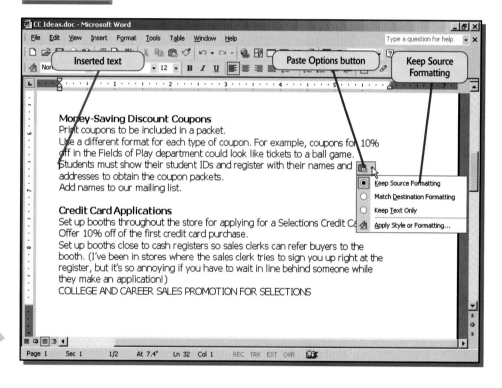

Figure 2-28

Troubleshooting
If you do not see a Paste Options button on your screen, choose **Tools**, **Options**, and click the **Edit** tab. Select the option **Show Paste Options buttons** and click **OK**.

9 Save the file.

Moving Text with Drag and Drop

It is a little easier to use the drag-and-drop method of copying or moving (though not mandatory) if both the original location and the new location are visible on the screen. When dragging and dropping in the same document, you can split the window if it is a very long document. Then you can scroll to the original location in one half of the window and scroll to the new location in the other half of the window. If you are dragging and dropping between two files, you can reduce the size of other document windows so that both documents display on the screen. In the next task, you will split the window to facilitate moving text with drag and drop.

Task 7:
To Move Text with Drag and Drop

1 Switch to Normal view.

2 Point to the border above the vertical scroll bar until the mouse pointer changes to a double arrow.

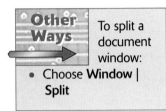

Other Ways

To split a document window:
- Choose **Window | Split**

Figure 2-29

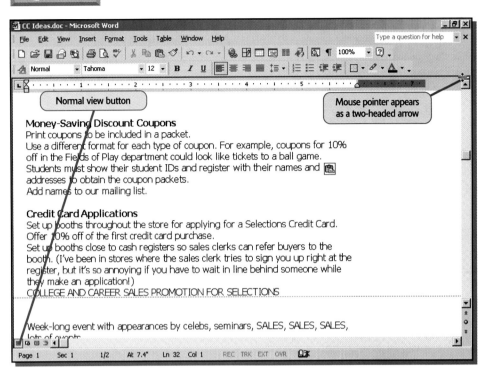

3 Double-click. The window splits into two separate panes.

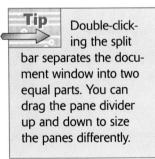

Tip Double-clicking the split bar separates the document window into two equal parts. You can drag the pane divider up and down to size the panes differently.

Figure 2-30

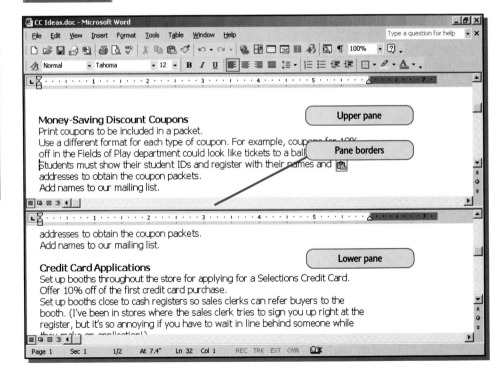

4 Scroll the document in the top pane until you can see the title at the top of Matthew's document and scroll the document in the bottom pane until the title of Rachel's document is at the top of the pane.

Tip
Because the window is divided into two panes, each pane has separate scroll bars that provide navigation tools for moving around the document and displaying different portions of the document in each pane.

Figure 2-31

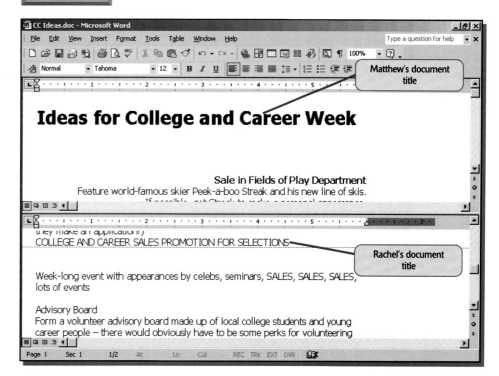

5 Select the text highlighted in Figure 2-32.

Troubleshooting
Remember that you are working with text from the same document but have split the screen so that you can display different portions of the document at the same time. Deleting or editing selected text in one pane affects the whole document.

Figure 2-32

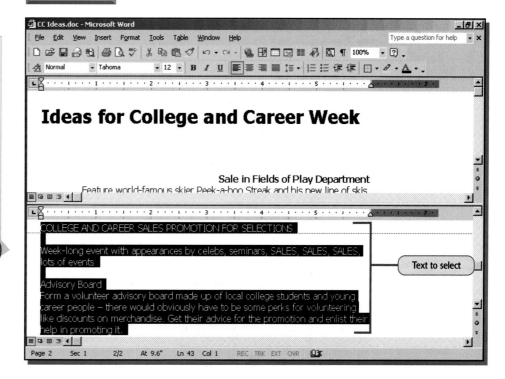

6 Drag the text into the top pane until you see a "ghost" insertion point just under Matthew's title and then drop the text. A ghost rectangle is attached to the pointer while you are dragging.

Tip If you want to copy the text instead of move it, press [Ctrl] while dragging. When you are copying, the ghost rectangle and a rectangle with a plus in it are attached to the cursor.

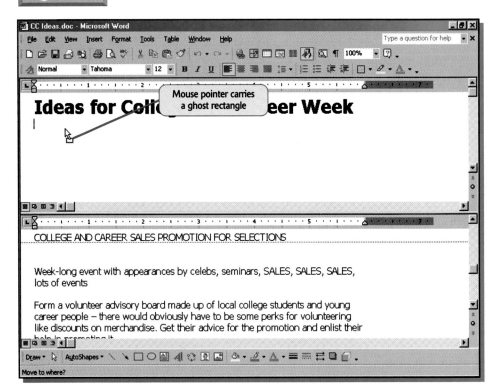

Figure 2-33

7 Delete Matthew's title and, if necessary, scroll down so you can see the space under the Advisory Board topic.

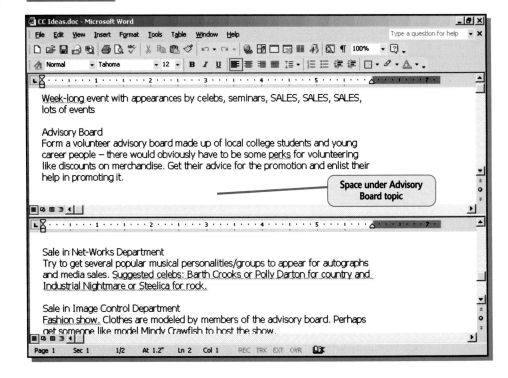

Figure 2-34

8 Scroll up in the bottom pane until you can see Matthew's topic on Career Day.

Troubleshooting
Because you're working in one document, the text on Career Day can be displayed in either pane. Be sure to scroll in the bottom pane rather than in the top pane.

Figure 2-35

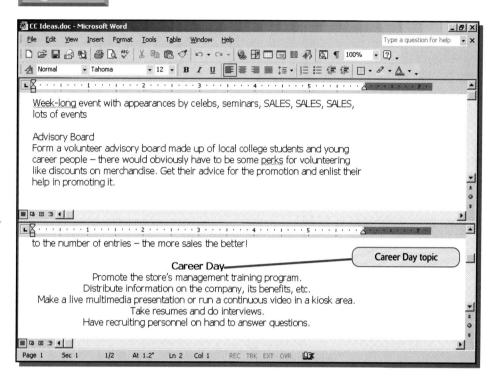

9 Select heading for the topic and all the text for the topic and drag it into the top pane just under the Advisory Board topic.

Tip If you press [Ctrl] as you drag the text to the new location, a copy of the text will appear at the new location and the text remains at its original location.

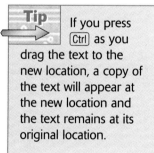

Figure 2-36

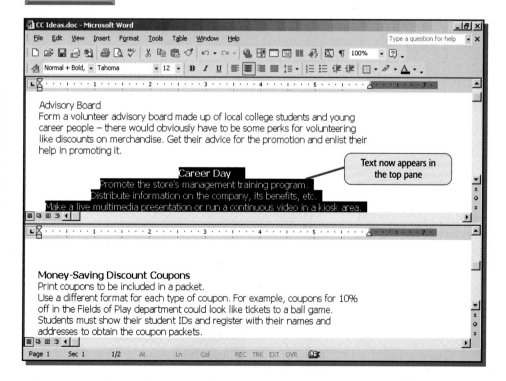

10 Point anywhere on the border that separates the two panes until the mouse becomes a double-headed arrow and double-click. The split is removed.

11 Save the file.

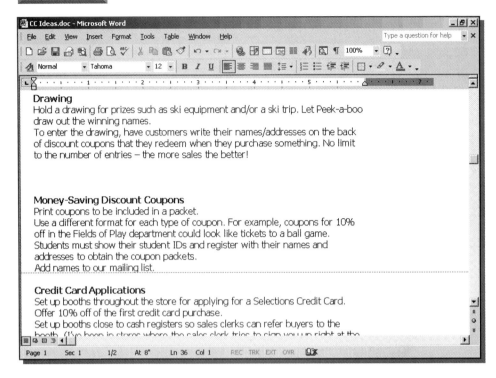

Figure 2-37

Copying Text with Paste Special

As mentioned earlier, the Paste Special command can specify how the text or object in the clipboard can be formatted before it is actually pasted in the new location. In the next task, you will copy data that is formatted very differently from the text in the location where you want to paste it. Because you know this ahead of time, you will use the Paste Special command to eliminate the formatting.

Task 8:
To Paste Text with Paste Special

1 Open *Advertising.doc.* Notice that the text uses an entirely different format from the text in the document you have been working on.

2 Select all the text by pressing Ctrl + A.

3 Click the Copy button to copy the text to the clipboard.

4 Close the document.

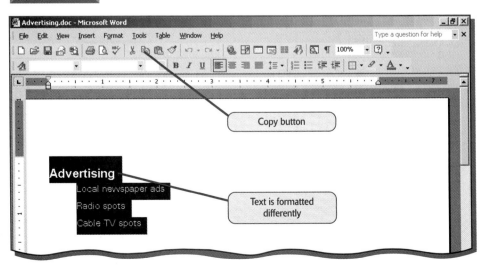

Figure 2-38

5 Press Ctrl + End to move to the end of the document.

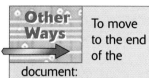

Other Ways

To move to the end of the document:

• Scroll using the vertical scroll bar until the end of the document appears.

Figure 2-39

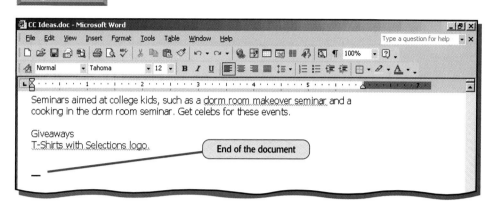

End of the document

6 Choose **Edit | Paste Special** to open the Paste Special dialog box.

Tip If you paste the text in the document you have been working on, the text will appear with its original format. Using Paste Special enables you to select the format you want to use to paste the text.

Figure 2-40

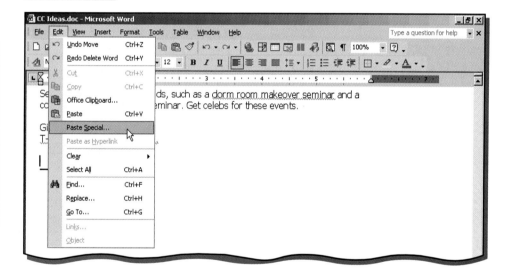

7 Select **Unformatted Text** from the **As** list.

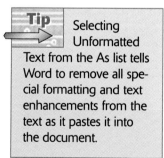

Tip Selecting Unformatted Text from the As list tells Word to remove all special formatting and text enhancements from the text as it pastes it into the document.

Figure 2-41

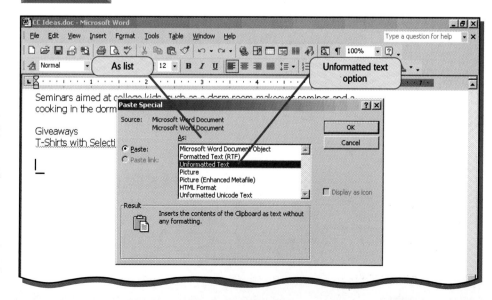

As list

Unformatted text option

8 Click **OK**. The text is pasted into the document without all the formatting that it had in the original document.

9 Save the file.

Figure 2-42

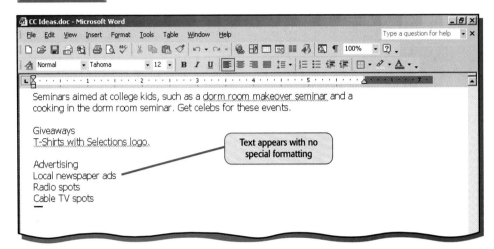

Text appears with no special formatting

Moving Text Using the Office Clipboard

As explained in Common Elements Project 2, the Cut and Copy buttons and menu commands store text or objects in the Windows Clipboard, which can hold only one item at a time. The *Office Clipboard*, on the other hand, can hold as many as 24 items. If you want the Cut and Copy buttons and menu commands to store to the Office Clipboard, you must either display the Office Clipboard or select the **Collect Without Showing Office Clipboard** option on the Office Clipboard Options list.

CHECK POINT

You learned about the Office Clipboard in Common Elements Project 2. Do you remember how to display the Office Clipboard? Choose **Edit | Office Clipboard** or press Ctrl + C twice. If the Office Clipboard is opened in any other Office application but is not open in Word, you can open it by double-clicking the icon in the system tray on the taskbar.

Task 9:
To Cut and Paste Using the Office Clipboard

1 Display the Office Clipboard and click the Clear All [Clear All] button to clear all snippets from the clipboard.

Figure 2-43

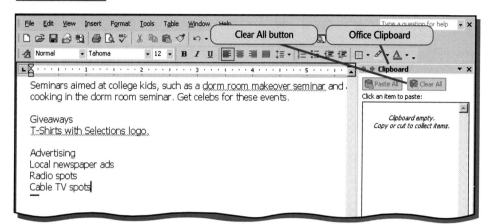

2 Press [Ctrl] + [Home] to move to the beginning of the document, select *Advisory Board* and the text below it, and click the Cut button to place the text on the clipboard.

Tip Explore the drop-down list that appears when you click the Options button down arrow to see settings you can change on the Office Clipboard.

Figure 2-44

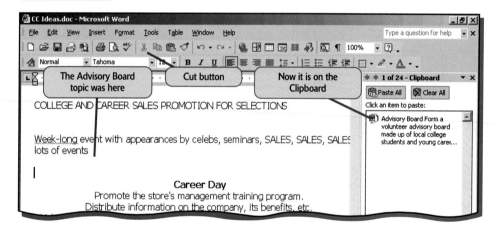

3 Select *Career Day* and the related text below it and cut it to the Office Clipboard.

Tip Notice that the text you cut and copy appears on the clipboard with the most recently added item at the top of the clipboard.

Figure 2-45

4 Continue selecting each heading and the text below it and cutting to the Office Clipboard. The remaining headings include:

- Sale in Fields of Play Department
- Drawing
- Money-Saving Discount Coupons
- Credit Card Applications
- Sale in Net-Works Department
- Sale in Image-Control Department
- Sale in Home Page Department
- Giveaways
- Advertising

Figure 2-46

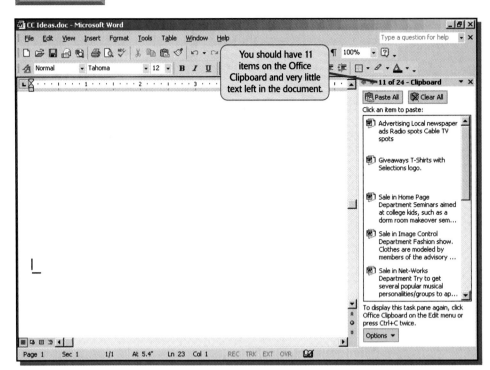

5 Press Ctrl + Home and then move the insertion point two lines below the text at the top of the document.

Figure 2-47

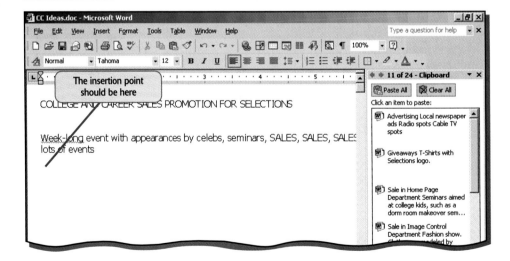

6 Click the Advertising item in the Clipboard. The item is pasted at the location of the insertion point.

Tip Notice that the Paste Options button appears each time you paste text from the Clipboard task pane. The same paste options are available when you paste using the Paste button on the Standard toolbar, the menu command, or the keyboard shortcut to paste the item that is stored on the Windows clipboard into the document.

Figure 2-48

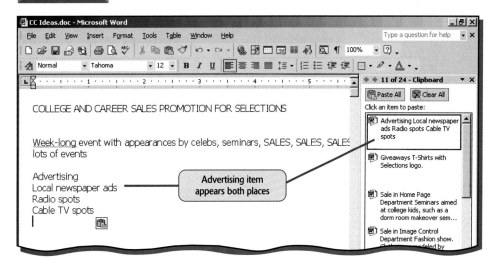

7 Paste the remaining items in the following order. Leave only one blank line between each item in the document.
- Advisory Board
- Career Day
- Drawing
- Money-Saving Discount Coupons
- Sale in Fields of Play Department
- Sale in Net-Works Department
- Sale in Image Control Department
- Sale in Home Page Department
- Giveaways
- Credit Card Applications

8 Save the file.

9 Close the task pane displaying the Office Clipboard.

Figure 2-49

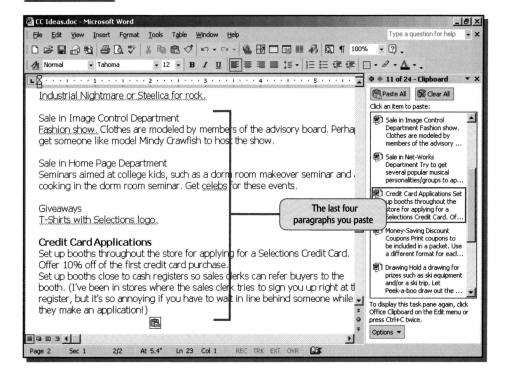

Finding and Replacing Text

The Find and Replace command is another editing technique that can be very helpful if you need to make the same correction several times in the same document. In the next task, you will use this technique to change the word *celebs* to *celebrities*.

Task 10:
To Find and Replace Text

1 Press Ctrl + Home.

2 Choose **Edit | Replace** to open the Find and Replace dialog box.

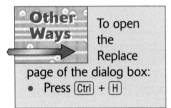

Other Ways To open the Replace page of the dialog box:
- Press Ctrl + H

Figure 2-50

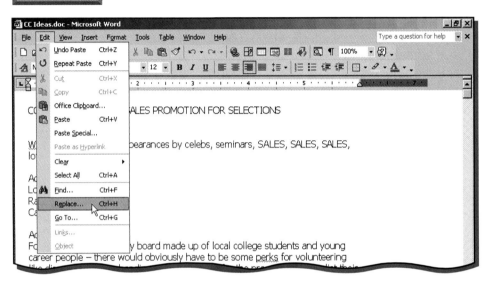

3 Click the Replace tab, if necessary, and type celebs for **Find what**, type celebrities for **Replace with**, and select **All** for **Search**, if necessary.

Tip The Replace tab should display automatically when you choose **Edit | Replace**.

4 Click **Replace All**. Word displays a message reporting how many changes were made.

Figure 2-51

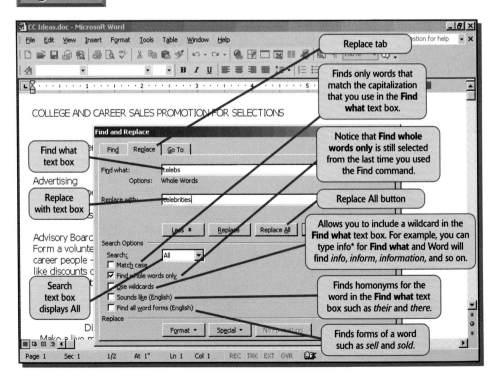

5 Click **OK** to acknowledge the message box, click Close to close the Find and Replace dialog box, and save changes to the file.

Figure 2-52

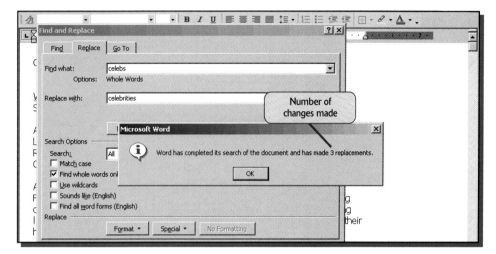

Number of changes made

Formatting Text

Word provides techniques for formatting characters, paragraphs, and entire sections of a document. In this project you will apply formats to characters, the most basic kind of formatting in Word. In Projects 3 and 4, you will learn to apply formats to paragraphs and sections.

Character formats include bold, italic, underline, font, font size, color, special effects, and *case* (upper and lower). You can use several different buttons in the Formatting toolbar to apply character formats, or you can use a *character style*, which is a named collection of character attributes. In this project you will change the default font, underline characters, add special effects to characters, apply and modify characters styles, and change the case of characters.

Tip Here's a keyboard shortcut for changing the font size: Select the text and press Ctrl + [to decrease the size one point or press Ctrl +] to increase the size one point. This is a nice method to use because you can see the text size increasing and decreasing onscreen.

Setting the Font Defaults

When you create a document by clicking the New Blank Document button, Word creates a document that uses Normal text. Normal text uses all the default font attributes, including the font, font style, size, color and underline; effects such as shadow and outline; character spacing; and text effects. You can set these defaults to whatever is best for your use. Changing the font defaults changes the text of the document that you are in and of all new blank documents created afterward.

Tip Word uses 12 point, Times New Roman as the default point size and font.

Task 11:

To Change the Font Defaults

1 Choose **Format | Font**. Notice that the font in use in this document is Tahoma.

Figure 2-53

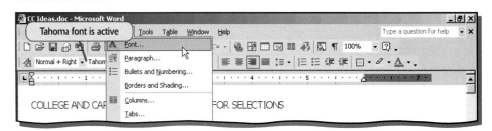

Figure 2-53

2 Select **Times New Roman** from the **Font** list and click **Default** to set the font as the default.

3 Click **Yes**.

Figure 2-54

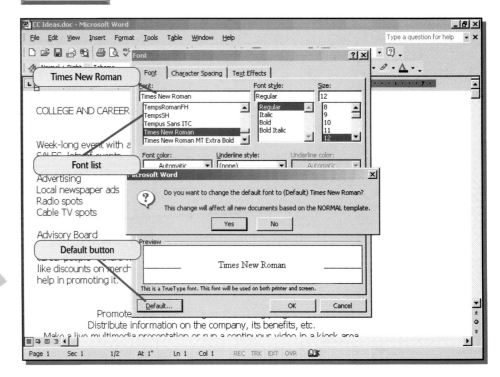

Troubleshooting

Times New Roman is a very common font that is available on most computers. If you do not see it in your font list, follow the direction of your instructor to apply a different font.

Underlining Text

To apply a single underline to text, you can use the Underline button in the Formatting toolbar. To apply a different kind of underline, such as a double underline, dashed line, or wavy line, you must use the Font dialog box.

Task 12:

To Apply an Underline

1 Use the **Find** command to locate *Sale in Net-Works Department.*

2 Choose **Format | Font**. The Font dialog box opens.

3 Select the double underline from the **Underline style** drop-down list, and click **OK** and save the file.

Figure 2-55

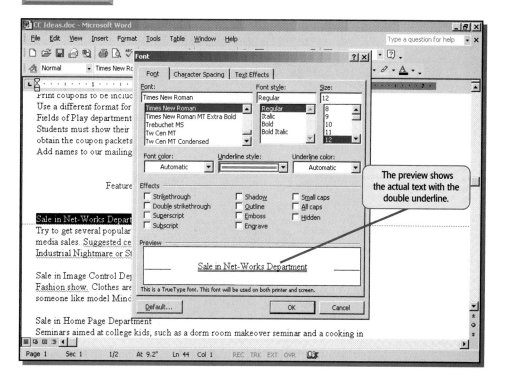

Tip The double-underline style is great for formatting text that represents a sum of values. Use it when you're creating balance sheets and income statements.

Applying Font Effects

Font effects include Strikethrough, Double strikethrough, Superscript, Subscript, Shadow, Outline, Emboss, Engrave, Small caps, All caps, and Hidden. Figure 2-56 illustrates all these font effects.

Tip Hidden text appears on the screen as shown in Figure 2-56 only when the display of Hidden text is activated by selecting it on the View tab of the Options dialog box. Otherwise, it is invisible. Hidden text also does not print unless you specifically choose the option to print it.

Figure 2-56

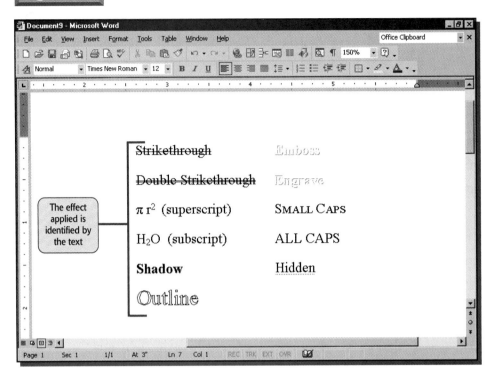

Task 13:

To Apply Font Effects to Text

1 Select the text that you underlined in the previous task, if necessary.

2 Choose **Format | Font**. The Font dialog box opens.

3 Select the **Small caps** effect.

4 Click **OK**.

Figure 2-57

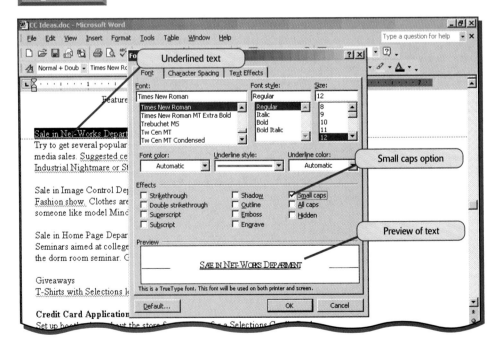

5 Use the **Find** command to find *Credit Card Applications* and experiment with an underline and a font effect of your choice.

Tip Small caps look better with an underline than upper/lowercase because there are no descenders for the underline to overstrike. Look at the preview in Figure 2-57 to see how the underline cuts through the descender in the letter *p* in *Department*. Then look at the same text in Figure 2-59.

CHECK POINT

If you've ever had to type a term paper or a paper for a math class that had raised and lowered characters, you'll appreciate Word's superscript and subscript formatting capabilities. To format text as superscript or subscript, follow these steps:

1. Type the text that needs to be raised or lowered and then select the individual character(s) that you want to format.

2. Choose **Format | Font** to open the Font dialog box, select the Superscript option to raise the characters above the line or the Subscript option to lower the characters below the line, and click OK.

Then you can apply the same format to other text characters that need to be raised or lowered by selecting the characters and pressing F4 to apply the formatting.

Modifying and Applying Character Styles

Word provides several default character formats called character styles. Two of these character styles that you might use frequently are called *Emphasis* and *Strong*. The Emphasis character style applies italic to text and the Strong character style applies bold.

You may have noticed while scrolling through the current document that some of the headings already have the Strong character format applied. In the next task, you will change the Strong format to a different font. This change will update the headings that already use the style. Then you will apply the modified style to the unformatted headings in the document.

Task 14:
To Modify and Apply a Character Style

1 Press Ctrl + Home and select the title of the document.

2 Click the Styles and Formatting ⚄ button on the Formatting toolbar. The Styles and Formatting task pane opens.

3 Compare your Styles and Formatting pane with the one in Figure 2-58. If necessary, choose **Available formatting** from the **Show** drop-down list at the bottom of the pane to display a list of available formats.

4 Scroll the **Pick formatting to apply** list until you see **Strong** listed.

5 Click **Strong** to apply it to the title of the document.

Tip Notice that the formatting of selected text appears in the box at the top of the task pane. The information in the Formatting of selected text box changes as you apply different formatting.

Figure 2-58

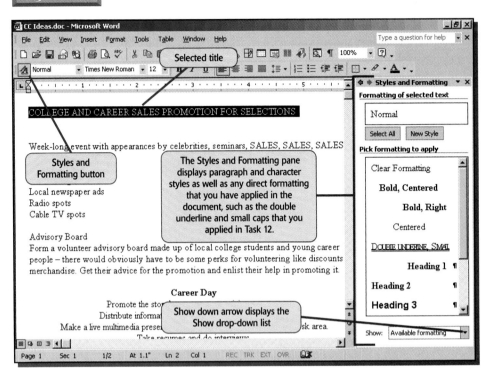

Figure 2-59

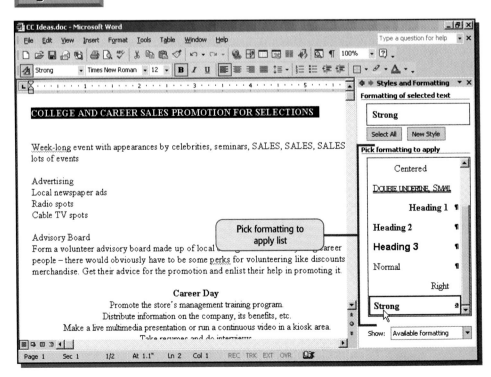

6 Right-click **Strong** in the task pane and select **Modify to open the Modify Style dialog box.**

Figure 2-60

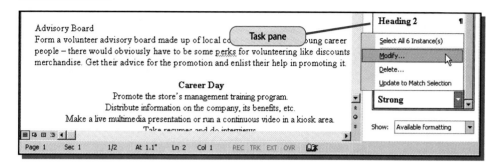

Troubleshooting
Be careful as you select Modify from the shortcut menu. If you accidentally select Delete, a message box opens and asks you if you want to delete the style. Select No.

7 Click the Bold button. Bold is no longer selected.

Figure 2-61

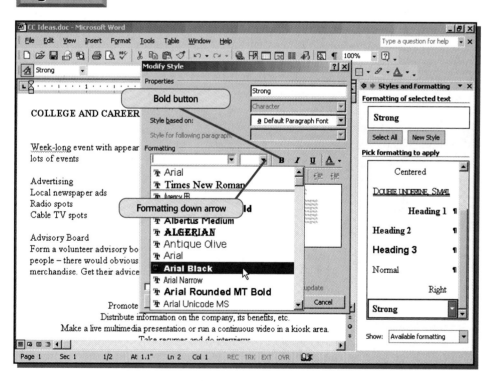

8 Click the down arrow for **Formatting** and choose **Arial Black.**

Tip To remove all formatting from text (i.e., to revert to Normal), select the text and press Ctrl + Spacebar.

9 Click **OK**. The font of the character style changes, and all text in the document that uses the style changes to the new font.

Figure 2-62

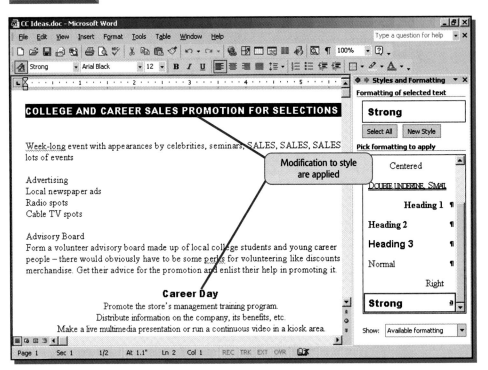

10 Click in the *Advertising* heading and click **Strong** in the task pane. The character style is applied.

11 Apply the Strong character style to the following headings:
- Advisory Board
- Sale in Net-Works Department
- Sale in Image Control Department
- Sale in Home Page Department
- Giveaways

12 Save the document and close the task pane.

Figure 2-63

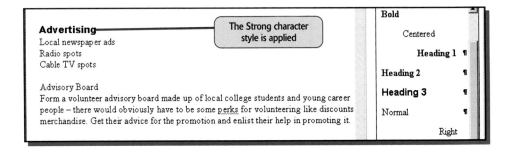

Tip To apply a character style to a single word, you can click in the word as in Step 10. To apply the style to more than one word, you must select all the words.

Changing Case

The Change Case command in Word has five options. Table 2-3 shows how each option would change the phrase *in the store*.

Table 2-3 Case Options		
Case options	**Example**	**Comment**
Sentence case	In the store	*Sentence case* capitalizes the first character of the first word. No other characters are changed.
Lowercase	in the store	*Lowercase* changes all characters to lowercase.
Uppercase	IN THE STORE	*Uppercase* capitalizes all characters.
Title case	In The Store	*Title case* capitalizes the first character of every word, even if the word is an article, preposition, or conjunction.
Toggle case	IN THE STORE	*Toggle case* reverses the case of every character. It is a quick way to correct text that has been typed with Caps Lock on by accident.

Task 15:
To Change the Case of Text

1 Choose **Edit | Find**. The Find and Replace dialog box opens.

2 Type **COLLEGE AND CAREER** in the **Find what** text box.

3 Click **More**, if necessary to extend the dialog box and display additional options.

4 Click **Match case**, click **Find Next**, and then close the dialog box.

Figure 2-64

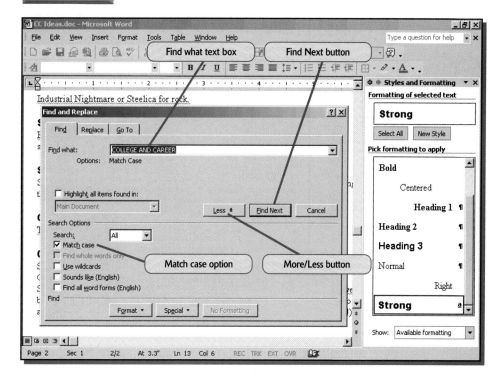

Tip The Find and Replace dialog box opens with the extended options displayed if there were displayed the last time you closed it. As a result, the Less button appears when the box is extended.

CHECK POINT

As you become more familiar with Word, you'll discover all sorts of neat effects you can apply to text. Among these special effects is one called text animation. Text animation enables you to emphasize text--words, sentences, or entire paragraphs--by making them flash, shimmer, light up, sparkle, and march! To apply text animation, follow these steps:

1. Select the text you want to format and choose Format | Font to open the Font dialog box.

2. Click the Text Effects tab, select the animation effection you want to apply from the Animation list, and click OK.

The Preview area of the dialog box demonstrates the selected effect. It's a great feature to have fun with!

5 Select all the text in the line containing the text COLLEGE AND CAREER in all caps.

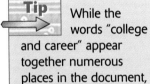

Tip While the words "college and career" appear together numerous places in the document, there is only one instance where they appear in all caps.

Figure 2-65

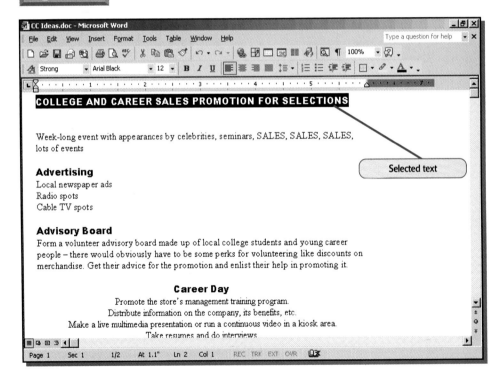

6 Choose **Format | Change Case** to open the Change Case dialog box.

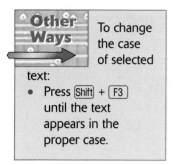

Other Ways
To change the case of selected text:
* Press Shift + F3 until the text appears in the proper case.

Figure 2-66

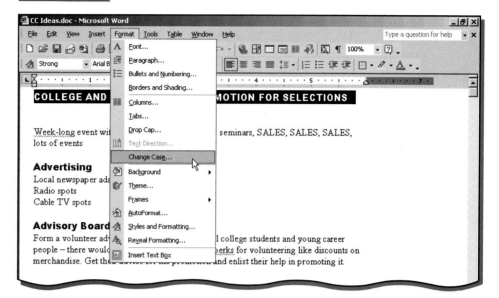

7 Select **Title Case** to apply the case to selected text and click OK.

Tip
Notice that the options in the Change Case dialog box are formatted to identify how text will appear if you select a particular option.

Figure 2-67

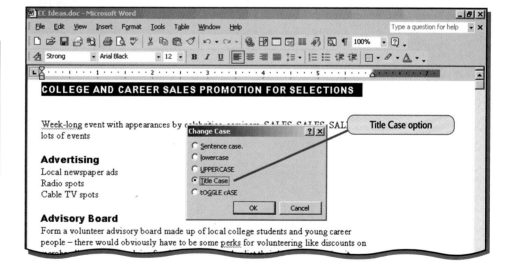

8 Change the words *And* and *For* to lowercase.

Figure 2-68

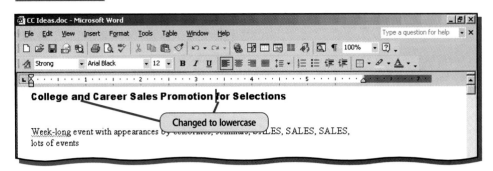

9 Select *SALES, SALES, SALES* in the next line.

Figure 2-69

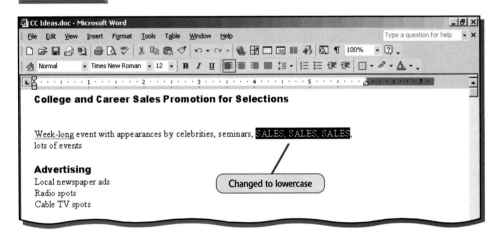

10 Press Shift + F3 several times to cycle through the case options and then change the text to lowercase.

Tip The Shift + F3 technique does not include Toggle case or Sentence case if the selected text does not have a period at the end.

Aligning Text

In a new document, the default *alignment* for paragraphs is left. The Formatting toolbar contains buttons for aligning text on the left margin, centering text between the margins, aligning text on the right margin, and aligning text on the left and right margins (like a newspaper column). The document you are working on has two sections in it that use an alignment other than the default left alignment. In the next task, you will change the alignment of these sections back to left.

Tip When using an alignment button, you can click anywhere in the paragraph. The alignment selected will apply to the entire paragraph.

Task 16:
To Align Text

1 Scroll to the *Career Day* heading in the document and click in the first line under the heading.

2 Click the Align Left button. The text aligns with the left margin and the Style control changes to Normal.

Figure 2-70

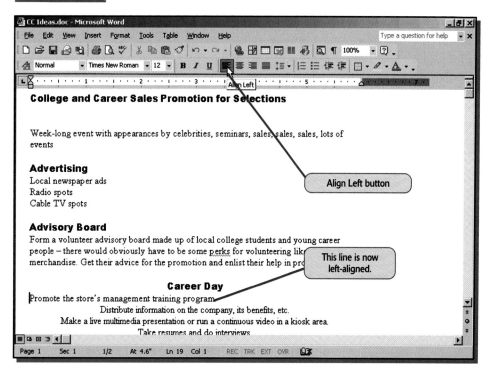

Align Left button

This line is now left-aligned.

3 Select from the line above the heading *Career Day* to the line below the text under that heading and apply left alignment.

Figure 2-71

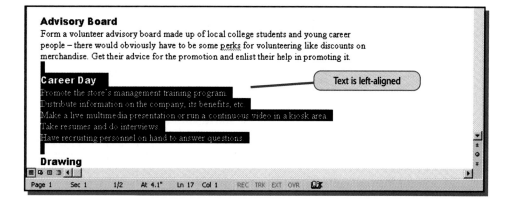

Text is left-aligned

4 Scroll down to the heading *Sale in Fields of Play Department*. Select all the way from the blank line above the heading to the blank line below all the text under that heading, and apply left alignment.

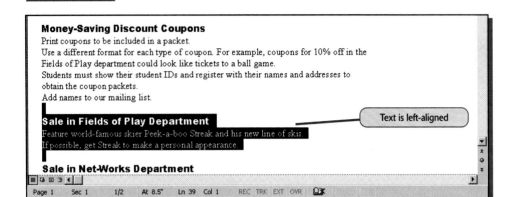

Figure 2-72

Money-Saving Discount Coupons
Print coupons to be included in a packet.
Use a different format for each type of coupon. For example, coupons for 10% off in the Fields of Play department could look like tickets to a ball game.
Students must show their student IDs and register with their names and addresses to obtain the coupon packets.
Add names to our mailing list.

Sale in Fields of Play Department
Feature world-famous skier Peek-a-boo Streak and his new line of skis.
If possible, get Streak to make a personal appearance.

> Text is left-aligned

Sale in Net-Works Department

Page 1   Sec 1   1/2   At 8.5"   Ln 39   Col 1   REC TRK EXT OVR

5 Click in the title *College and Career Sales Promotion for Selections* at the top of the report and click the Center ☰ button to center the title.

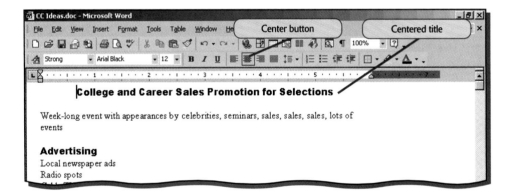

Figure 2-73

CC Ideas.doc - Microsoft Word

File Edit View Insert Format Tools Table Window He

> Center button

> Centered title

Strong   Arial Black   12   **B** *I* <u>U</u>

College and Career Sales Promotion for Selections

Week-long event with appearances by celebrities, seminars, sales, sales, sales, lots of events

Advertising
Local newspaper ads
Radio spots

6 Delete the blank line above the title, if you have one.

7 Save the document.

Highlighting Text

The *Highlight* button in the Formatting toolbar marks text with color just like a highlighting pen. Use this feature when you want to call attention to text. The default highlight color is yellow, but you can choose from among several different colors, including bright green, turquoise, pink, blue, red, dark blue, teal, green, violet, dark red, dark yellow, two shades of gray, and black.

Tip If you print a document on a black-and-white printer, text that is highlighted prints with gray shading. Yellow highlighting usually prints as light gray shading, but other colors may print as gray shading that is too dark to read.

Task 17:
To Highlight Text

1 Press Ctrl + End and scroll up if necessary to see the last paragraph.

2 Click the Highlight 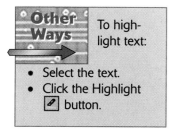 button and drag the pointer through the entire parenthetical text in the last paragraph.

Other Ways To highlight text:

- Select the text.
- Click the Highlight button.

3 Press Esc. The pointer changes back to an I-beam.

Figure 2-74

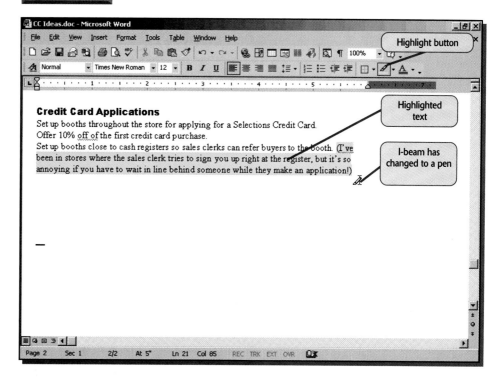

Credit Card Applications
Set up booths throughout the store for applying for a Selections Credit Card.
Offer 10% off of the first credit card purchase.
Set up booths close to cash registers so sales clerks can refer buyers to the booth. (I've been in stores where the sales clerk tries to sign you up right at the register, but it's so annoying if you have to wait in line behind someone while they make an application!)

Highlight button

Highlighted text

I-beam has changed to a pen

Tip To remove highlighting, click the down arrow on the Highlight button, select **None**, and then drag the pointer through the highlighted text.

Using Writing and Proofing Tools

The writing and proofing tools provided by Word help polish your documents and give them a professional look. The basic proofing tool is the Spelling and Grammar tool, which you have already used several times. You should use this tool in almost every document you create.

The basic writing tools include the Thesaurus and the Hyphenation tool. Use the Thesaurus to choose just the right word, and use the Hyphenation tool to make the right margin of a document look less "ragged."

Tip Word also provides an advanced writing tool that reports statistics such as word count and sentence complexity and scores the text on readability and grade level. To use this tool, simply select the option **Show readability statistics** on the **Spelling & Grammar** tab of the Options dialog box. Each time you check the spelling of the document, the readability statistics will display when the spelling checker is complete.

Checking Spelling and Grammar

As you already learned in Common Elements Project 2 and the Introduction to Word, Word can check your spelling and grammar as you type. When this option is activated, you will see the Spelling and Grammar Status icon in the status bar. A pencil moves back and forth across the pages of the book icon as you type. When Word finds a mistake in your document, the icon displays a red *X*. If no mistakes have been found, a red check mark appears. As you will see in the next task, you can use the Spelling and Grammar icon to go to each mistake and then make the correction.

Troubleshooting Before you start the next task, it is important that the appropriate options are set on your computer. **Choose Tools | Options,** click the Spelling and Grammar tab, and set the following options:
- Check spelling as you type
- Always suggest corrections
- Ignore words in UPPERCASE
- Ignore words with numbers
- Ignore Internet and file addresses
- Check grammar as you type
- Check grammar with spelling

Then select Grammar Only from the Writing style drop-down list, if necessary, and clear the checkmarks from all other options on this page of the dialog box. When your settings are complete, click OK.

Task 18:
Using the Spelling and Grammar Icon to Move to Mistakes

1 Look at the **Spelling and Grammar Status** icon in the status bar to see that errors appear in the document.

2 Press Ctrl + Home so you can begin at the top of the document.

3 Double-click the **Spelling and Grammar Status** icon in the status bar. The insertion point moves to the first error and automatically displays the shortcut menu.

Figure 2-75

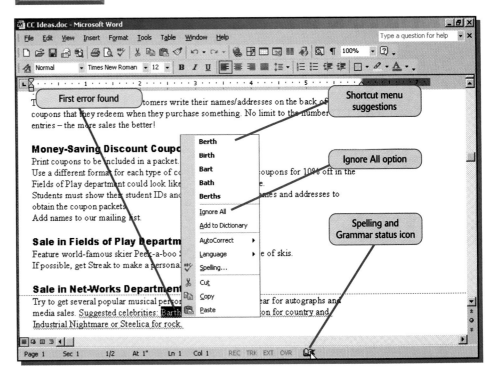

4 Click **Ignore All**.

5 Double-click the icon again.

6 Press [Esc] so you can correct the fragment.

Figure 2-76

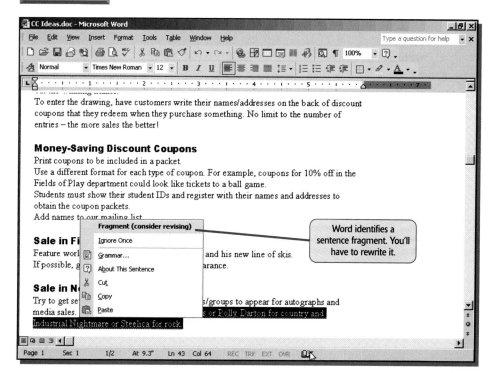

Word identifies a sentence fragment. You'll have to rewrite it.

7 Select *Suggested celebrities:* and type **We could invite celebrities such as** so that the fragment is a complete sentence.

Figure 2-77

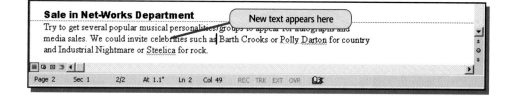

Sale in Net-Works Department
Try to get several popular musical personalities/groups to appear for autographs and media sales. We could invite celebrities such as Barth Crooks or Polly Darton for country and Industrial Nightmare or Steelica for rock.

New text appears here

8 Continue double-clicking the Spelling and Grammar Status icon to complete checking the document, taking the following actions:
- Select Ignore All for Darton and Steelica
- Change the next fragment to say *Have a fashion show*
- Change the last fragment to say *Give away the T-shirts with the Selections logo*

9 Press [Ctrl] + [Home] and edit the text under the title so it says the following: *The College and Career promotion is a week-long event with appearances by celebrities, seminars, sales, and various events.*

10 Save the file.

Tip Word did not flag the fragment at the top of the page because it had no period after it.

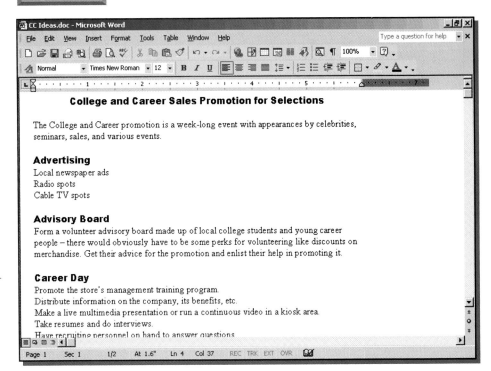

Figure 2-78

Using the Thesaurus

The electronic *Thesaurus* in Word can suggest *synonyms* (words with similar meanings) or *antonyms* (words with opposite meanings) for a word in a document and then automatically replace the selected word with the word you choose.

WEB TIP

To improve your vocabulary and have some fun too, visit the Merriam-Webster Web site and play the word game of the day.

Task 19:

To Replace a Word Using the Thesaurus

1 Find and select the word *advice* and then choose **Tools | Language** to display the language tools list.

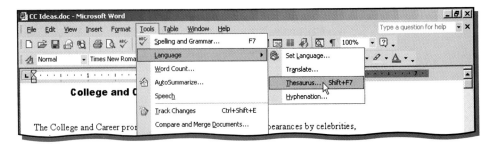

Figure 2-79

2 Click **Thesaurus** to open the Thesaurus.

Figure 2-80

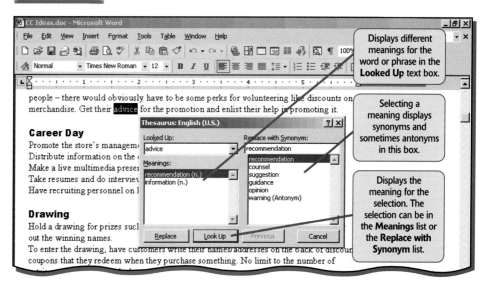

3 Select *opinion* in the **Replace with Synonym** list and click **Look Up**. The Thesaurus looks for *opinion*.

4 Click **Previous**. The Thesaurus looks up *advice* again.

5 Click **Replace**. The Thesaurus closes and replaces *advice* with *recommendation*.

Figure 2-81

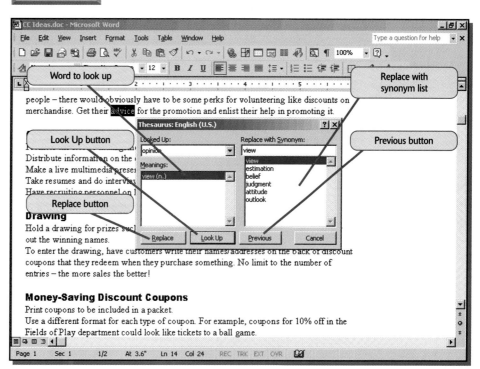

Hyphenating a Document

When the *Hyphenation* feature is activated, Word hyphenates a word at the end of a line if the word falls within the hyphenation zone. A larger zone results in more words being hyphenated; a smaller zone results in fewer words being hyphenated. Because Word constantly checks for words that should be hyphenated, adding and deleting text in a document may change the hyphenation of certain words.

Tip

It is advisable to use hyphenation with justified text. Word justifies text by adding additional spaces in each line to force the text to extend to the right margin. The additional spaces added to the lines of text can be very noticeable on a page that contains nothing but text. The spaces create what is referred to as "rivers of white" that flow through the text. Hyphenating justified text can alleviate obvious rivers of white by forcing more text on a line and using less white space to justify the line.

Task 20:

To Hyphenate a Document

1 Choose **Tools | Language | Hyphenation** to open the Hyphenation dialog box.

Figure 2-82

2 Select **Automatically hyphenate document** to set the automatic hyphenation feature, select **3** for **Limit consecutive hyphens to** to limit the number of consecutive rows Word hyphenates to 3, and click **OK**. Word hyphenates eligible words.

Figure 2-83

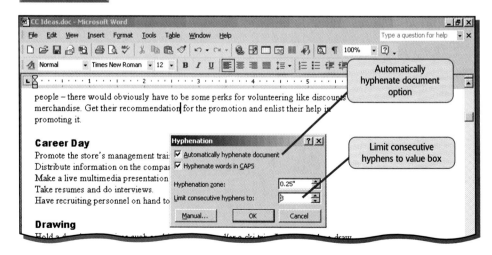

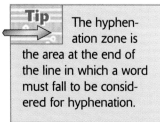

Tip The hyphenation zone is the area at the end of the line in which a word must fall to be considered for hyphenation.

3 Scroll through the document to see the hyphenated lines.

4 Save the document and close it.

Figure 2-84

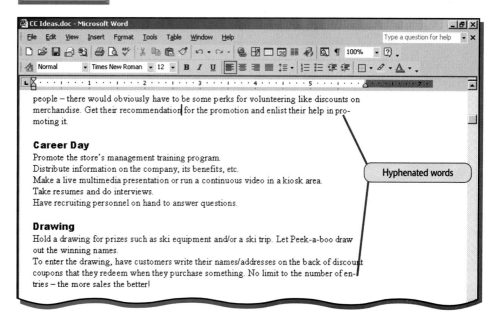

Career Day
Promote the store's management training program.
Distribute information on the company, its benefits, etc.
Make a live multimedia presentation or run a continuous video in a kiosk area.
Take resumes and do interviews.
Have recruiting personnel on hand to answer questions.

Drawing
Hold a drawing for prizes such as ski equipment and/or a ski trip. Let Peek-a-boo draw out the winning names.
To enter the drawing, have customers write their names/addresses on the back of discount coupons that they redeem when they purchase something. No limit to the number of entries — the more sales the better!

SUMMARY AND EXERCISES

SUMMARY

- It is easier to insert a file than to open the file, copy and paste it into another file, and then close the file.
- You can navigate in a document with keystrokes, the mouse, the Browse objects, the Go To command, or the Find command.
- You can copy and move text with the Copy, Cut, and Paste buttons or the Copy, Cut, Paste, and Paste Special commands, or you can use drag and drop or the Office Clipboard.
- An easy way to move text in the same document is to split the window and drag the text across the split.
- The Find and Replace command replaces a word or phrase found multiple times in the same document with the specified replacement text.

- Word uses a default font and a default font size.
- You can apply additional underlining styles and font effects from the Fonts dialog box.
- Word provides several default character formats called character styles.
- Word can change the case of text to sentence case, all uppercase, all lowercase, or title case, or it can toggle the case, reversing the case of each character.
- In a new document, the default alignment for paragraphs is left.
- The Highlight button in the Formatting toolbar marks text with color just like a highlighting pen.
- Word can constantly check your spelling and your grammar as you type.
- The Thesaurus in Word looks up synonyms or antonyms for words.
- Hyphenating a document makes the right margin less ragged.

KEY TERMS & SKILLS

KEY TERMS

alignment (p. 2-44)	Highlight (p. 2-46)
antonyms (p. 2-50)	hyphenation (p. 2-52)
case (p. 2-33)	Office Clipboard (p. 2-28)
character style (p. 2-33)	Paste Options button (p. 2-19)
Find command (p. 2-14)	Select Browse Object (p. 2-10)
font effects (p. 2-35)	synonyms (p. 2-50)
Go To command (p. 2-13)	Thesaurus (p. 2-50)

SKILLS

Align text (p. 2-45)	Highlight text (p. 2-47)
Apply a character style (p. 2-38)	Hyphenate (p. 2-52)
Apply bold (p. 2-33)	Insert a file (p. 2-5)
Browse by object (p. 2-11)	Look up a word in the Thesaurus (p. 2-50)
Change case (p. 2-41)	
Check grammar (p. 2-48)	Modify a character style (p. 2-33)
Check spelling (p. 2-48)	Move text (p. 2-19)
Copy text (p. 2-19)	Navigate a document (p. 2-8)
Cut text (p. 2-20)	Paste special (p. 2-26)
Drag and drop (p. 2-22)	Paste text (p. 2-20)
Find (p. 2-16)	Select text (p. 2-14)
Find and replace (p. 2-32)	Underline (p. 2-35)
Go to (p. 2-13)	

STUDY QUESTIONS

MULTIPLE CHOICE

1. Word can check constantly for
   a. words that should be hyphenated.
   b. spelling errors.
   c. grammar errors.
   d. All of the above.

2. Which dialog box has a button that changes from More to Less and vice versa?
   a. Font
   b. Find and Replace
   c. Open
   d. Save As

3. "Rivers of white"
   a. are caused by hyphenation.
   b. may appear in left-justified text.
   c. are caused by spaces that are added in lines of justified text.
   d. refer to text that looks washed-out when printed.

4. The button that splits the screen is located on the
   a. Formatting toolbar.
   b. horizontal scroll bar.
   c. vertical scroll bar.
   d. Standard toolbar.

5. The Thesaurus displays
   a. only antonyms.
   b. only synonyms.
   c. only homonyms.
   d. synonyms and antonyms (as available).

6. To move to the end of a document, press
   a. End.
   b. Ctrl + End.
   c. Delete + End.
   d. Ctrl + Shift + End.

7. When Word finds a misspelled word in a document, it marks a red *X*
   a. before the word.
   b. after the word.
   c. on the Spelling and Grammar Status icon.
   d. beside the word in the Spelling and Grammar dialog box.

8. Which of the following does not move the insertion point?
   a. Ctrl + Home
   b. scrolling with the vertical scroll bar
   c. clicking the mouse
   d. Shift + F5

9. The hyphenation zone
   a. is located in the left margin.
   b. is located in the right margin.
   c. determines the words that are eligible for hyphenation.
   d. is 20 characters.

10. The Select Browse Object button is located on the
    a. Formatting toolbar.
    b. horizontal scroll bar.
    c. vertical scroll bar.
    d. Standard toolbar.

SHORT ANSWER

1. How do you move to the last revision?
2. When do the Browse buttons automatically reset to Next Page and Previous Page?
3. What happens if you double-click the page number in the status bar?
4. How can you quickly go to a spelling or grammar error?
5. How do you insert a file?
6. What is the hyphenation zone and how does it work?
7. How do you look up a synonym for a word?
8. Name some of the colors available for the highlight option.
9. Which option in the Find dialog box looks for homonyms?
10. How do you turn on automatic hyphenation in a document?

FILL IN THE BLANK

1. Press [Shift] + _____ to change the case of selected text.
2. When you select an item from the Browse Object palette, the arrows on the browse buttons change from black to _____.
3. Press _____ to quickly display the Go To tab.
4. To find all occurrences of Ray and skip all the occurrences of ray, choose _____ in the Find dialog box.
5. To go to the end of a line, press _____.
6. You can apply a double underline from the _____ dialog box.
7. Word uses Times New Roman and _____ point for the font defaults.
8. Navigation keystrokes move the _____, but the scroll bars do not.
9. To copy text when dragging, press the _____ key.
10. Basic writing and proofing tools include the Thesaurus, the _____ tool, and the Spelling and Grammar tool.

DISCUSSION

1. Discuss the Select Browse Object feature, how it is used, and what effect it has on screen elements.
2. Compare and contrast moving the insertion point with keystrokes and with the mouse.
3. Discuss the options that you can use in the Find dialog box.
4. Compare the Go To command with the Select Browse Object palette.
5. Compare and contrast two ways of moving text in a document.

GUIDED EXERCISES

1 EDITING THE FASHION SHOW DOCUMENT

Rachel is formalizing her ideas on the fashion show that will be held during the College and Career Week promotion. In this exercise you will edit the document she has started on the subject.

Figure 2-85

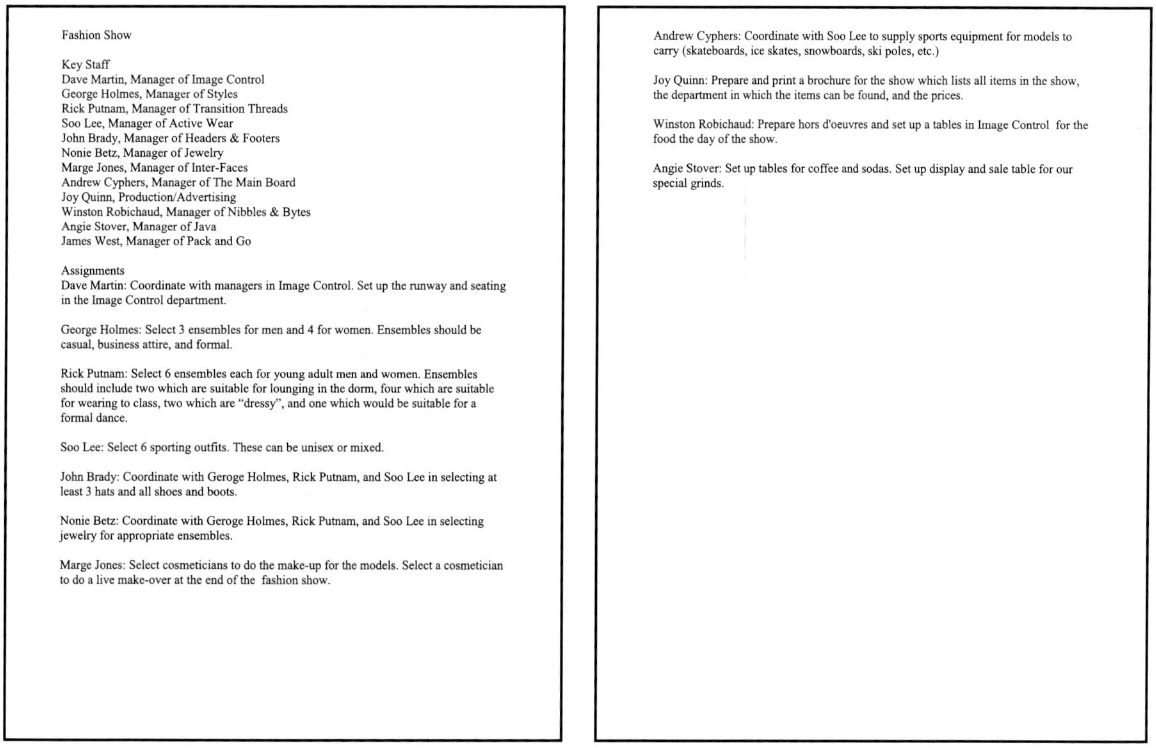

Fashion Show

Key Staff
Dave Martin, Manager of Image Control
George Holmes, Manager of Styles
Rick Putnam, Manager of Transition Threads
Soo Lee, Manager of Active Wear
John Brady, Manager of Headers & Footers
Nonie Betz, Manager of Jewelry
Marge Jones, Manager of Inter-Faces
Andrew Cyphers, Manager of The Main Board
Joy Quinn, Production/Advertising
Winston Robichaud, Manager of Nibbles & Bytes
Angie Stover, Manager of Java
James West, Manager of Pack and Go

Assignments
Dave Martin: Coordinate with managers in Image Control. Set up the runway and seating in the Image Control department.

George Holmes: Select 3 ensembles for men and 4 for women. Ensembles should be casual, business attire, and formal.

Rick Putnam: Select 6 ensembles each for young adult men and women. Ensembles should include two which are suitable for lounging in the dorm, four which are suitable for wearing to class, two which are "dressy", and one which would be suitable for a formal dance.

Soo Lee: Select 6 sporting outfits. These can be unisex or mixed.

John Brady: Coordinate with Geroge Holmes, Rick Putnam, and Soo Lee in selecting at least 3 hats and all shoes and boots.

Nonie Betz: Coordinate with Geroge Holmes, Rick Putnam, and Soo Lee in selecting jewelry for appropriate ensembles.

Marge Jones: Select cosmeticians to do the make-up for the models. Select a cosmetician to do a live make-over at the end of the fashion show.

Andrew Cyphers: Coordinate with Soo Lee to supply sports equipment for models to carry (skateboards, ice skates, snowboards, ski poles, etc.)

Joy Quinn: Prepare and print a brochure for the show which lists all items in the show, the department in which the items can be found, and the prices.

Winston Robichaud: Prepare hors d'oeuvres and set up a tables in Image Control for the food the day of the show.

Angie Stover: Set up tables for coffee and sodas. Set up display and sale table for our special grinds.

1 Open *Fashion Show.doc*.

2 Using the keyboard shortcut, change the case of *FASHION SHOW* to title case.

3 Click on the line after John Brady's assignment and add an assignment for Nonie Betz. Nonie will be working with the same people as John Brady, so you can type her name and then copy the appropriate text from John Brady's assignment. Nonie's assignment should look like this:

Nonie Betz: Coordinate with George Holmes, Rick Putnam, and Soo Lee in selecting jewelry for appropriate ensembles.

4 Change the order of the names listed at the top of the document to the order in which the names appear in the Assignments section. List James West (who is not in the Key Staff list) last. (Hint: It will be easier to do this if you split the screen.)

5 Insert a page break by pressing Ctrl + Enter before the paragraph that begins *Andrew Cyphers* so that more text appears on the second page.

6 Preview the file and then print it.

7 Save the file as *Fashion Show Edited*.

8 Close the document.

2 POLISHING THE FASHION SHOW DOCUMENT

The Fashion Show document has been through another round of edits and it needs some polishing with Word writing tools. In this exercise, you will use the Thesaurus and the Spelling and Grammar tool.

1 Open *Assignments.doc*.

2 Find *seating* and look it up in the Thesaurus. Replace it with a synonym.

3 Select the word *Staff* in the Key Staff heading and replace it with an appropriate synonym.

4 Choose **Tools | Options** and click the **Spelling & Grammar** tab. Change the **Writing style** to **Grammar & Style**, if necessary. Click **Settings**. Select **always** for **Comma required before last list item**. Select **inside** for **Punctuation required with quotes**. Click **OK** to close the Grammar Settings dialog box. Click **OK** to close the Options dialog box.

5 Scroll through the document and look for one occurrence of text that has a wavy, green line. Right-click the text and choose an appropriate replacement.

6 Press Ctrl + Home to return to the top of the document in preparation for checking the spelling. (Word begins checking from the position of the insertion point.)

7 Click the Spelling and Grammar button. Select appropriate responses for spelling and grammar errors. Continue until the check is complete and then click **OK**. (Hints: [1] Most proper names appear at least twice in the document. You might want to click **Ignore All** when the spelling checker finds names that are not in its dictionary. [2] You may need to consult a grammar textbook for the proper use of *which* and *that*.)

8 Save the document as *Fashion Show Edited 2*.

9 Close the document.

3 FORMATTING THE FASHION SHOW DOCUMENT

The Assignments document has been edited yet another time. The content is finally just what we want. Now it needs some formatting.

1 Open *Fashion Show Assignments.doc*.

2 Select the title.

3 Choose **Format | Font**. Change the color of the text to blue and select **Outline** for **Effects**. Click **OK**.

4 The title should still be selected. Press Ctrl + [ ] until the font size reaches 24 point. (Tip: Watch the font size control in the Formatting toolbar.)

5 Center the title.

6 Modify the Strong character style so that it is bold, blue, and 16 points.

7 Apply the Strong character style to the headings *Key Personnel* and *Assignments*. (Note: The heading *Key Staff* was changed using the Thesaurus. You may have used another word in the previous instead of *Personnel*.)

8 Use the Find command to search for the following three portions of text and highlight them:

- Ensembles should be casual, business attire, and formal.
- Ensembles should include two that are suitable for lounging in the dorm, four that are suitable for wearing to class, two that are "dressy," and one that would be suitable for a formal dance.
- These can be unisex or mixed.

9 View the two pages of the document in Print Preview and then close Print Preview.

10 Save the document as *Fashion Show Final* and close the document.

4 EDITING AND HYPHENATING A PROPOSAL

One of Rachel's ideas is to give away a Fashion scholarship. She has done some research on several colleges and institutions that specialize in Fashion Design and written a report with a recommendation. In the next exercise, you will edit and format the report.

Figure 2-86

Fashion Scholarship Proposal

Introduction We might want to give away a scholarship to a college or institute that offers a degree in or specializes in fashion design. I have researched several institutions: the Fashion Institute of Design & Merchandising, the Helen Lefeaux School of Fashion Design, the Shannon Rodgers and Jerry Silverman School of Fashion Design and Merchandising, the Whitehouse School of Fashion, and Otago Polytechnic.

The Fashion Institute of Design & Merchandising (FIDM)

This is a co-educational, private college that offers Associate of Arts, Professional Designation and Advanced Study Degree programs in Fashion Design, Interior Design, Fashion Merchandise Marketing, Textile Design, Visual Communications, Graphic Design, Cosmetics & Fragrance Merchandising, Theatre Costume, International Manufacturing & Product Development, and Apparel Manufacturing Management. The college has campuses in Los Angeles, San Francisco, San Diego, and Orange County, California.

FIDM has an enrollment of 4000 full-time students. Promotional material for the college says, "Over the last 30 years, FIDM has built an alumni network in excess of 25,000 graduates around the world. The college's alumni base, and industry-wide reputation for excellence, give our students an exceptional network of contacts and resources when they enter into the marketplace."

Helen Lefeaux School of Fashion Design (HLSFD)

Located in Vancouver, British Columbia, Canada, the Helen Lefeaux School of Fashion Design has a 39 week course that is divided into three 13-week periods. Promotional material about HLSFD says, "Theoretical design is important, but just as important or more so, is the ability to take a design idea through all its stages to the finished product. The main objective of the Fashion Design Program is to enable the student to interpret ideas in a professional manner from concept through illustration, pattern, and the finished garment including its presentation." The classes are very small—a maximum of 15 students per class—and the total enrollment averages 60 to 75 students.

Shannon Rodgers/Jerry Silverman School of Fashion Design and Merchandising (SRJSSFDM)

The Shannon Rodgers/Jerry Silverman School of Fashion Design and Merchandising has multiple links to the fashion industry through its advisory board and the school's internships and externships. People and organizations in the industry assist the school with curricular, scholarship, and technological support. Promotional material for SRJSSFDM says, "The school enjoys a successful internship/externship program, providing student interns for top designers and stores."

The Whitehouse School of Fashion

Named for its principal owner, Leanne Whitehouse, the Whitehouse School of Fashion, located in Australia offers a comprehensive program in design and technical aspects. Promotional material for WSF says, "It is the purpose of the school to provide students with quality education and training programs, developing each student's individual talents and interests, while at the same time responding to the needs, practices, and techniques of the fashion industry. The school aims to develop the skills of designer, artist, and manager while encouraging personal growth. In doing this, students understand that all experiences—including physical, psychological, aesthetic, are within the province of their design development."

Otago Polytechnic (OP)

Located in Dunedin, New Zealand, Otago Polytechnic offers a two-year certificate and a three-year diploma in Fashion and Design. A collection of each student's garments is given an outing on the catwalk at the "Collections" event at the end of each year. Promotional material on OP says, "The course covers both the theoretical and practical sides of fashion, with the aim of providing in-depth industry and marketing knowledge, while nurturing your individuality and creativity."

Recommendation I recommend Otago Polytechnic. Of the schools that I researched, it seemed to have the most comprehensive course of study. The following outlines the topics studied in each year of the three-year program.

Year one:
Garment construction
Patternmaking
Design and drawing
Industrial machining
Life drawing
Textile technology
Textile creation
History of fashion
The apparel industry
Millinery
Computer-aided patternmaking
Personal development

Year two:
Garment construction
Patternmaking
Design and drawing, including use of Photoshop software
Textile printing
Computer-aided patternmaking
Millinery
Apparel marketing and manufacturing
Industry field trip to Christchurch

Year three:
Garment construction
Patternmaking
Design and drawing, including use of Photoshop software
Industrial cutting
Computer-aided patternmaking
Professional studies
Photography and display Work placement

1 Open *Fashion Scholarship Proposal.doc*. Notice that the document has justified text.

2 Choose **Tools | Language | Hyphenation**. Select **Automatically hyphenate document** and specify **3** for **Limit consecutive hyphens to.** Clear the check box for **Hyphenate words in CAPS.** Click **OK.**

3 Apply the Strong character style to the headings with the names of each college or institution.

4 Find the phrases *Year one, Year two,* and *Year three* and apply the Strong character style to each.

5 Find the words *Introduction* and *Recommendation* and apply the Emphasis character style. (Hint: Select **All styles** for **Show** in the Styles and Formatting task pane.)

6 Modify the Strong character style and change the font to Arial.

7 Modify the Emphasis character style and add bold.

8 Check the spelling and grammar.

9 Save the document as *Fashion Scholarship Proposal Edited*.

10 Close the document.

ON YOUR OWN

The difficulty of these case studies varies:
are the least difficult; are more difficult; and are the most difficult.

---

1 EDITING THE SKI TRIP DOCUMENT

Matthew has created a document that explains the drawing that will be held for the ski trip. Open *Ski Trip.doc* and search the Web using keywords such as ski resort, skiing, and skiing vacation. Using the information that you find, add at least three more suggested ski resorts to the file. Write your descriptions in a similar manner to the ones that are included in the file. Check the spelling and grammar. Save the file as *Ski Trip Revised* and close the file.

2 BROWSING THROUGH DOCUMENTS

Open the document named *Grand Resort.doc*. Using the Select Browse Object, browse the document first by heading and then by table. Close the document when finished or leave it open for the next exercise.

3 USING THE OFFICE CLIPBOARD

Open the *Grand Resort.doc* file. Copy the first paragraph, copy the first graphic, and then copy the first table. The Office Clipboard should appear automatically. Create a new document. Paste the first object, paste the second object, paste the third object, and then paste all objects at once. Clear the Office Clipboard. Close all files without saving.

4 CREATING A REPORT ON YOUR IDEAL VACATION SPOT

Create a document that describes your ideal vacation spot. You might want to take a cue from the Grand Resort document for content or do a little research on the Internet. Use different fonts and font effects to format the text. Cut text and move it around. Use the Thesaurus and other writing tools, such as the Spelling and Grammar tool, to polish the document. Save the file as *Ideal Vacation Spot*.

5 IMPROVING YOUR WORK

Open a document that contains a paper you have written for any class. Print the document as is. Use the Thesaurus, the Spelling and Grammar tool, and the Hyphenation tool to improve the paper. Print the revised document.

6 GRADING READABILITY

Open one of your documents that contains a paper you have written for class. At the bottom of the last page, type the following text:

Initial Readability Statistics
Passive Sentences
Flesch Reading Ease
Flesch-Kincaid Grade Level

Improved Readability Statistics
Passive Sentences
Flesch Reading Ease
Flesch-Kincaid Grade Level

Turn on the Show readability statistics option, if necessary. Check the spelling and grammar, but choose Ignore All for all suggested changes. When the Readability Statistics dialog box appears, make note of the three statistics at the bottom of the dialog box. Type the readability statistics for the three items under *Initial Readability Statistics* on the last page of your document. See if you can improve the readability score by revising the document. Use the Spelling and Grammar tool to help you improve the writing style. Type the new statistics for the items under *Improved Readability Statistics*. Save and print the revised version (including the readability scores).

PROJECT 3

Creating a Brochure

W ord recognizes three levels of formatting—character, paragraph, and section. In previous projects, you learned techniques for formatting at the character level. In this project you will focus mainly on the techniques for formatting at the paragraph level. Before you begin formatting the paragraphs, you will define the page setup options for a three-column brochure.

OBJECTIVES

After completing this project, you will be able to:

• Define the page setup

• Create and revise columns

• Apply formatting to paragraphs

• Create bulleted and numbered lists

• Find and replace formatting

• Apply, create, and modify paragraph styles

• View formatting information

• Insert WordArt and graphics

e-selections **Running Case**

The College and Career Week promotion idea is a big hit with the store managers. Plans for the event are in full swing. Rachel and Matthew have come up with all the details on the "Remodeling Your Dorm Room on a Budget" seminar that will be given during the promotion. Now they must format the information into a handout that can be distributed.

Playing by the Rules

The design capabilities of Word are many and diverse. You can use different fonts, apply borders and shading, insert clip art, create WordArt, draw your own line art, create backgrounds with gradients or textures, and apply different colors to just about everything. With all these choices, you must use some accepted design rules to ensure that your printed message is effective, easy-to-read, and credible. Roger C. Parker, author of *One-Minute Designer*, says, "The correctness of every design decision you make is solely related to how effectively the design solution you choose enhances your reader's willingness and ability to understand your message."

Before you start formatting a Word document, ask yourself what the purpose of the design is. Is the purpose to attract attention or to make the document easier to read and assimilate? If you are creating a poster, then using a design with striking colors and visual images will certainly draw attention. On the other hand, if you are creating a long and complex report, your design should be transparent to the reader.

Let's take a look at some good rules of thumb:

1. Begin by organizing the information in the document so that it flows in a logical, meaningful order. Readers are more likely to respect the message contained in an organized document than in a disorganized document.

2. Restrict the number of fonts used in a design. Use standard fonts such as Times New Roman and Arial when designing for transparency. Trendy typefaces can overshadow the message by calling too much attention to the fonts.

3. To make long blocks of text easier to read, break them up with subheadings. Use different font sizes to indicate the hierarchy of the headings. For example, use 14 points for a first level heading and 12 points for a second level heading.

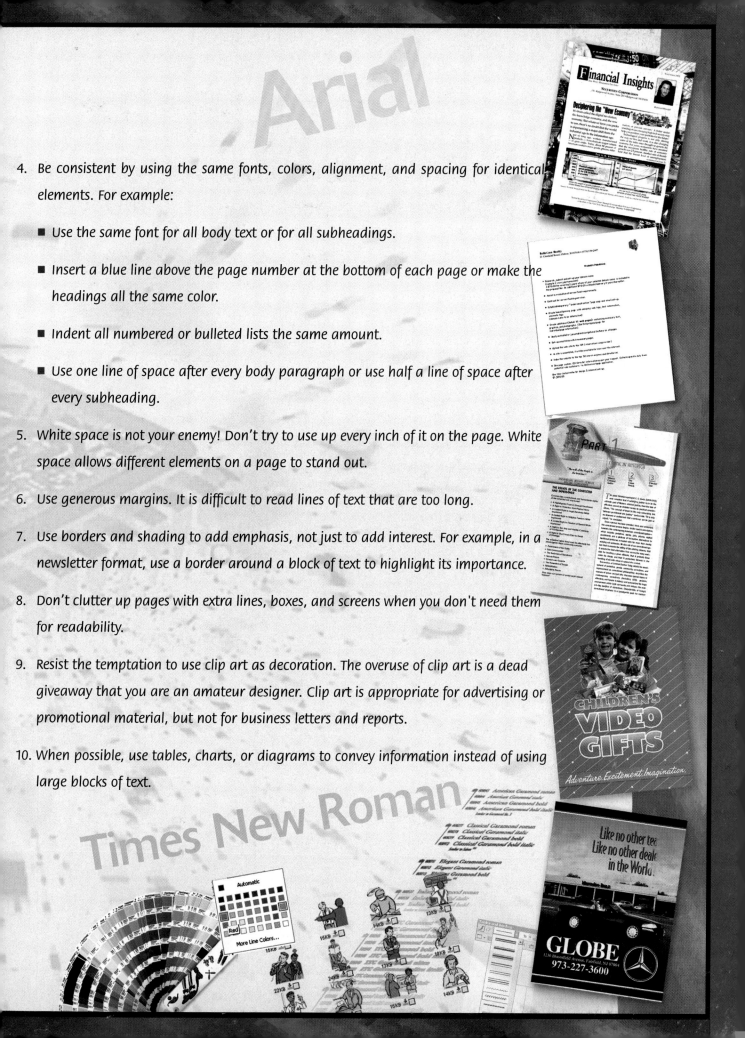

4. Be consistent by using the same fonts, colors, alignment, and spacing for identical elements. For example:

   ■ Use the same font for all body text or for all subheadings.

   ■ Insert a blue line above the page number at the bottom of each page or make the headings all the same color.

   ■ Indent all numbered or bulleted lists the same amount.

   ■ Use one line of space after every body paragraph or use half a line of space after every subheading.

5. White space is not your enemy! Don't try to use up every inch of it on the page. White space allows different elements on a page to stand out.

6. Use generous margins. It is difficult to read lines of text that are too long.

7. Use borders and shading to add emphasis, not just to add interest. For example, in a newsletter format, use a border around a block of text to highlight its importance.

8. Don't clutter up pages with extra lines, boxes, and screens when you don't need them for readability.

9. Resist the temptation to use clip art as decoration. The overuse of clip art is a dead giveaway that you are an amateur designer. Clip art is appropriate for advertising or promotional material, but not for business letters and reports.

10. When possible, use tables, charts, or diagrams to convey information instead of using large blocks of text.

Creating a Brochure

The Challenge

Because of your artistic ability, Rachel and Matthew have given you all the information and asked you to come up with a layout for the handout. You have decided that the best format is a tri-fold brochure that can be printed on 8 1/2-by-11-inch paper.

The Solution

You will use page formats to set the page orientation to landscape (11 inches wide by 8 1/2 inches high) and create three columns in the document to accommodate the tri-fold for the brochure. To make your work easier, you will apply paragraph styles to format the text and apply direct formatting when creating a style would be unnecessary. Figure 3-1 shows the front and back of the brochure.

Figure 3-1

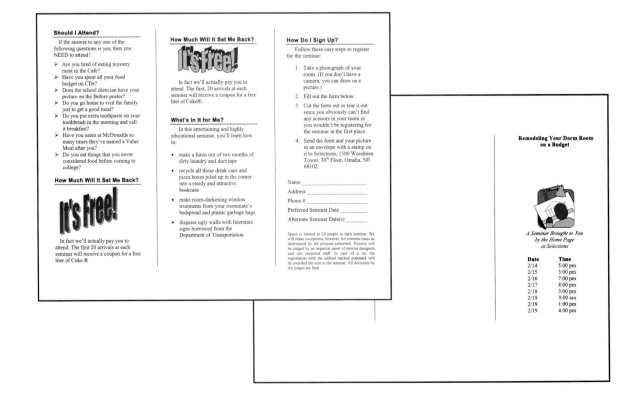

Defining the Page Setup

The settings that determine the setup of a page include the following:

- Margins (the amount of white space at the top, bottom, and sides of the paper)
- Orientation (the direction in which text prints on the page)
- Paper size
- Paper source (the locations (drawers or bins) in the printer from which the paper will come for the printing of the first page and for the following pages)
- Layout options such as headers and footers, vertical alignment on the page, line numbers, and borders

When you create a new document using the New Blank Document button, Word uses a paper size of 8 1/2 inches by 11 inches, portrait orientation, top and bottom margins of 1 inch, and left and right margins of 1.25 inches.

Task 1:

To Define the Page Setup

1. Start Word and open *Remodel.doc* and save the file as *Remodel Revised*.

Figure 3-2

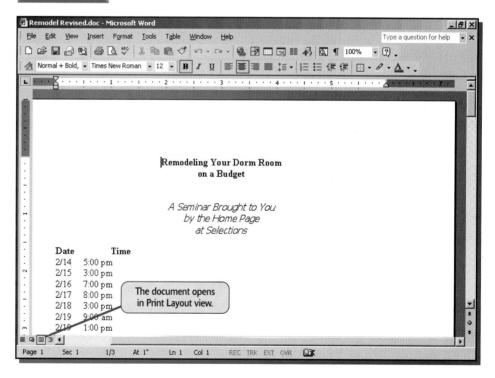

The document opens in Print Layout view.

2 Review the document and then press Ctrl + Home to move the insertion point to the top of the first page.

3 Choose **File | Page Setup** to open the Page Setup dialog box.

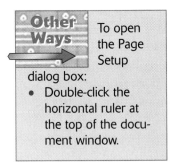

Other Ways To open the Page Setup dialog box:
- Double-click the horizontal ruler at the top of the document window.

Figure 3-3

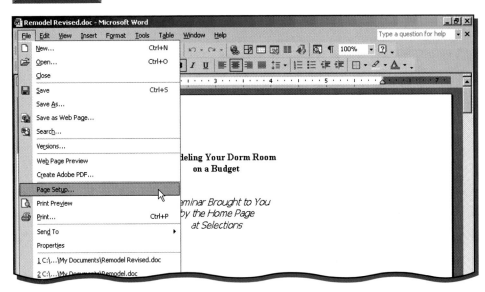

4 Click the **Margins** tab, if necessary and change the top, bottom, left, and right margins to 0.5".

5 Select **Landscape** and click **OK** to change the paper orientation.

6 Click the Print Preview button to display the document in the Print Preview window.

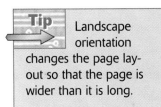

Tip Landscape orientation changes the page layout so that the page is wider than it is long.

Figure 3-4

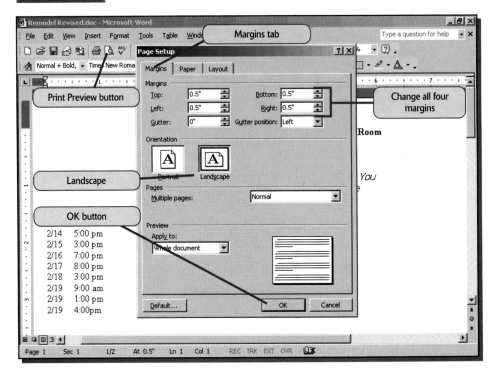

7 Click the Close **Close** button in the Preview toolbar to close the preview window.

Tip You might like to know about one page format that you won't be using in this brochure. It's the page border. Check it out by choosing **Format | Borders and Shading** and clicking the Page Border tab.

Figure 3-5

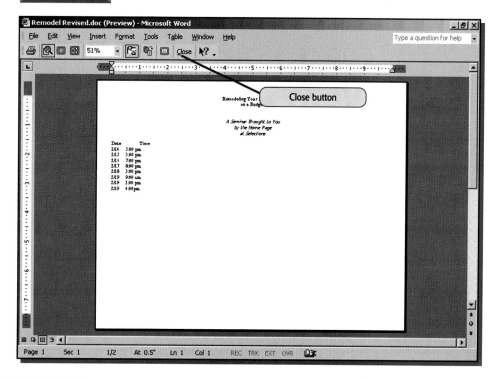

Close button

CHECK POINT

What page orientation default does Word use? It is called Portrait, and it orients the page layout to 8 1/2 inches wide and 11 inches long.

Creating and Revising Columns

In Word, you can create two kinds of columns—newspaper columns, which wrap from the bottom of one column to the top of the next, and parallel columns, which are created with tables. In this project, you will create and revise newspaper-style columns.

Tip Column settings are section formats; therefore, if you want to change the number of columns used, you must insert a section break between the sets of columns. For example, if you want to use two columns, followed by three columns, you must insert a section break after the two-column format.

Creating Columns

Word can create newspaper-style columns of equal width or different widths with or without a vertical line between the columns.

Task 2:
To Format the Page with Equal-Width Columns

1 Click the Columns 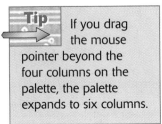 button to display the columns palette.

2 Click the second column of the pop-up palette. Word applies a two-column format to the entire document.

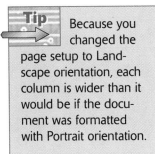

Tip If you drag the mouse pointer beyond the four columns on the palette, the palette expands to six columns.

Figure 3-6

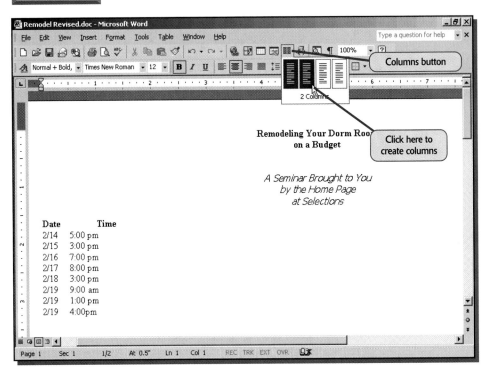

3 Go to page 2 to get a better idea of the format.

Tip Because you changed the page setup to Landscape orientation, each column is wider than it would be if the document was formatted with Portrait orientation.

Figure 3-7

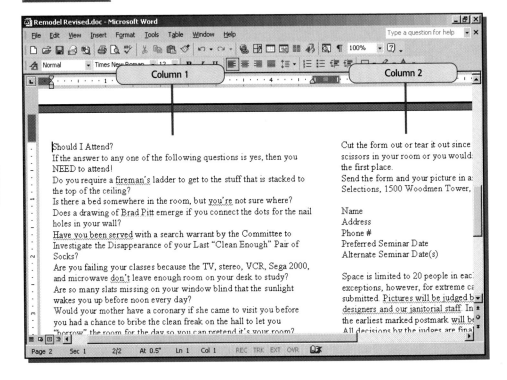

Changing the Column Structure

You can change the structure of columns by changing the width or the number of columns.

Task 3:
To Change the Column Structure

1 Choose **Format | Columns** to open the Columns dialog box.

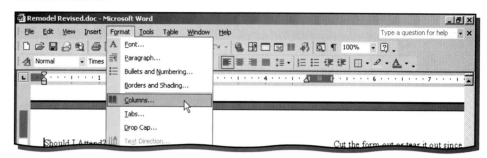

2 Select **Three** for **Presets** and notice that the columns are equal width.

3 Specify 1" for **Spacing** for the first column. The Spacing for column 2 changes to 1" also. The Preview shows how the page will look.

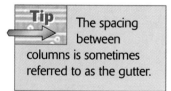

Tip The spacing between columns is sometimes referred to as the gutter.

4 Select **Line between** and then click **OK**.

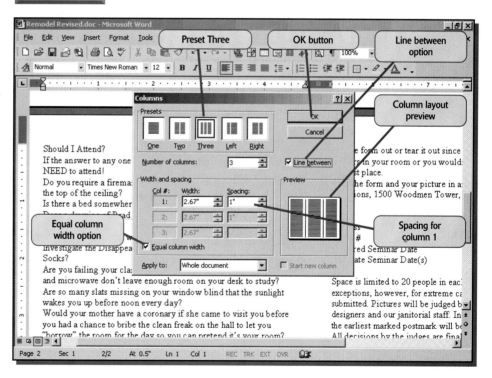

5 Save the file.

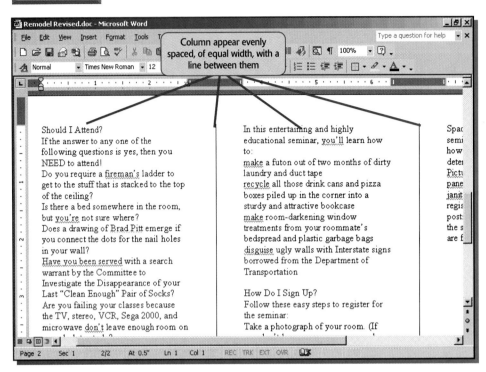

Figure 3-10

Inserting Column Breaks

Text in newspaper-style columns automatically wraps from the bottom of one column to the top of the next. Sometimes, however, you may not want the text to fill a column. If you want a portion of text in one column to go to the next column, you must insert a column break before the text.

Task 4:
To Insert Column Breaks

1 Go to the top of page 1 and choose **Insert | Break** to open the Break dialog box.

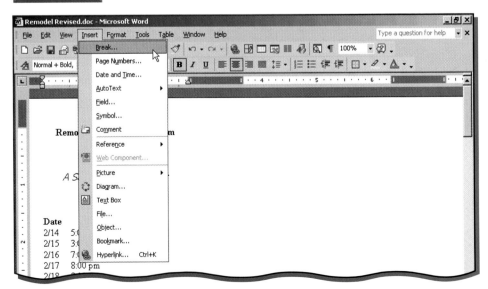

Figure 3-11

2 Select **Column break** to identify the break type and click **OK**. The text moves to the second column.

Tip Inserting a column break is a good way to create space for a brochure title or specific item that you want to position in a column. It is also a good way to distribute text across columns so that the columns end evenly at the bottom of the page.

Figure 3-12

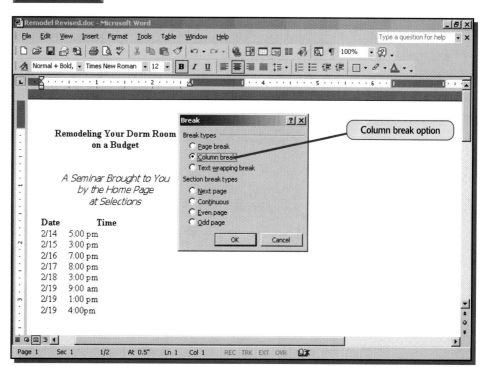

3 Insert another column break at the same location. The text moves over to the third column.

Tip Text that appears in the third column will appear on the front of a printed page when it is tri-folded.

Figure 3-13

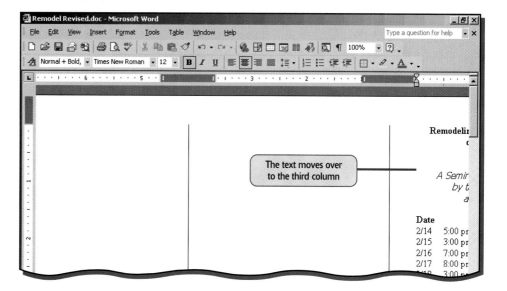

4 Go to page 2 and click before the text *How Much Will It Set Me Back?* at the bottom of the first column and insert a column break. The text moves to the top of the second column.

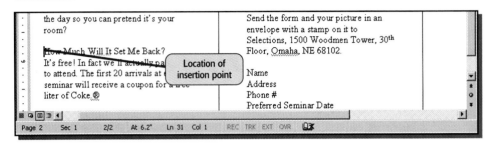

Figure 3-14

5 Click before *How Do I Sign Up?* in the middle of the second column and insert another column break. The text moves to the top of the third column.

6 Save the file.

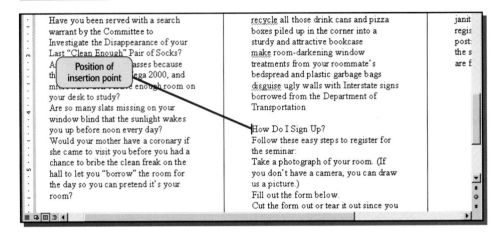

Figure 3-15

Applying Formatting to Paragraphs

Now that you have set up the page and created the columns, you'll turn your attention to formatting the paragraphs in the brochure. All the paragraphs in the document are currently formatted with the Normal style. You can change the appearance of the paragraphs by modifying the Normal style, applying a different style, or applying formatting directly to the paragraph. First you will apply formatting directly to selected paragraphs; then, later in this project, you will modify styles and apply styles to format paragraphs.

Paragraph formats that you can apply directly include tabs, alignment, indentations, and spacing. When you apply direct formatting to a paragraph, the formats apply only to that paragraph. The formats can be carried forward to the next paragraph by pressing Enter anywhere in the paragraph or at the end of the paragraph. For example, if you apply center alignment to a paragraph and press Enter at the end of the paragraph, the next paragraph will also be centered.

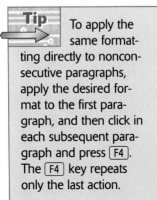

Tip To apply the same formatting directly to nonconsecutive paragraphs, apply the desired format to the first paragraph, and then click in each subsequent paragraph and press F4. The F4 key repeats only the last action.

Other Ways

To apply the same formatting to nonconsecutive paragraphs:
- Select the first paragraph and press Ctrl as you select the other paragraphs. Then apply the format to all selected paragraphs at once.

Setting Tabs

When you want text to align in a particular way at a specific location on a line, you can use a tab stop, which is set on the ruler. When you press the [Tab] key, the insertion point moves to the column on the line that aligns with the tab stop on the ruler. When you type, the text aligns on the tab. Table 3-1 describes the different types of tab stops available in Word and shows the symbol that is displayed for the tab stop in the ruler. The Leader tab does not have a symbol in the ruler.

Table 3-1	Types of Tab Stops	
Type	**Symbol**	**Description**
Left	⌊	Aligns text on the left
Center	⊥	Centers text on the tab.
Right	⌋	Aligns text on the right
Decimal	⊥	Aligns text on the decimal
Bar	!	Inserts a vertical bar at the tab stop (used for drawing vertical lines). The bar tab inserts a bar automatically. It is not necessary to tab to the bar tab stop unless the bar tab stop is set beyond where the line of text ends.
Leader		Inserts a series of specified characters (usually periods) before the tab stop. Leaders can be added to all types of tabs except the bar tab. Frequently, leaders are used before the page numbers in a table of contents.

CHECK POINT

By now you have most likely explored the Click and Type feature and discovered that each document contains numerous zones. When you use it to type in zones 3 and 5 of a blank area, a left tab is automatically set on the ruler at those locations.

Figure 3-16 shows the five different tab symbols on the ruler and the way text lines up on each. By default, Word sets a left tab on the ruler every half-inch, but no symbols appear on the ruler for default tabs. When a user sets a tab, the default tabs to the left are disabled. For example, if you set a left tab at 2 inches, the default tabs at .5 inch, 1 inch, and 1.5 inch are disabled.

Figure 3-16

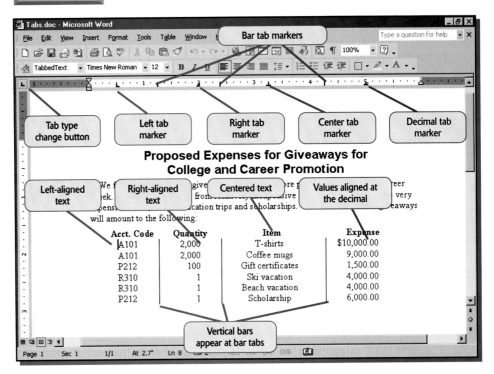

When working with tabs and indents, you might find it helpful to display the nonprinting characters by clicking the Show/Hide ¶ button so you can see where the Tab key has been pressed. The nonprinting character for a tab is an arrow that points to the right.

In this task, you will set two right tabs—one with and one without a leader character.

Leaders are generally used to help the reader's eye relate the text at the beginning of a line with the text at the end of the line, such as a page number in a table of contents. The period is the character that is used most frequently as a leader and it is referred to as a "dot leader." In Word, you can use a period or any other punctuation mark that you specify.

Task 5:

To Set Right Tabs and Tabs with Leaders

1 Select the paragraphs for the dates and times on the first page.

2 Click the **Tab** button until it displays a right tab ⌐, then point to the 2.5-inch mark on the ruler in the third column, and click.

Figure 3-17

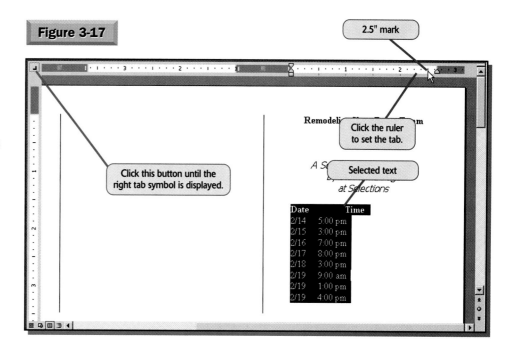

2.5" mark

Click the ruler to set the tab.

Click this button until the right tab symbol is displayed.

Selected text

3 Click the Show/Hide ¶ button to show the paragraph and tab markers and notice that there are two tab characters before the word *Time*.

4 Delete one of the tabs and click the Show/Hide ¶ button again to hide the paragraph and tab markers.

Figure 3-18

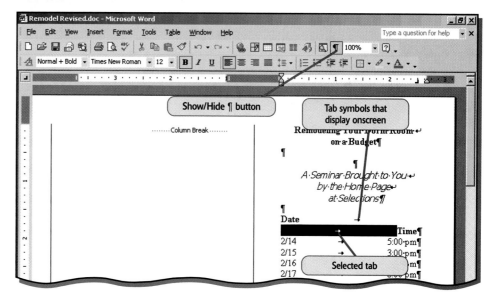

Show/Hide ¶ button

Tab symbols that display onscreen

Selected tab

5 Select the paragraphs in the registration form in the third column of the second page.

6 Choose **Format | Tabs** to open the Tabs dialog box.

Tip The Tabs dialog box enables you to set additional features and to more precisely position tabs.

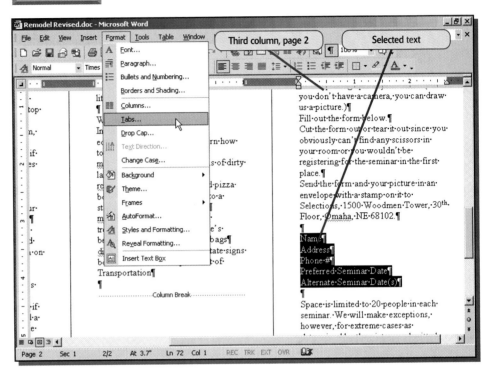

Figure 3-19

7 Type **2.5** in the **Tab stop position** text box, select **Right** for **Alignment**, and select option **4** for **Leader**.

8 Click **Set** and click **OK**. The Ruler displays a right tab at the 2.5-inch mark in the third column.

Tip Leaders are characters that fill the space before the set tab. In this case, if you type text before the tab you set at the 2.5" mark and then press [Tab], the character identified in in leader 4 will fill the space to the 2.5" tab marker.

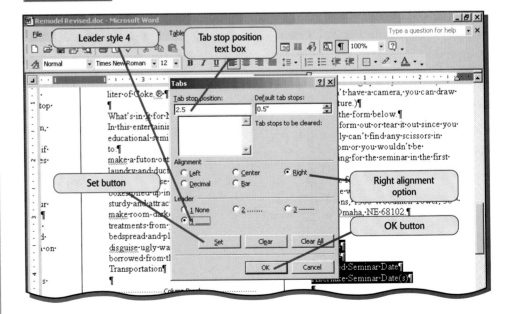

Figure 3-20

9 Click the insertion point after Name and press Tab. A line is created because the underline character was selected as the tab leader.

10 Repeat the procedures identified in Step 9 to create underlines for each additional form line, as shown in Figure 3-21.

11 Click the Show/Hide button again to turn it off and save the file.

Figure 3-21

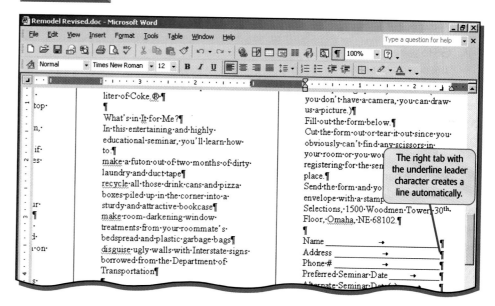

Tip The right indent is generally used only in combination with a right indent.

Setting Indents

You can format paragraphs with several types of indents—a first line indent, a left indent, a right indent, and a hanging indent. Figure 3-22 shows examples of each type of indent.

Figure 3-22

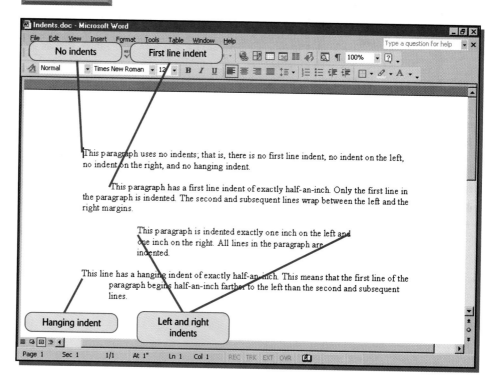

7 Click the insertion point anywhere at the top of the second column in the sentence *It's free!* and press F4.

Troubleshooting
Remember that this keyboard shortcut repeats the last action. Since the last action was setting the first line indent to .25 inches, this key sets the same indent for the current paragraph.

8 Using F4 again, indent the first line of the paragraph that begins *In this entertaining and highly…* in the second column and the paragraph that begins *Follow these easy steps to register…* in the third column.

9 Save the file.

Figure 3-27

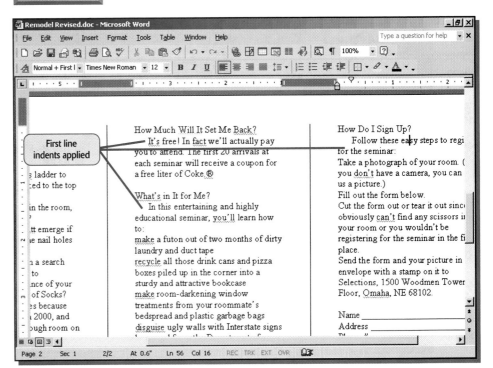

Tip: Because F4 only repeats the last action, you may want to use the Format Painter button in the Standard toolbar to apply a format that has more than one setting. To use the Format Painter, select the text that has the formatting, click, and then select the text to which you want to apply the format.

Setting Paragraph and Line Spacing

Paragraph spacing adds space above or below a paragraph; line spacing adds space between the lines in the paragraph. By default, a Normal paragraph has no space above it or below it, and the lines are single-spaced. Paragraph spacing is measured in points. (Twelve points equal a line and there are 72 points in an inch.) Line spacing includes single, double, and 1.5. Additionally, line spacing can be set to an exact measurement, a minimum measurement, and a multiple measurement.

Task 7:
To Set Paragraph Spacing

1 Select the five paragraphs on page 2 in the third column that make up the registration form (Name, Address, Phone #, Preferred Seminar Date, and Alternate Seminar Date).

2 Choose **Format | Paragraph** to open the Paragraph dialog box.

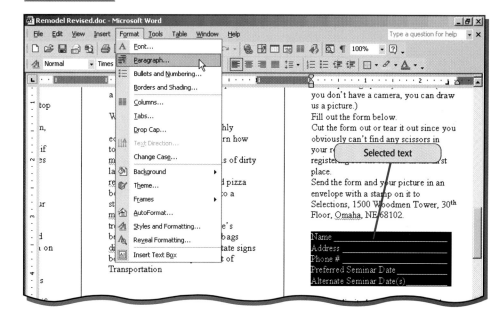

Figure 3-28

3 Type **6** for **After**.

4 Click **OK**. The paragraph spacing increases.

5 Go to page 1 and position the insertion point in the title shown in the third column.

6 Repeat the procedures outlined in Steps 2-4 to add 66 points after the title and save changes to the file.

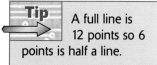

Tip A full line is 12 points so 6 points is half a line.

Figure 3-29

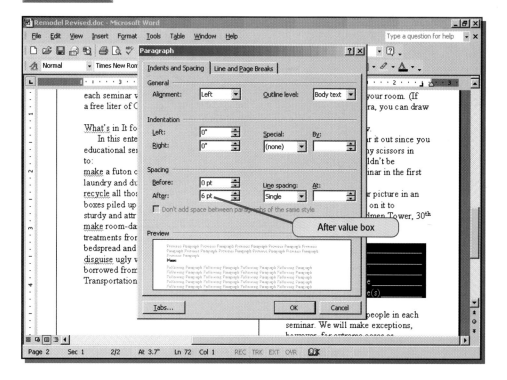

Creating Bulleted and Numbered Lists

To draw attention to paragraphs in a list, you can bullet the list or number it. A bullet is a symbol (usually a filled circle) that precedes the text in the list. Bulleted and numbered lists generally use a hanging indent, in which the second and subsequent lines of a paragraph are indented more than the first line of a paragraph. You don't have to know how to set a hanging indent because the Bullets button and the Numbering button do it for you.

> **Tip**
> Items in a list that have no particular order should be bulleted instead of numbered.

Task 8:
To Create Bulleted and Numbered Lists

1 Use the Find command to find the text *make a futon out of.*

2 Select the paragraphs as shown in Figure 3-30.

3 Click the Bullets button to format the paragraphs with bullets and click the Decrease Indent button once to move the bulleted items to the left.

Figure 3-30

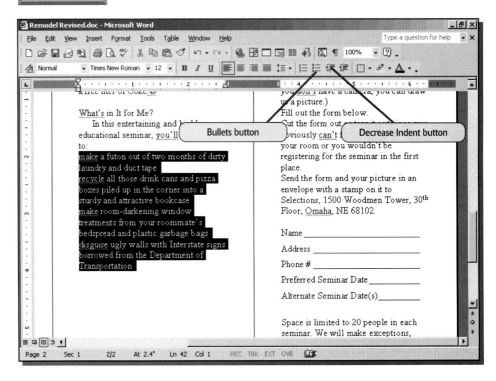

4 Apply bullets to the paragraphs in the first column of page 2 (right after the sentence *If the answer to any one of the following question is yes, then you NEED to attend!*) and decrease the indent.

Figure 3-31

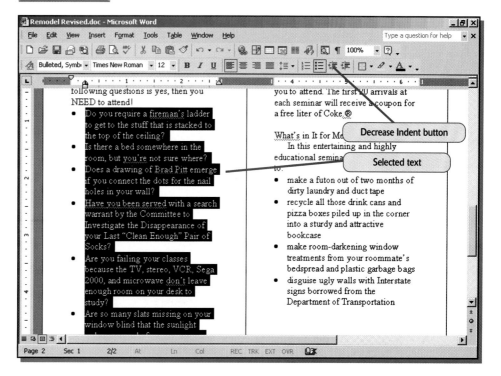

5 With the paragraphs still selected, choose **Format | Bullets and Numbering** to open the Bullets and Numbering dialog box.

Tip The Bullets and Numbering dialog box contains options for setting specific bullet and numbering formats.

Figure 3-32

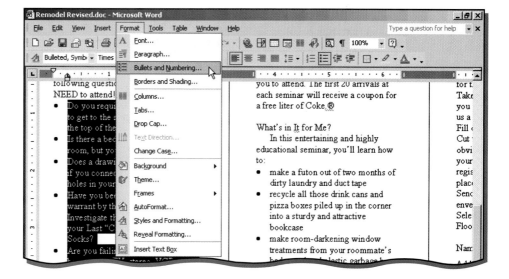

6 Select the check-mark bullets and click **OK**. The bullets change to checkmarks.

Troubleshooting

Because bullets can be customized, your dialog box may show different bullets in different positions. If you do not have the check-mark bullets, select a different bullet.

Figure 3-33

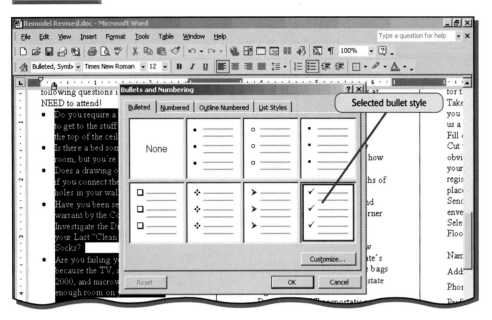

7 Find the text *Follow these easy steps to register* and select the paragraphs immediately below the text.

Figure 3-34

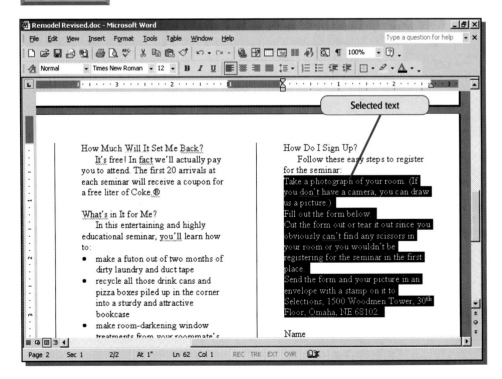

8 Click the Numbering ☷ button and set the paragraph spacing to 6 points for **After**.

9 Use F4 to set the paragraph spacing for the bulleted paragraphs in the first and second columns and save the file.

Troubleshooting
As long as text is selected, you can continue to make format changes. When you have completed the formatting, be sure to de-select the text.

Figure 3-35

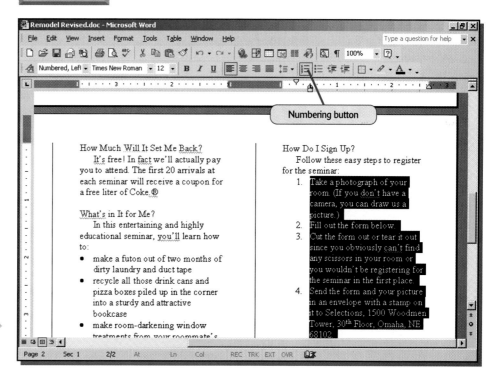

Numbering button

Finding and Replacing Formatting

By now, you have most likely learned how to use the Find and Replace feature to locate and replace document text. In the next task you will learn how to use the Find and Replace command to replace formatting. On the cover of the brochure, the font of the text *A Seminar Brought to You by the Home Page at Selections* is Tahoma. All of the text in the brochure should be Times New Roman. To change all text that might be using the Tahoma font, you will use the Find and Replace command.

Task 9:
To Find a Font and Replace It with Another Font

1 Press Ctrl + Home and then choose **Edit | Replace**. The Find and Replace dialog box opens and displays the Replace page.

Figure 3-36

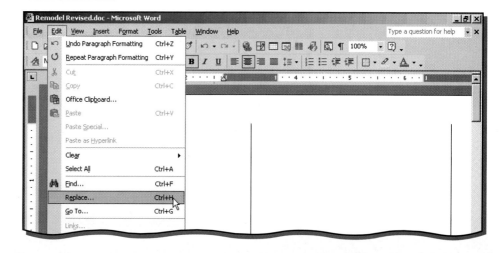

2 Delete any text that appears in the **Find what** and **Replace with** text boxes and then click in the **Find what** text box.

3 Click **More**, if necessary, click **Format**, and select **Font**. The Replace Font dialog box opens.

> **Tip**
> Review the other features on the Format menu. Word provides a number of different items you can search for and replace.

4 Select **Tahoma** for **Font** and click **OK** to find the first occurrence of the font.

> **Tip**
> To locate specific text formatted with a specific font, type the text you want to locate in the Find what text box.

Figure 3-37

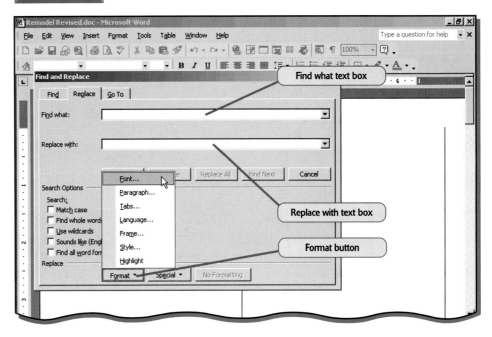

Figure 3-38

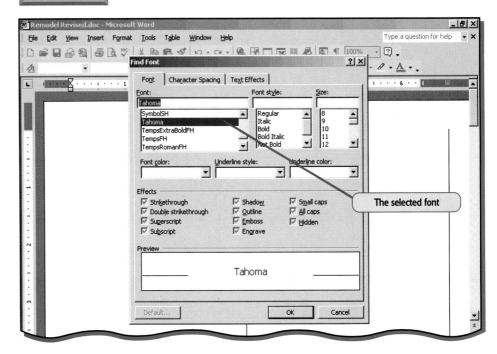

5 Tab to the **Replace with** text box, click **Format | Font**, and set Times New Roman as the font.

6 Select **All** in the **Search** list box, if necessary, and then click **Replace All**. Word reports that it has replaced the Tahoma font with Times New Roman in one location.

Tip Leaving the Find what and Replace with text boxes blank allows Word to replace all the Tahoma font with the Times New Roman font throughout the document.

Figure 3-39

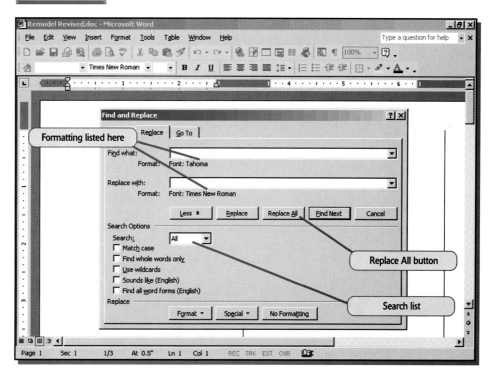

Troubleshooting The next time you use Find or Find and Replace, you will have to remove the formatting options from the **Find what** and **Replace with** text boxes.

7 Click **OK** to acknowledge the message and then click **Close**. The Find and Replace dialog box closes.

Figure 3-40

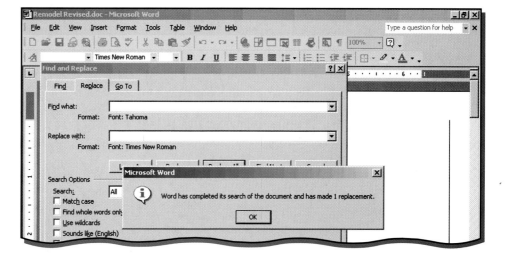

Applying, Creating, and Modifying Paragraph Styles

A paragraph style, like a character style, is a named collection of format settings. When you apply a style to a paragraph, the text of the paragraph takes on the format settings stored in the style.

All new blank documents use the Normal paragraph style. The default Normal style uses the following settings:

- Times New Roman font, 12-point size, with no attributes
- Single spacing with no space before or after the paragraph
- No indents
- Left alignment
- Left tabs every half-inch

When you want to use a format that is different from the settings used by Normal, you can do one of the following:

- Apply direct formatting
- Modify the Normal style
- Apply a different style
- Modify and apply a different style

Knowing when to use direct formatting and when to use a style is the trick. Without going into the complex details of how Microsoft "builds" a document, it is sufficient to say that it is best to use direct formatting sparingly. In addition to being better for the document, it is generally more efficient for the user to apply styles instead of direct formatting. If you use styles to format paragraphs, you can make changes to multiple paragraphs at one time by changing the style that is applied to them. If you use direct formatting, you have to change every paragraph individually.

Applying a Style

Word provides several methods of applying a style. You can apply a style from the Style control in the Formatting toolbar, from the Styles and Formatting task pane, or by using various keyboard shortcuts (such as Ctrl + Alt + 1 to apply the Heading 1 style). In the next task, you will apply a style from the Styles and Formatting task pane. In later tasks, you will use additional methods.

Task 10:
To Apply a Style

1 Press [Ctrl] + [F] to display the Find and Replace dialog box and notice that the formatting option for the Tahoma font is still active.

2 Click **No Formatting** and then type Space is limited in the Find what text box.

3 Click **Find Next** and close the dialog box.

4 Click in the paragraph and then click the Styles and Formatting 🖉 button to open the Styles and Formatting task pane.

5 Select **All styles** from the **Show** drop-down list in the task pane.

Figure 3-41

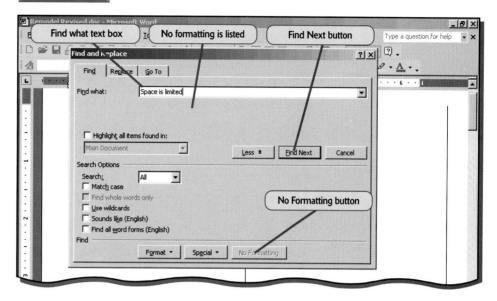

Figure 3-42

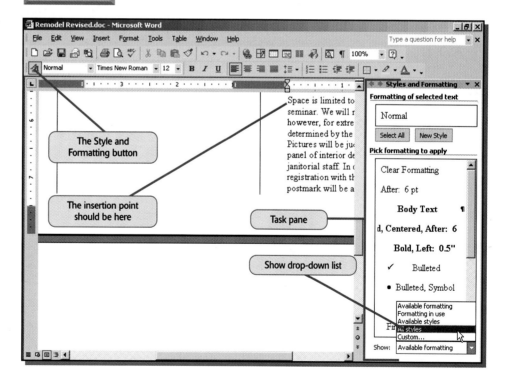

6 Scroll the list of styles if necessary and select **Body Text 3** to apply the style to the paragraph.

7 Close the task pane and save the file.

Tip The styles displayed in the Styles and Formatting list may be different on your machine because of settings that are active on your computer. Most of the styles displayed in Figure 3-43 are included in the document.

Figure 3-43

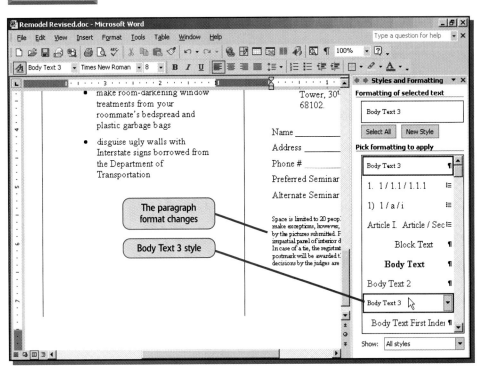

Creating a Style by Example

A simple way to create a new style is to format a paragraph just the way you want it using direct formatting and then use the paragraph as the example of the new style. This is called "creating a style by example."

Task 11:

To Create a Style by Example

1 Select the first paragraph on page 2, *Should I Attend?*

2 Change the font to **Arial** and click the Bold **B** button to bold the text.

Figure 3-44

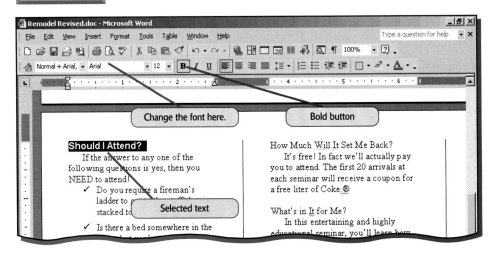

3 With the paragraph still selected, choose **Format | Paragraph** to open the Paragraph dialog box, type **3** for **After** to set 3 points of spacing after the paragraph, and click **OK**.

Tip Three points of spacing equals only 1/4 line. While this may seem to be very little spacing, it serves to set off the paragraph appropriately.

Figure 3-45

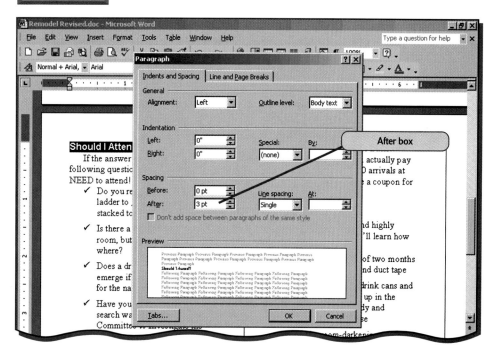

4 With the paragraph still selected, choose **Format | Borders and Shading** to open the Borders and Shading dialog box.

Figure 3-46

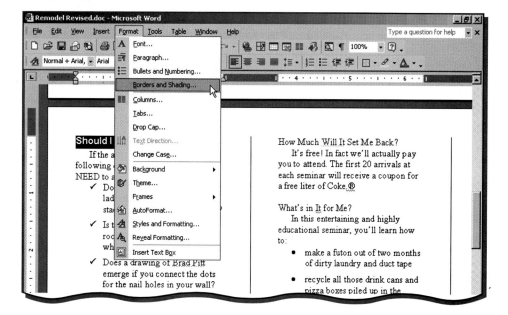

5 Click the **Borders** tab, if necessary.

6 Select **1 pt** from the **Width** drop-down list to change the size of the border line and click the bottom border on the Preview to place a border at the bottom of the document page only.

7 Click **Options** to open the Border and Shading Options dialog box.

Tip When you become more comfortable with formatting paragraphs, you will want to explore more of the options in this dialog box. You'll be amazed at the different effects you can create by simply using borders.

8 Type **2** for **Bottom**, click **OK** to close the Border and Shading Options dialog box, and click **OK** again to close the Borders and Shading dialog box.

Tip Settings in this dialog box control the distance between the text and the border. The higher the number, the greater the distance between the text and the border.

Figure 3-47

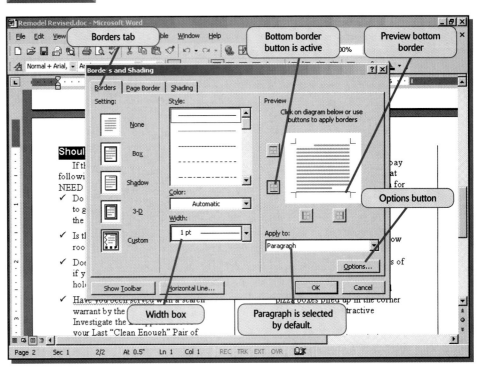

Figure 3-48

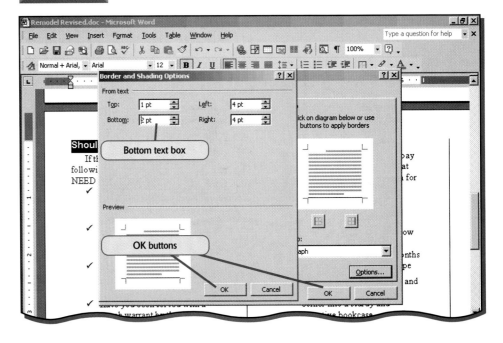

CHECK POINT

In addition to applying borders to paragraphs, you can also shade paragraphs to make them stand out. Shading paragraphs can be very effective when you print brochures and other documents on a color printer. To apply shading to a paragraph, select the paragraph, display the Borders and Shading dialog box, and click the Shading tab. Then select the color you want to apply to the paragraph from the Fill color palette and the depth of color to apply from the Style drop-down list. Review the Preview area of the dialog box and make necessary adjustments to the color and then click OK.

Tip

Underlining text sometimes cuts through the descenders (the part of a character that extends below the baseline, as in the letters *j* and *y*). By using a border instead of an underline, you have the option of specifying a distance from the text to the line so the line will not cut through the descenders.

9 Click in the paragraph *What's in It for Me?* and click the down arrow on the Style button in the Formatting toolbar.

10 Scroll until you see the Question style and click it. The style is applied to the paragraph.

Figure 3-49

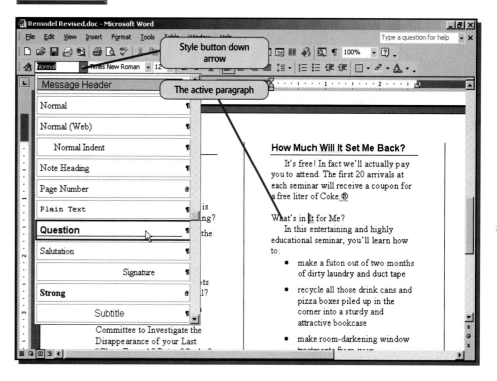

11 Apply the Question style to the *How Do I Sign Up?* paragraph at the top of the third column using the method of your choice.

Figure 3-50

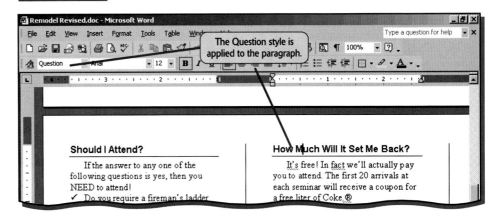

> **Tip** If you want to use a style that exists in another document, you can copy the style easily by copying a paragraph formatted with the style (or just the paragraph mark) and pasting it into the desired document.

12 Click in the paragraph *Follow these easy steps to register for the seminar* (just below the insertion point's current position).

13 Add 12 points of spacing after the paragraph and then using the formatting of this paragraph, create a style by example and name it *Intro*.

14 Apply the new style to the first paragraph under each Question heading on page 2. Page 2 should look like Figure 3-51.

15 Save the file.

Figure 3-51

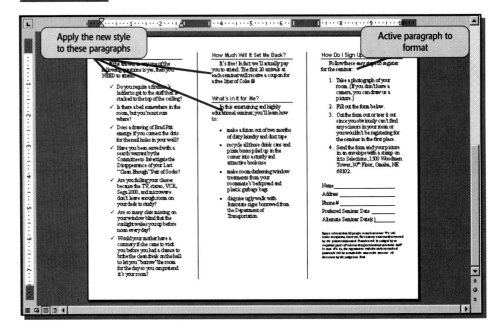

Modifying a Style

Sometimes a style is almost what you want, but not quite. When this is the case, you can modify the style so that it is exactly what you want.

Task 12:
To Modify a Style

1 Click the Styles and Formatting **A** button. The Styles and Formatting task pane opens.

2 Press Ctrl + End. The insertion point moves to the last paragraph and its style (Body Text 3) is selected in the task pane.

3 Click the style's down arrow and select **Modify**.

4 Select **9** for **Font size** and click **OK**. The text in the last paragraph, which is formatted with the Body Text 3 style, changes to 9 point.

5 Save the file.

Figure 3-52

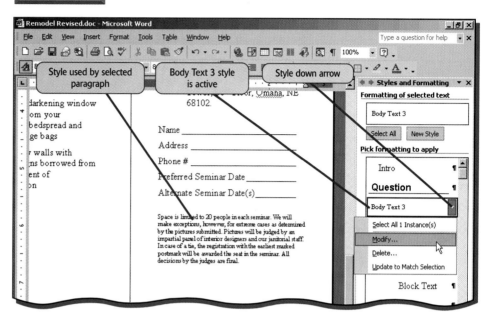

Figure 3-53

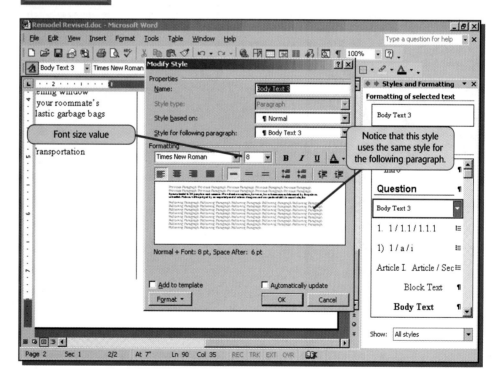

Viewing Formatting Information

The new Reveal Formatting command in Word shows the formatting of selected text in the task pane so you can see exactly what the format settings are for the font, the paragraph, and even the section of the document. In the next task, you will use the Reveal Formatting command to not only view formatting information, but to modify it.

Task 13:
To Reveal Formatting

1 Choose **Format | Reveal Formatting** to open the Reveal Formatting task pane.

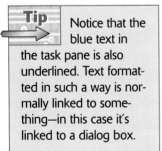

Troubleshooting
If you do not see blue text under Font or Paragraph, click the plus sign in the box before the heading to expand the heading.

2 Click the blue text that says *Alignment*. The Paragraph dialog box opens.

Tip
Notice that the blue text in the task pane is also underlined. Text formatted in such a way is normally linked to something—in this case it's linked to a dialog box.

Figure 3-54

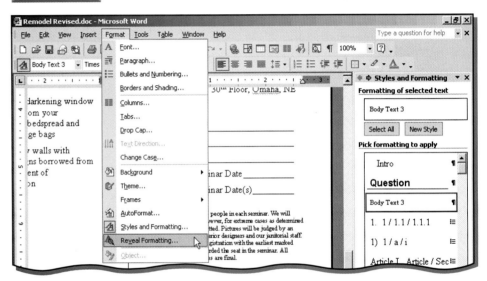

Figure 3-55

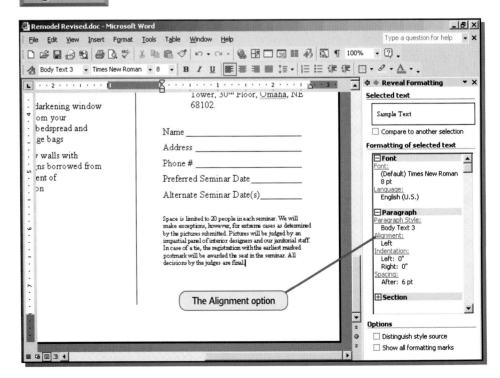

The Alignment option

> **Tip** Justified alignment positions text evenly down both the left and right margins or column boundaries.

3 Select **Justified** for **Alignment** and click **OK**. The Body Style 3 style changes to justified alignment.

4 Click the insertion point in the text *Alternate Seminar Date(s)* just above the current paragraph and notice the difference in the format settings in the task pane.

5 Close the task pane.

6 Save the file.

Figure 3-56

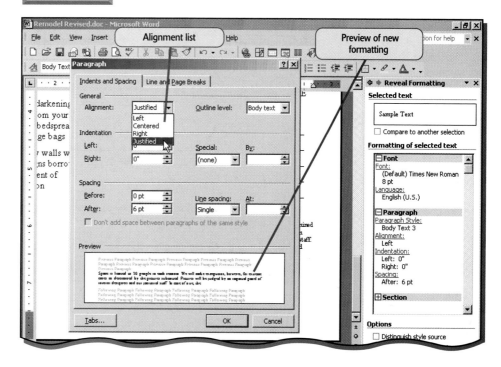

Inserting WordArt and Graphics

In Project 3 of Common Elements, you inserted graphic images and created WordArt. In this task, you will use what you learned in that project to finalize the remodeling brochure.

Task 14:
To Insert WordArt

1 Delete the text *It's free!* at the top of the second column.

2 Click the Drawing button. The Drawing toolbar displays.

> **Tip** By default, the Drawing toolbar displays at the bottom of the screen. If you move the Drawing toolbar to a different location, it will redisplay in the new each time it is opened.

3 Click the Insert WordArt button to open the WordArt Gallery dialog box.

4 Select the WordArt style shown in Figure 3-57 and click **OK**.

5 Type **It's Free!** and click **OK**. The WordArt is inserted.

Figure 3-57

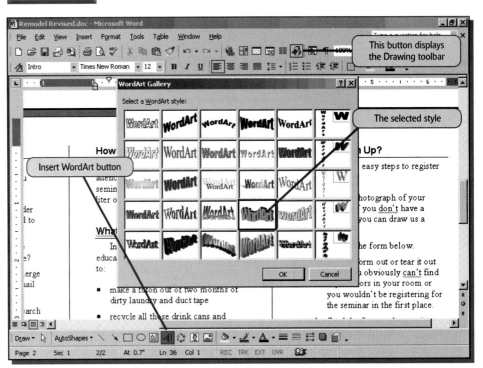

Figure 3-58

6 Press Enter to move the paragraph below the WordArt and save the file.

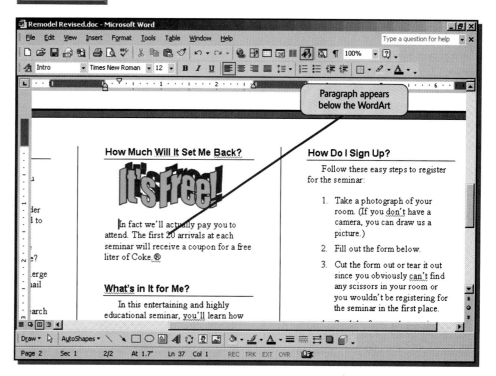

Figure 3-59

Task 15:
To Insert a Graphic

1 Go to the top of the third column on page 1.

2 Click in the blank line above *A Seminar Brought to You.*

3 Choose **Insert | Picture | From File** to open the Insert Picture dialog box.

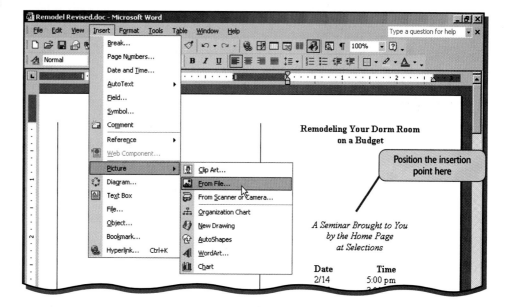

Figure 3-60

4 Navigate to the folder where you keep the files for this book and double-click *Remodel.wmf.*

5 Save the file and close it.

Figure 3-61

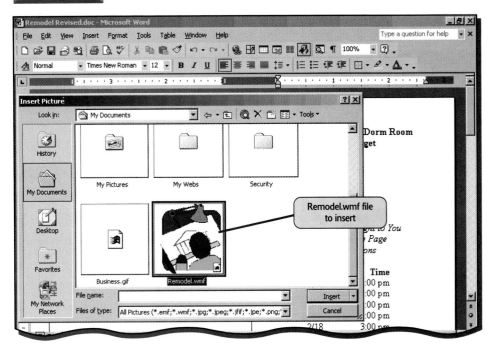

Remodel.wmf file to insert

Tip By default, WordArt and graphics are inserted inline with text. To make a WordArt or a graphic float, right-click the WordArt or graphic and choose **Format WordArt** or **Format Picture**. Click the **Layout** tab and select any option for **Wrapping style** except **In line with text**. Then click **OK**.

WEB TIP

Would you like to create your own brochure, a business card, or a Christmas card? Check out the PaperDirect Web site for a huge selection of predesigned papers, including letterhead, brochures, business cards, labels, invitations, holiday designs, and other helpful ready-made paper products.

SUMMARY AND EXERCISES

SUMMARY

- Page Setup options include margins, headers and footers, orientation, paper size, paper source, and layout options such as vertical alignment, line numbers, and borders.
- In Word, you can create two kinds of columns—newspaper columns and parallel columns.
- Paragraph formats include tabs, alignment, indentations, line spacing, and spacing before and after the paragraph.
- Tabs align text in specific ways, depending on the type of tab.
- You can format paragraphs with a first line indent, a left indent, a right indent, and a hanging indent.
- You can format paragraphs with spacing before or spacing after, in addition to spacing between the lines.
- Word provides the Numbering button and the Bullets button for quickly creating simple numbered or bulleted lists.
- The Find and Replace command can find and replace formatting as well as characters.
- A style is a collection of character and paragraph formats.
- The Reveal Formatting command shows the formatting in selected text by displaying a list of the formats in the task pane.
- By default, WordArt and graphics are inserted inline with text.

KEY TERMS & SKILLS

KEY TERMS

bar tab (p. 3-13)	leader (p. 3-13)	paper size (p. 3-5)
border (p. 3-5)	left indent (p. 3-17)	paper source (p. 3-5)
bullet (p. 3-22)	left tab (p. 3-13)	paragraph spacing
bulleted list (p. 3-22)	line spacing (p. 3-20)	(p. 3-20)
center tab (p. 3-13)	margin (p. 3-5)	paragraph style (p. 3-28)
column (p. 3-7)	newspaper columns	parallel columns
column break (p. 3-7)	(p. 3-7)	(p. 3-7)
decimal tab (p. 3-13)	Normal style (p. 3-12)	portrait (p. 3-5)
first line indent (p. 3-17)	numbered list (p. 3-22)	right indent (p. 3-17)
hanging indent (p. 3-17)	orientation (p. 3-5)	right tab (p. 3-14)
landscape (p. 3-6)	page setup (p. 3-5)	tab stop (p. 3-13)

SKILLS

Apply a border (p. 3-5)
Apply a style (p. 3-29)
Apply direct formatting to a
    paragraph (p. 3-12)
Create a bulleted list (p. 3-22)
Create a numbered list (p. 3-22)
Create a style by example (p. 3-30)
Create columns (p. 3-7)

Find and replace formatting (p. 3-25)
Indent (p. 3-17)
Insert a graphic (p. 3-39)
Insert WordArt (p. 3-38)
Modify a style (p. 3-35)
Reveal formatting (p. 3-36)
Set margins (p. 3-5)
Set tabs (p. 3-13)

STUDY QUESTIONS

MULTIPLE CHOICE

1. When you modify a style,
   a. the format changes aren't reflected in the paragraphs that already use the style.
   b. the format changes are reflected in the paragraphs that already use the style.
   c. you must give the style a new name.
   d. you must reapply the style to paragraphs that already use the style.

2. You can create newspaper columns of unequal width
   a. by clicking the Columns button.
   b. by choosing Format, Columns.
   c. by clicking the Insert Tables button.
   d. by dragging the column guidelines.

3. To repeat the last typing or operation, press
   a. F3.
   b. F4.
   c. F5.
   d. F6.

4. If you use Click and Type, in what zones are left tab stops automatically set on the ruler?
   a. 1 and 3
   b. 2 and 4
   c. 3 and 5
   d. 4 and 6

5. Instead of applying formats directly to selected paragraphs, you can
   a. choose **Format | Paragraph**.
   b. choose **Format | Font**.
   c. click appropriate buttons on the Formatting toolbar.
   d. apply styles.

6. What is the default top margin?
   a. 1"
   b. 1.25"
   c. .5"
   d. 1.5"

7. How would you define the word *gutter*?
   a. The space between columns.
   b. The space above or below a paragraph.
   c. Additional space added to margins for the purpose of binding.
   d. Additional space on the screen on the left and right of the text.

8. How many points are in an inch?
   a. 12
   b. 48
   c. 72
   d. 96

9. Tab stops are used to align text
   a. on a specific character.
   b. at a specific location.
   c. instead of default tabs.
   d. on an indention.

10. When a style is applied to a paragraph,
    a. the name of the style appears in the selection bar.
    b. the paragraph takes on the formatting of the style.
    c. the paragraph can't be edited.
    d. the formatting of the paragraph can't be changed.

SHORT ANSWER

1. List at least three line spacing options available.
2. What is a bullet?
3. Where is the Tab selector button located?
4. Explain one way to apply a style.
5. When is it better to bullet a list than to number it?
6. How do you create a style by example?
7. What is the difference between paragraph spacing and line spacing?
8. How do you add a line that is not an underline under a heading?
9. How do you change the style of a bullet?
10. How does the Show/Hide ¶ button help when you are using tabs?

FILL IN THE BLANK

1. In Word, you can create two kinds of columns—newspaper columns and _____ columns.
2. A column _____ causes text in one column to move to the top of the next column.
3. Word uses a(n) _____ indent in a numbered list formatted with the Numbering button.
4. Space before a paragraph is measured in _____.
5. A _____ is a collection of character and paragraph formats.
6. If you press Enter at the end of a centered paragraph, the next paragraph will be _____.
7. Instead of using the underline feature, you can use a(n) _____ to draw a line under text.
8. The _____ tab creates a vertical line.
9. You set top and bottom margins in the _____ dialog box.
10. Click the _____ button in the Find and Replace dialog box to see additional options.

FOR DISCUSSION

1. Describe some scenarios in which you would use the Find and Replace command to replace one type of formatting with another type of formatting.
2. Discuss the advantage of using styles to format paragraphs.
3. Discuss the advantage of using space before or space after a paragraph instead of adding space by pressing Enter.
4. Compare the two methods of setting tabs (i.e., using the ruler and using the dialog box).

5. List and briefly describe at least four features provided by Word that auto-mate the formatting process.

GUIDED EXERCISES

1 **SETTING TABS**

Matthew and Rachel have to estimate how much the company should spend on promotional giveaways. You will type the columnar text shown in Figure 3-62.

Figure 3-62

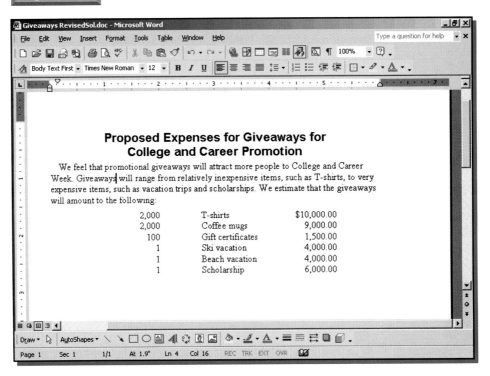

1 Open *Proposed Expenses for Giveaways.doc.*

2 Click the insertion point on the blank line under the first paragraph.

3 Set the following tabs: Right tab at 2 inches; Left tab at 3 inches; Decimal tab at 5 inches.

4 Type the following text using the tabs you have set:

2,000	T-shirts	$10,000.00
2,000	Coffee mugs	9,000.00
100	Gift certificates	1,500.00
1	Ski vacation	4,000.00
1	Beach vacation	4,000.00
1	Scholarship	6,000.00

5 Select all the lines in the table you just typed and drag the left tab to 2.75 inches.

6 Apply the Body Text First Indent style to the paragraph under the title.

7 Save the file as *Giveaways Revised* and close it.

2 **FORMATTING THE CAREER DAY BROCHURE**

Matthew is designing the Career Day informational brochure that will go in the student packets. In this exercise, you will format the brochure as shown in Figure 3-63.

Figure 3-63

Career Day

Tours
Martha Brown will give tours of the administrative offices from 10:00 am – 11:00 am and Heidi Pennypacker will give tours from 2:00 pm – 4:00 pm. The tour will also include the employee dining room and the executive dining room.

Kiosks
The kiosk will have a continuously running slide show presentation about Selections. Someone in Marketing will set up the slide show. Bob Fleischman will man the booth from 10:00 am - 2:00 pm and Tricia Patton will be in the booth from 2:00 pm – 9:00 pm.

Employment Counseling
Miller Payne will be available from 10:00 am – 12:00 pm to answer questions about employment at Selections. Pam Taylor will be available for consulting with students on their resumes from 12:00 pm – 9:00 pm.

Recruiting Booth
Rachel Crawford and Matthew Brainard, the originators of College and Career Week, will man the recruiting booth and talk to prospects about the Management Program. Rachel will be in the booth from 10:00 am – 2:00 pm and Matthew will be in the booth from 2:00 pm – 9:00 pm.

1 Open *Career Day.doc*.

2 Insert the graphic *Business.gif* above the title and use the size handles to make the graphic larger to match the graphic in Figure 3-63.

3 Select the title, center it, and choose **Format | Font**. Select **Comic Sans MS**, **48** point. Select the Character Spacing tab. Select **Expanded** for **Spacing** and specify 4 points for **By**.

4 Currently, the document uses Heading 1 style for the headings. Create a style by example named Activities, based on the Heading 1 style, that uses Comic Sans MS regular (not bold). Apply the style to Tours, Kiosks, Employment Counseling, and Recruiting Booth.

5 Select all the text from *Tours* to the end of the document and make it two columns. (Note: When you select the text, the title and graphic are not included.)

6 Insert a column break before *Employment Counseling*.

7 Save the file as *Career Day Formatted* and close it.

3 **FORMATTING A SPRING BREAK VACATION FLYER**

Matthew is also designing a Spring Break vacation flyer that will go in the student packets. In this exercise you will format the flyer as shown in Figure 3-64.

Figure 3-64

Picture Yourself Here

One lucky person will win a roundtrip flight and one week, all-expenses-paid vacation in Daytona Beach, Florida for Spring Break! You will stay at the luxurious Edgewater Beach Resort located in the center of all the Spring Break activities, including the weeklong, live telecast of MTV's *Spring Break-athon.* You must be 18 to enter the drawing, and you must be present at the drawing to win.

Spring Break on the Beach

Fill this out and drop it in the Spring Break Drawing boxes in any department.

Name _____

Address _____

City, State, Zip _____

1 Open *Spring Break.doc*.

2 Apply the following direct formatting to the title *Picture Yourself Here*:

24 point, bold, gold, shadow, Comic Sans MS

center alignment

12 points of space after

3 Apply the Body Text style to the paragraphs below the title.

4 Modify the Body Text style so that it has the following attributes:

11 point Comic Sans MS font

Line spacing of 1.5 inches

5 Click in the paragraph that begins *Fill this out…* Choose **Format | Borders and Shading** and click the **Borders** tab, if necessary. Select **1 pt** for **Width** and select the dashed line for **Style**. Click **None** for **Setting** and then click the upper border in the **Preview** and click **OK**.

6 With the same paragraph selected, add 72 points of space before the paragraph and 12 points of space after the paragraph.

7 Press [Ctrl] + [End] and type the following, using a right tab with an underline leader at 6 inches to create the line:

Name _____

Address _____

City, State, Zip _____

Phone Number _____

8 Add 12 points of space after each paragraph typed in step 7.

9 Refer to Figure 64 and insert the appropriate WordArt for *Spring Break on the Beach* below the last paragraph and above the dotted line. Center it by centering the paragraph.

10 Save the file as *Spring Break Revised* and close the file.

4 FORMATTING THE COOKING SEMINAR BROCHURE

Rachel is responsible for the cooking seminar brochure, which is essentially the same format as the remodeling brochure designed in this project. In this exercise, you will format the brochure as shown in Figure 3-65.

Figure 3-65

Cooking in the Dorm Room

*A Seminar Brought to You by the
Home Page
for College and Career Week at
e-Selections*

Date	Time
2/14	1:00 pm
2/15	7:00 pm
2/16	9:00 am
2/17	1:00 pm
2/18	7:00 pm
2/19	3:00 pm

Should I Attend?

If the answer to any one of the following questions is yes, then you NEED to attend!

➢ Are you tired of eating mystery meat in the Cafe?
➢ Have you spent all your food budget on CDs?
➢ Does the school dietician have your picture on the Before poster?
➢ Do you go home to visit the family just to get a good meal?
➢ Do you put extra toothpaste on your toothbrush in the morning and call it breakfast?
➢ Have you eaten at McDonalds so many times they've named a Value Meal after you?
➢ Do you eat things that you never considered food before coming to college?

How Much Will It Set Me Back?

In fact we'll actually pay you to attend. The first 20 arrivals at each seminar will receive a coupon for a free liter of Coke.®

What's in It for Me?

In this delicious and fun-filled seminar, you'll learn how to:

• grill sandwiches with your iron
• roast hot dogs over your Halogen light
• harvest the mushrooms growing under your bed
• turn leftover pizza crust into a tasty Italian treat

How Do I Sign Up?

Follow these easy steps to register:

1. Send us your favorite recipe that has one of the following ingredients: chewing gum, breath mints, candy bars, or potato chips.

2. Fill out the form below.

3. Send the form and your recipe to Selections, 1500 Woodmen Tower, 30th Floor, Omaha, NE 68102.

Name _____

Address _____

Phone # _____

Preferred Seminar Date _____

Alternate Seminar Date(s) _____

Space is limited to 20 people in each seminar. We will make exceptions, however, for extreme cases as determined by how bizarre your favorite recipe is. An impartial panel of chefs from various school cafeterias will judge recipes. In case of a tie, the registration with the earliest marked

postmark will be awarded the seat in the seminar. All decisions by the judges are final.

Featured Seminar Recipe

The following recipe will be demonstrated in the seminar. If you're not able to attend, please **do not** attempt to cook this recipe in your dorm room. This recipe should only be used by trained professionals.

1 Open *Cooking Seminar.doc*. View the two pages in Print Preview, and then close Print Preview.

2 Set the top, bottom, left, and right margins to .5″ and change the page orientation to Landscape.

3 Format the document with three equal columns. Change the column spacing for the first column to 1 inch, and use a line·between the columns.

4 On the first page, insert two column breaks before the title.

5 Open *Remodel Revised.doc*. Select the paragraph on the first page with the headings Date and Time. Click the Format Painter button. Switch to the Cooking Seminar window and select the same text on the first page. The format is copied.

6 Using the same procedure, copy the format of the first paragraph under the heading (Date and Time) in *Remodel Revised* and apply it to all the date/time paragraphs in the *Cooking Seminar* window.

7 In *Remodel Revised*, click the Show/Hide ¶ button and then copy the paragraph mark after the text *Should I Attend?* at the top of the first column on page 2. Close the document without saving changes. Click the Show/Hide ¶ button in *Cooking Seminar*, select the paragraph mark after *Should I Attend?*, and paste. The Question style is applied to the text in *Cooking Seminar*.

8 Apply the Question style to *How Much Will It Set Me Back?*, *What's in It for Me?*, *How Do I Sign Up?*, and *Featured Seminar Recipe*.

9 Apply the default style, Body Text First Indent, to the first paragraph under each heading (formatted with the Question style).

10 Insert a column break before *What's in It for Me?* and *Featured Seminar Recipe*.

11 Using Figure 3-65 as your guide, bullet or number the paragraphs under the headings *Should I Attend?*, *What's in It for Me?*, and *How Do I Sign Up?*. Decrease indents as necessary to match the figure. f

12 Delete "It's Free!" in the text and replace it with the appropriate Word Art (refer to Figure 3-65).

13 Log onto the Internet and go to the HGTV Web site or to the Food Network Web site. Find an appropriate recipe to include in the third column of the brochure. Type and format the recipe appropriately.

14 Save the file as *Cooking Seminar Formatted* and close it.

ON YOUR OWN

The difficulty of these case studies varies: ⚑ are the least difficult; ⚑⚑ are more difficult; and ⚑⚑⚑ are the most difficult.

1 MAKING SIGNS

⚑ Using page borders, styles, Word Art, and graphics, make a variety of signs for the door of your room, such as Do Not Disturb, Donations are Tax Deductible, Don't Feed the Animals, Men Working, Women Working, and I'd Rather Be Surfing (Fishing, Sky-Diving, and so on).

2 DESIGNING AND PRINTING A PARTY INVITATION

⚑ You're having a party. First decide on a theme for the party, and then be creative and design a unique invitation that illustrates the theme.

③ CREATING WORD PUZZLES WITH GRAPHICS

If you can't find anything better to do at your party, use this activity to create some party games. Create a file and type the title **Word Puzzles** at the top. Using Word ClipArt or graphics you find on the Web, create at least three pictorial word puzzles, such as: In 1998 this state elected a retired Navy Seal and WWF wrestler as governor.

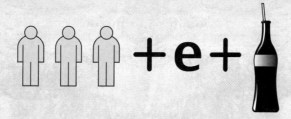

You might have to do a little research in Help on the topic of "wrapping" to get the graphics positioned correctly. Save the puzzles in a file named *Puzzles*. By the way, the answer to the example puzzle is Minnesota. Can you name the governor? It's Jesse "The Body" Ventura, who now likes to be called Jesse "The Brain" Ventura.

④ DESIGNING AND PRINTING GIFT CERTIFICATES

Create at least four gift certificates for your friends and family to give away as prizes at your party. The certificates should be worded something like the following: "This certificate entitles the bearer to one free car wash by <your name>." Choose **Custom size** for paper size and specify 4.25" by 5.5." Print four pages per sheet. Experiment with different page borders and create appropriate styles for the text.

⑤ DESIGNING AND PRINTING YOUR OWN GREETING CARDS

Create your own greeting cards to send to your friends and family. If you use 8 1/2-by-11-inch paper, you can fold the paper in quarters to create the card. The document should be two pages and use two columns. The front of the card should print in the bottom right corner of the first page. After printing the first page, you should turn it over and send it through the printer to print the inside page. Positioning the inside page will be the challenging part. Good luck! (Hint: Check out the animated greeting cards at the Blue Mountain Web site for ideas.)

6 **CREATING A TEMPLATE FOR RESEARCH PAPERS**

When writing research papers, it is likely that you have been told to follow the guidelines set forth by a style manual such as the *MLA Handbook for Writers of Research Papers* or the *Chicago Manual of Style*.

Refer to the style guidelines that you are required to use and create a document that uses the prescribed formats. Set the appropriate margins, modify the default Normal or Body Text style so that it uses the proper font, font size, line spacing, indentation, and paragraph spacing. Modify the default Footnote, Header, and Footer styles so that they use the proper font, font size, line spacing, indentation, and paragraph spacing. Create pages with sample text for the required elements, such as a title page and bibliography. Save the document as a template by selecting **Document Template (*.dot)** in the **Save as type** list box in the Save As dialog box. To use the template when you want to write a new paper, choose **File | New**. Click General Templates in the task pane. Select the template from the **General** tab and click **OK**.

Photospread credits pages 3-2 & 3-3

©EyeWire; ©Pearson Education, © Lorraine Castellano

P R O J E C T **4**

Working with Multipage Documents

Multipage documents often require what might be considered more advanced formatting, such as section breaks, headers, and footers—formatting that is more complex than character or paragraph formatting. Longer documents may require additional navigation techniques. In this project you will learn techniques for working with longer documents and some features, such as outlines and footnotes that are frequently associated with longer documents.

OBJECTIVES

After completing this project, you will be able to:

• Compare and merge documents

• Create a title page

• Create sections

• Create an outline

• Create and modify headers and footers

• Create footnotes

• Use the Document Map to navigate

• Print specific pages

e-selections) **Running Case**

Matthew has electronic files for all of the events and details concerning College and Career Week. He wants to put all the files into one document and organize them into a professional-looking report, with a title page, that will be printed on both sides of the paper and bound.

Formatting a Research Paper

It's 2:00 A.M. and there are just six more hours until your first English term paper is due. You calculate that you have just enough time to finish—if the coffee holds out and your computer cooperates. You've done all your research and typed up most of your notes, but you still have to edit and format the paper and create a list of your sources. Your English professor requires that you format the paper using the Modern Language Association (MLA) of America standards. You look around for your *MLA Handbook for Writers of Research Papers,* but all you can find is a copy of *Publication Manual for the American Psychological Association* (APA) that belongs to your roommate (a psych major). You're wondering whether you should continue your search or if you can just use the guidelines in your roommate's book. After all—they couldn't be that different, could they?

Well, the answer is yes! The guidelines put forth by the MLA are quite a bit different from the guidelines of the APA. It's not that one set of guidelines is more correct than the other is. They're simply used by different disciplines. The MLA standards are used most frequently in the humanities, in the study of English and other languages, for example. The APA standards are used most frequently in the social sciences, such as the study of education and psychology. What it really boils down to, however, is the preference of the professor or the department as a whole.

The MLA and APA guidelines concerning the order and punctuation of sources listed in the bibliography are quite different. You should consult your particular guidelines for details. Both handbooks now include rules for listing electronic and media sources as well as books, periodicals, research papers, pamphlets, etc.

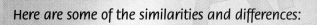

Here are some of the similarities and differences:

	MLA	APA
Margins	1" for all margins	1.5" for all margins
Paragraph indent	1/2"	1/2"
Paragraph spacing	Double-spaced	Double-spaced
Title page	Not required; name and course information (professor's name and course name) and date appear in a block 1" from the top on the left margin of the first page	Required
Page numbers	Insert your last name followed by the page number in the upper-right margin, 1/2" from the paper's edge. Your name and the page number appears on all pages.	On all pages, including the title page, insert the page number in the upper-right margin, two lines below a summary of the paper's title.
Author references	Placed in the body of the text in parentheses; footnotes are used only for explanatory notes	Placed in the body of the text in parentheses
Bibliography	Sources for the paper are listed in alphabetical order by author's last name at the end of the paper on a separate page with the title "Works Cited."	Sources for the paper are listed in alphabetical order by author's last name at the end of the paper on a separate page with the title "References."

Working with Multipage Documents

The Challenge

It is your responsibility as the administrative assistant to make sure that the formats in the document are ready for printing, the pages are numbered correctly, and all the documents are inserted in the right place. You will also have to solve a problem that Matthew has created. He actually has two files for one of the documents—a file he created at home and one that he created at work. You will have to compare the two files and decide which one to use or use the best text from each file.

The Solution

Before you begin the report, you will solve the problem of the two files by using Word's Compare and Merge Documents feature. Once you have merged the changes, you will be ready to tackle the report. You will begin the report by creating a title page, followed by an outline that will serve as an executive overview of what is in the file. Then you will insert the various files following the outline. So that you can start page numbering with the first page of the outline and not the title page, you will have to insert a section break before the outline. To number the outline, you will begin using lowercase Roman numerals and then start numbering the actual report pages with Arabic numbers (starting with one). To restart the numbering on the report pages and change the format of the page number, you will also have to insert a section break after the outline. Figure 4-1 shows the first few pages of the report.

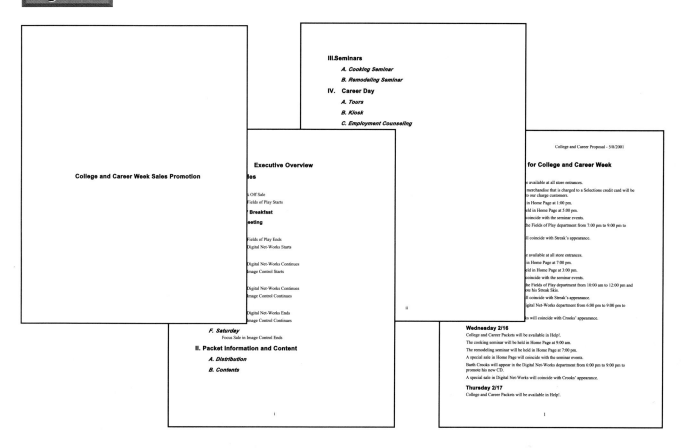

Comparing and Merging Documents

Matthew has given you two versions of the Seminars file and you don't know if they are the same or not. One way to find out is to let Word mark the differences in the documents with the Compare and Merge Documents command.

When you use this command, Word compares the documents and merges the changes into one or the other of the two documents or into a new document. You can go to each change and accept it or reject it using the Reviewing toolbar.

Task 1:
To Compare and Merge Two Documents

1 Open Word and then open *Seminars.doc*.

2 Choose **Tools | Compare and Merge Documents** to open the Compare and Merge Documents dialog box.

3 Navigate to the location where you are storing your files for this class and select *Seminars2.doc*.

4 Click the down arrow on the Merge button and select **Merge into new document**. The differences in the two documents are marked in the merged document.

Figure 4-2

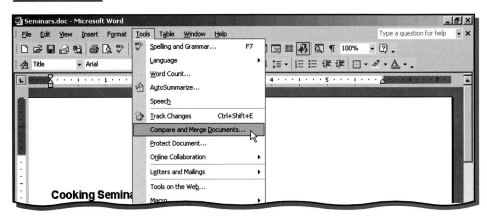

Figure 4-3

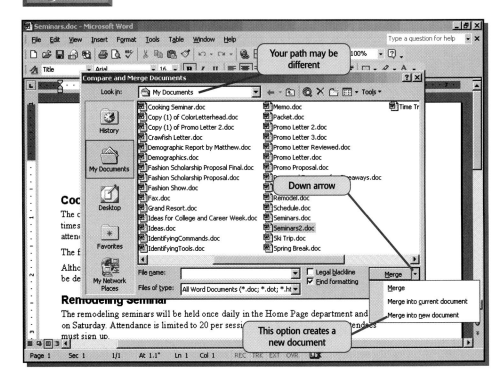

5 Click the Next button in the Reviewing toolbar. Next to the triangle you can see that the word *held* was used in the other source document. Now you must make a decision. Do you want to use the word *scheduled* or *held* in the sentence? If you decide to use *scheduled*, you must reject the deletion of the word *scheduled* and reject the insertion of the word *held*. If you decide to use *held*, you must accept the deletion of *schedule* and accept the insertion of *held*.

Figure 4-4

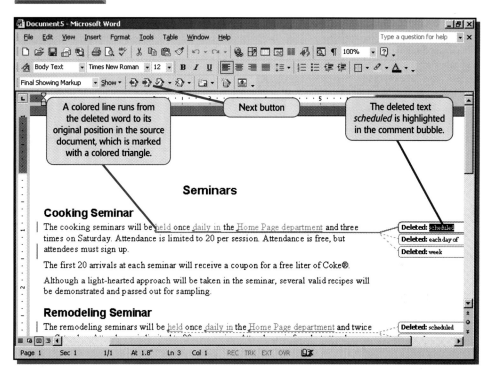

6 Click the Reject Change/Delete Comment button to reject the change. The word *scheduled* is reinserted in the sentence.

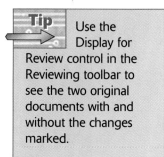

Tip Use the Display for Review control in the Reviewing toolbar to see the two original documents with and without the changes marked.

7 Click the Next button to move to the next change inserted word *held* highlighted.

8 Click the Reject Change/Delete Comment button to delete the word *held*.

Figure 4-5

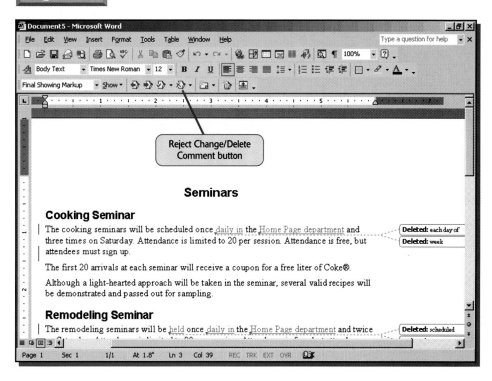

9 Click the Next button. The deleted phrase *each day of* is highlighted.

10 Click the Accept Change ✔ ▾ button to accept the deleted phrase. The marked phrase is deleted.

11 Continue reviewing changes and make the following edits:
- Keep the change for the inserted text *daily in*
- Accept the deletion of the word *week*
- Accept the change to insert the phrase *Home Page department*
- Reject the *Not Italic* change

Use Figure 4-7 as a guide to complete your review.

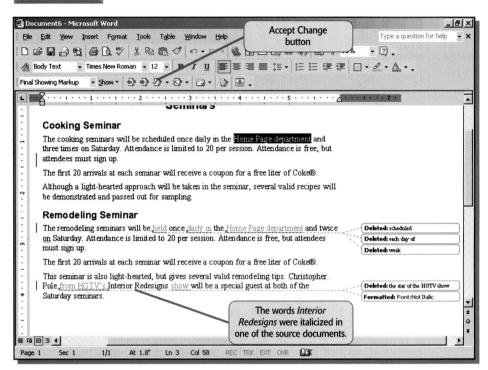

Figure 4-6

Troubleshooting
Sometimes you may make a change accidentally. If this happens and you want to reverse a change, click the Undo ↩ ▾ button.

12 Save the file as *SeminarsMerged* and close both files when you are finished.

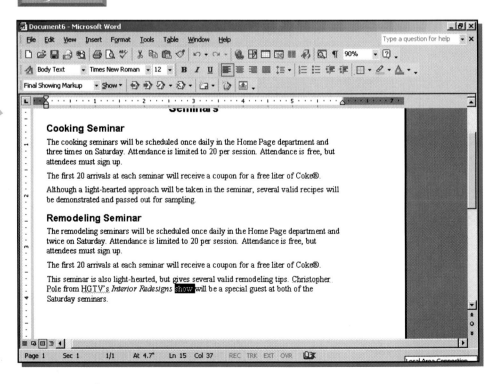

Figure 4-7

Creating a Title Page

A title page is the first page of a report and it is not numbered. The text of a title page is generally centered on the page vertically. Instead of pressing [Enter] until you think you have reached the vertical center of the page, you can simply select a layout option that automatically centers text on the page.

Task 2:

To Create a Title Page

1 Create a new document and switch to Print Layout view, if necessary.

2 Type College and Career Week Sales Promotion, and press [Enter].

3 Apply the Title style to the text.

Figure 4-8

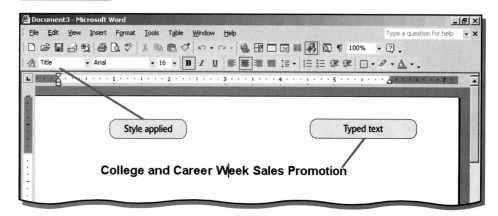

4 Choose **File | Page Setup** to open the Page Setup dialog box.

 CHECK POINT

To apply styles, you can use the Styles and Formatting task pane or the Styles drop-down list in the Formatting toolbar. The Styles and Formatting button in the Formatting toolbar displays the Styles and Formatting task pane.

Figure 4-9

5 Click the **Margins** tab, if necessary. Set the **Left** and **Right** margins at 1" and set **Gutter** at .5".

Tip The gutter spacing on documents formatted with multiple columns sets the spacing between columns. Setting a gutter on a document formatted with no columns sets extra spacing for binding down the left margin. When Normal is selected from the Multiple pages drop-down list, the Gutter position defaults to Left.

Figure 4-10

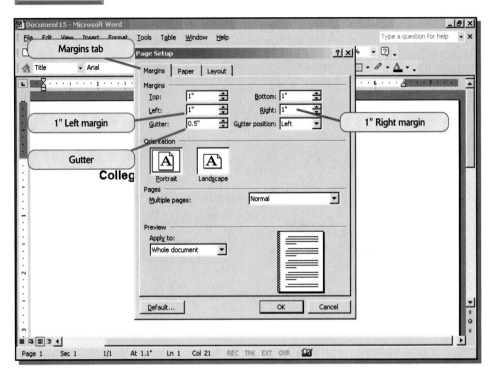

6 Click the **Layout** tab.

7 Select **Center** from the Vertical alignment drop-down list to set vertical centering on the page.

8 Click **OK**. The title moves to the vertical center of the page.

Figure 4-11

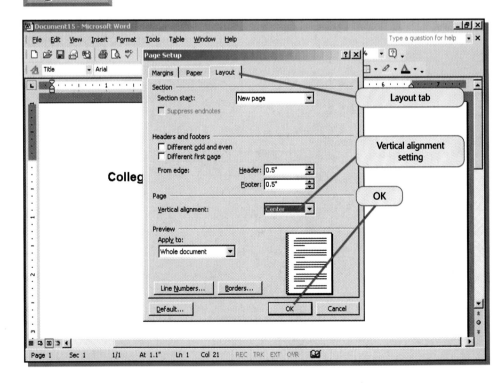

9 Press Ctrl + End to move to the end of the document and press Ctrl + Enter to insert a page break below the title.

Tip Because you will be printing the report on both sides of the paper, referred to as *duplex printing*, you need a blank page following the title page so that the next section, the outline, can begin on a right-hand page.

10 Save the file as *C & C Promo Proposal*.

Figure 4-12

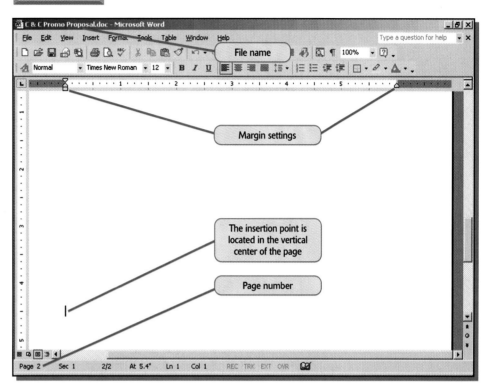

Creating Sections

Section breaks divide a page or a document into independent parts. Word uses four types of section breaks: next page, continuous, even page, and odd page. A continuous section break divides a page into sections and allows each section to have different left and right margins and a different number of columns.

The other types of section breaks (next page, even page, and odd page) divide the document into sections by using page breaks. When one of these section breaks is inserted, each section can have a different page setup. Each section can have a different paper size, different orientation, different vertical alignment, different margins, and different headers and footers.

Table 4-1 describes section break options.

Table 4-1 Types of Section Breaks	
Section Break	**Description**
Next page	Breaks the page and starts the new section on the next page.
Continuous	Starts the new section on the same page; does not create a page break.
Odd page or Even page	Breaks the page and starts the new section on the next odd-numbered or even-numbered page.

In the next task you will insert a section break to begin a new section so that you can use top alignment instead of center alignment. Inserting the section break will also allow you to start numbering the pages in the new section without numbering the title page and the blank page that follows it.

Task 3:
To Insert a Section Break

1 Choose **Insert | Break** to open the Break dialog box.

Figure 4-13

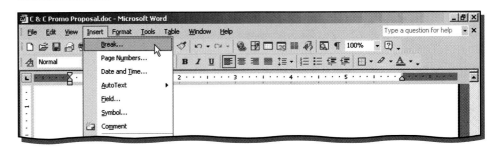

2 Select **Next page** and click **OK**. Word inserts a section break and creates a new page.

Figure 4-14

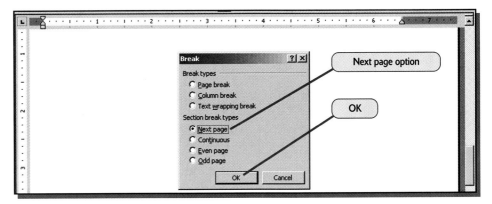

Tip Notice in the status line that you now have three pages. The new page uses center alignment because the new section copies the formatting of the previous section.

3 Switch to Normal view and scroll up with the vertical scroll bar to see the section break.

Figure 4-15

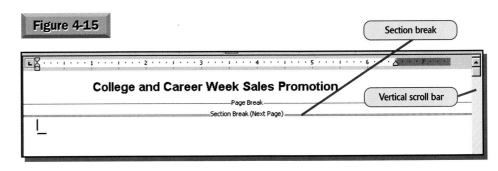

Troubleshooting
Do not move the insertion point. Press [Ctrl] + [End] if you have moved it.

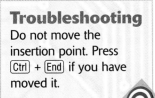

4 Switch back to Print Layout view and choose **File | Page Setup**. The Page Setup dialog box displays the Layout tab because it was the last tab used in the dialog box.

5 Select **Top** for **Vertical alignment**; under **Apply to**, verify that **This section** is selected; and click **OK**. The insertion point (on page 3 in section 2) moves to the top of the page.

6 Save the file.

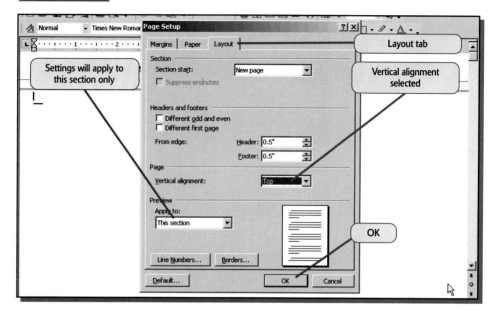

Figure 4-16

Creating an Outline

The *outline numbering* feature in Word numbers each topic for you automatically. It also renumbers the topics if you add additional topics or delete topics. Several default outline numbering styles are available, and you can create your own style.

WEB TIP

Did you know that the Microsoft Support Web site maintains an extensive collection of help articles called a Knowledge Base? To learn more about outline numbering, go to the Microsoft Web site and click Support. Navigate to the Knowledge Base and search for the phrase *outline numbering*.

Task 4:

To Create an Outline

1 Type **Executive Overview** and press Enter. Then apply the Title style to the text.

2 Press Ctrl + End to move to the end of the document and then choose **Format|Bullets and Numbering** to open the Bullets and Numbering dialog box.

3 Click the **Outline Numbered** tab and select the style that uses I. A. 1. for the headings.

Troubleshooting
If the selected style shown in Figure 4-18 doesn't match the style in your dialog box, select the style and click the Reset button.

4 Click **OK**. The Roman numeral *I.* appears in the document.

Figure 4-17

Figure 4-18

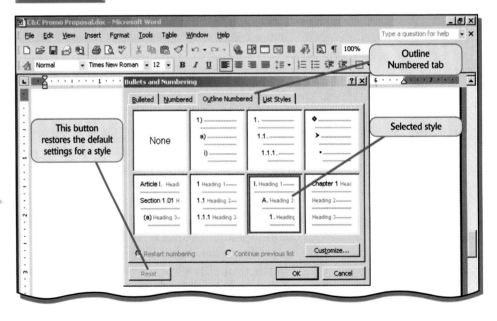

Outline Numbered tab

Selected style

This button restores the default settings for a style

5 Switch to Outline view. The Outline toolbar appears.

Tip The buttons on the left side of the Outline toolbar are the ones that you'll use when creating an outline. The buttons on the right side of the tool-bar are used when cre-ating master documents and subdocuments.

Figure 4-19

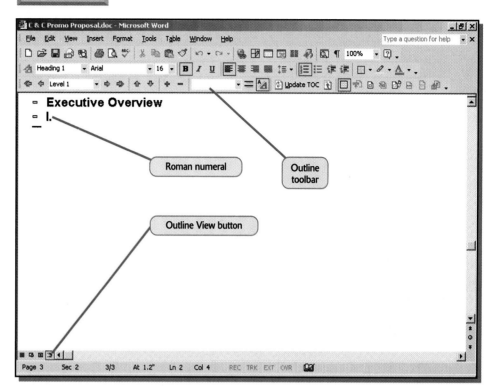

Roman numeral

Outline toolbar

Outline View button

6 Type Schedule of Sales, press Enter, and then press Tab to demote the heading to the next lower level.

7 Type Monday and press Enter. When you press Enter, Word inserts the next letter on this level (B.)

Figure 4-20

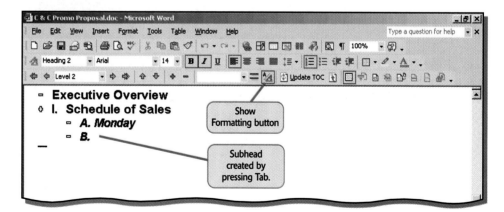

Show Formatting button

Subhead created by pressing Tab.

Troubleshooting If you do not get the next Roman numeral when you press Enter or the let-ter A when you press Tab, you forgot to switch to Outline view. Press Backspace to return to the end of the line "Schedule of Sales," switch to Outline view, and repeat the correct steps.

Troubleshooting If the text on your screen is not formatted and does not look like Figure 4-20, click the Show Formatting button to activate the formatting.

8 Press Tab, type Kick-off Breakfast, and press Enter.

9 Type Team Meeting and press Enter.

10 Press Shift + Tab to move to the previous tab. Word promotes the heading to the next higher level.

11 Type Tuesday and press Enter.

12 Repeat step 11, substituting the remaining days of the week through Saturday, as shown in Figure 4-21, and be sure to press Enter after typing Saturday.

13 Press Shift + Tab. The insertion point moves to the left margin and the *G* changes to *II*.

14 Type the remaining headings as shown in Figure 4-22 and after the last heading, press Enter, and then press Bksp. The outline number is erased on the new line.

Figure 4-21

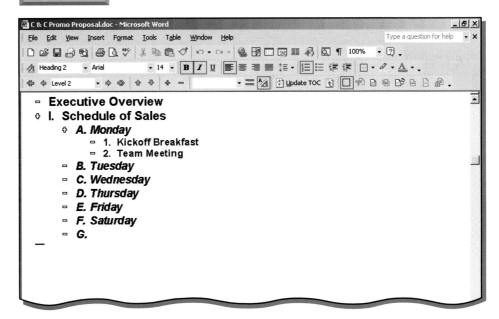

To promote a heading:
- Click the Promote ⇦ button.

Figure 4-22

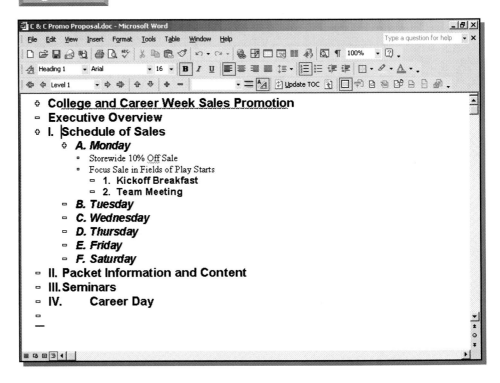

15 Click the Show Formatting 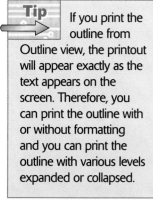 button on the Outline toolbar to turn off text formatting. The formatting is removed from the text and more text displays on the screen.

16 Save the file.

Figure 4-23

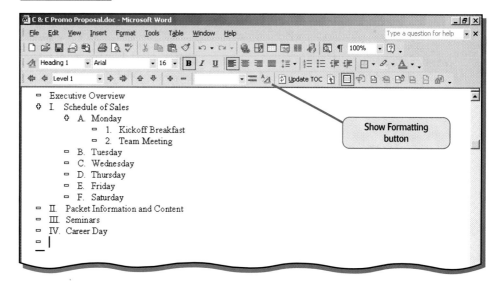

> **Tip**
>
> If you print the outline from Outline view, the printout will appear exactly as the text appears on the screen. Therefore, you can print the outline with or without formatting and you can print the outline with various levels expanded or collapsed.

Typing Body Text

In an outline, body text is text that does not have an outline level. Word automatically applies the Normal style to outline body text instead of a heading style. Do not confuse outline "body text" with the style called "Body Text."

 CHECK POINT

By now you have most likely learned how beneficial using AutoText entries can be. Look at the repetitive text (*Focus Sale in*) that you must type in Step 5 of the next task. Perhaps you will want to create an AutoText entry for the text. To do that, type the text the first time and then select it. Press [Alt] + [F3], give the entry a short name, and then click **OK**. To use the AutoText, type the short name and press [F3].

Task 5:

To Type Body Text

1   Click the insertion point after the *y* in *Monday* and press Enter.

2   Click the Demote to Body Text button. The outline numbering is removed and the Body text level is applied.

3   Type Storewide 10% Off Sale, press Enter, and then type Focus Sale in Fields of Play Starts.

4   For each of the remaining days of the week, click the insertion point after the "y," press Enter, and demote the heading to Body text. Type the Body text shown in Figure 4-25.

Figure 4-24

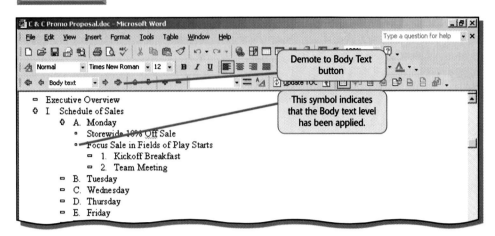

Figure 4-25

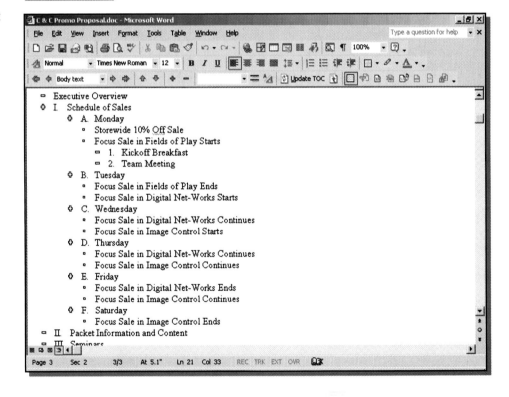

5 Type the remaining subheadings under headings II, III, and IV as shown in Figure 4-26.

6 Save the file.

Figure 4-26

```
  ⊕  II.  Packet Information and Content
         ▫  A.  Distribution
         ▫  B.  Contents
  ⊕  III.  Seminars
         ▫  A.  Cooking Seminar
         ▫  B.  Remodeling Seminar
  ⊕  IV.  Career Day
         ▫  A.  Tours
         ▫  B.  Kiosk
         ▫  C.  Employment Counseling
         ▫  D.  Recruiting Booth
  ▫
```

Collapsing and Expanding an Outline

One of the most convenient features about an outline is the ability to collapse (hide) and expand (show) various levels in the outline.

Task 6:

To Collapse and Expand an Outline

1 Press Ctrl + Home to go to the top of the document and click the down arrow in the Show Level drop-down list.

2 Select **Show Level 1**. The outline collapses, showing only the paragraphs formatted with the Titles style and the headings at the first level.

3 Click anywhere in the heading *Schedule of Sales* and click the Expand ✚ button once. Only that heading displays its next level of headings.

Troubleshooting
Do not confuse the Expand button with the plus to the left of the text in the outline. If you try to click the plus next to the text, you will select the text.

Figure 4-27

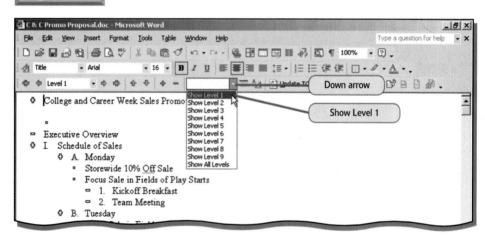

Figure 4-28

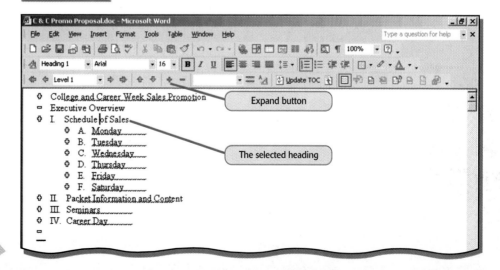

4 While the insertion point is still in the same heading, click the Expand ✚ button again. Only this heading displays the next heading level.

Figure 4-29

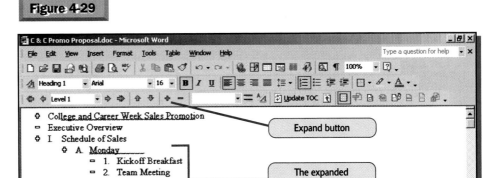

5 Without moving the insertion point, click the Expand ✚ button one more time. This time the body text displays (only for this heading) because there are no more subhead levels to display.

Figure 4-30

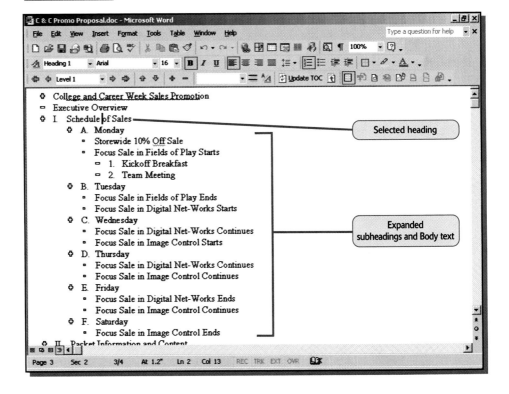

6 With the insertion point still in the *Schedule of Sales* heading, click the Collapse ➖ button once. Word hides the body text under the heading.

7 Click the Collapse ➖ button twice. All sub-headings for this topic collapse.

8 Click the down arrow in the Show Level drop-down list and select **Show Level 2**.

Figure 4-31

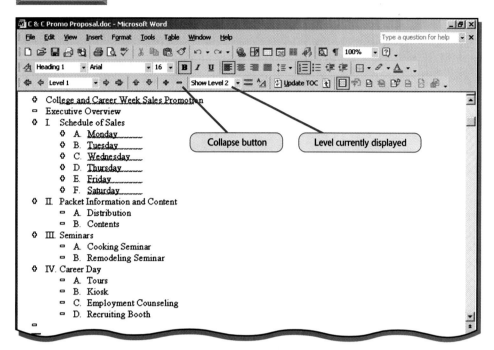

9 Click the Print Layout View ⊟ button. The full document appears in Print Layout view.

Troubleshooting
The paragraphs are not indented as you would expect. You can enhance the appearance of the outline by modifying the styles.

Figure 4-32

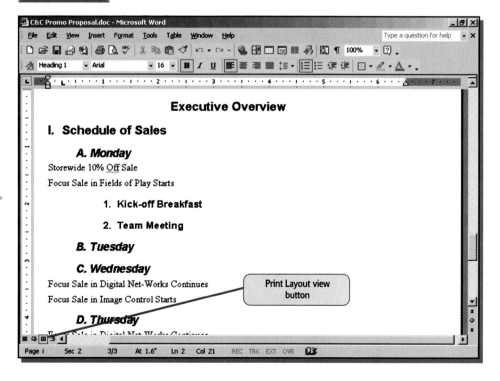

10 Select all the text that does not have an outline level (the text that uses the Body text level) and apply the Block Text style.

Troubleshooting

If you are a "formatting purist," you will not be happy with the way Word formats the numbers in an outline. Notice that the Roman numerals are not aligned on the decimal point. This causes the space between the decimal point and the text to vary. (Compare headings II and III.) You can improve the look of the formatting in one of two ways. If you are a "purist," you should modify all the Heading styles and change the number alignment to **Right**. If you are satisfied to "get by," you can simply change the tab following the number in Heading 1 style to .5".

Figure 4-33

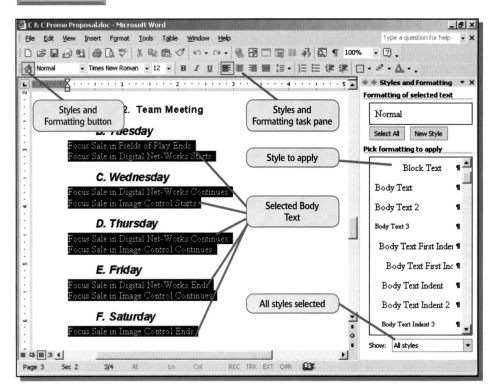

Tip After selecting the first paragraphs, press Ctrl while selecting all the other paragraphs so you can apply the style to all text at one time.

Tip To apply a style after selecting the text, click the Styles and Formatting button to display the task pane. If necessary, select **All Styles** for **Show** and then click the Block Text style.

11 Check with your instructor to see if and how you should modify the formatting of the numbers.

12 Insert a page break before the *Seminars* heading.

13 Save the file.

Figure 4-34

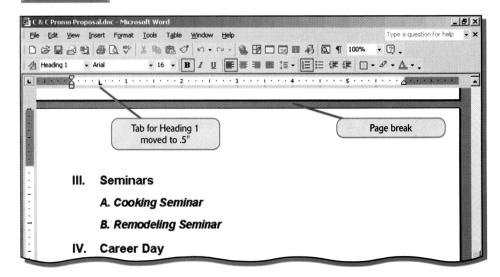

In the next task, you will insert the new file that you merged from two files and the three other files that Matthew created separately.

CHECK POINT

Do you remember the steps for inserting a file? Choose **Insert | File**, select the file, and then click **Insert**.

Task 7:
To Create the Next Section

1 Press Ctrl + End to move to the end of the document and insert a Next page section break. A new page and a new section are created.

2 Insert the following files in this document and insert a page break after each file except the last one:
Schedule.doc
Packet.doc
SeminarsMerged.doc
CC Day.doc

3 Save the file. You should now have a 9-page document with three sections.

Figure 4-35

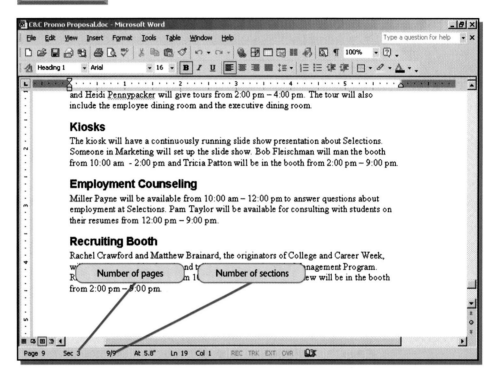

Creating and Modifying Headers and Footers

A *header* is text that prints at the top of every page in a section. A *footer* is text that prints at the bottom of every page in a section. The header prints within the default 1-inch top margin, a 1/2 inch from the top edge of the paper. The footer prints in the default 1-inch bottom margin, a 1/2 inch from the bottom edge of the paper.

Creating Headers and Footers

Every document contains a blank header and footer space. To create a header or a footer you open the header or footer space and enter text. By default, the header and footer space both have a center tab and a right tab.

Task 8:
To Create Headers and Footers

1 Go to the first page (the title page) and choose **View | Header and Footer**. The header space opens and the Header and Footer toolbar appears.

Figure 4-36

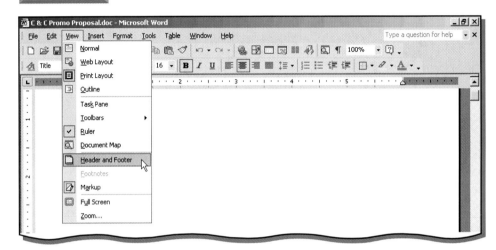

Tip

The Header and Footer toolbar contains buttons to insert page numbers, format page numbers, insert the date, insert the time, format the page, show or hide the text on the page, create or break a link to the previous header or footer, navigate between the header and footer, and navigate between the sections.

2 Click the Page Setup  button on the Header and Footer toolbar to open the Page Setup dialog box.

3 Select **Different odd and even** to create headers and footers that have different text on alternating pages and click **OK**. The Header—Section 1 changes to Odd Page Header—Section 1.

Figure 4-37

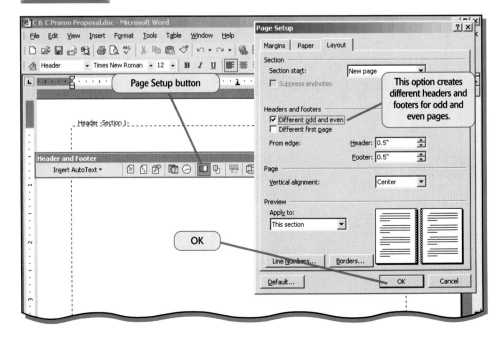

4   Click the Show Next
🖳 button twice. The
Odd Page header - Section 2
opens.

Figure 4-38

5   Click the Same as
Previous 🖳 button.
The link between this header
and the header in section 1 is
broken and the "Same as
Previous" indicator disappears.

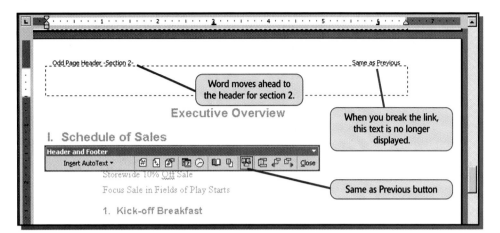

Figure 4-38

6   Click the Switch
Between Header and
Footer 🖳 button. The Odd
Page Footer - Section 2
opens.

7   Click Same as Previous
🖳 button. The link
between this footer and the
footer in section 1 is broken.

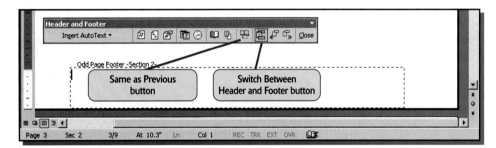

Figure 4-39

8   Leave this footer open
for the next task.

Inserting and Formatting Page Numbers

Page numbers in headers or footers can be formatted to use different number
formats or include text.

Task 9:

To Insert and Format Page Numbers

1 The insertion point should still be positioned in the footer for section 2. Press `Tab`, and click the Insert Page Number button. The page number is centered in the footer.

2 Click the Format Page Number button to open the Page Number Format dialog box, select **i, ii, iii…** from the **Number format** drop-down list, select **Start at**, and click **OK**. The number in the footer changes to "i".

3 Click the Show Next button to move to the Even Page Footer for section 2 and click the Same as Previous button to break the link between this footer and the previous footer.

4 Press `Tab` and click the Insert Page Number button. The Roman numeral *ii* is inserted in the center of the footer.

Figure 4-40

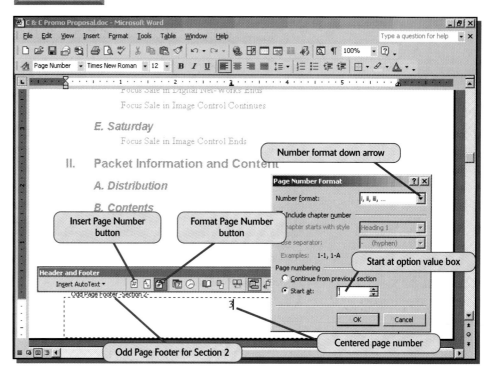

Figure 4-41

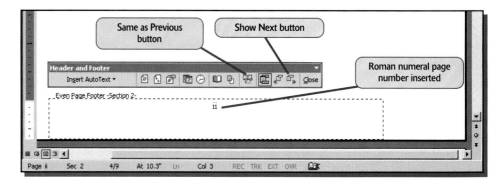

5 Click the Switch Between Header and Footer 🔲 button to go to the Even Page Header for section 2 and then click the Same as Previous 🔲 button.

6 Click the Show Next 🔲 button to go to the Odd Page Header for section 3, click the Same as Previous 🔲 button, press Tab twice, and then type College and Career Proposal.

Figure 4-42

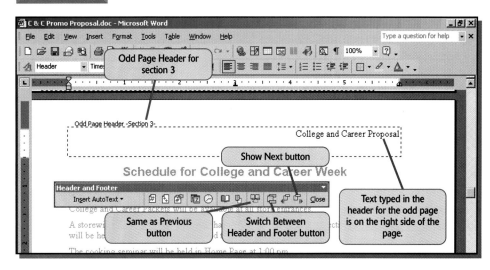

7 Click the Show Next 🔲 button to go to the next section, click the Same as Previous 🔲 button, and type College and Career Proposal.

Figure 4-43

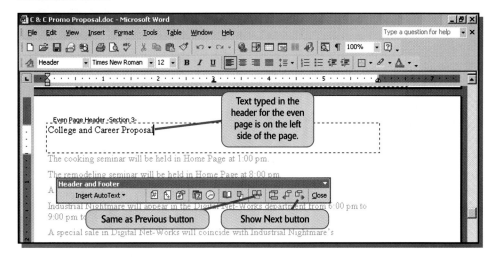

8 Click the Switch Between Header and Footer ⌨ button. The Even Page footer for section 3 displays.

9 Click the Same as Previous ⌨ button.

10 Click the Format Page Number ⌨ button, select **Start at**, and click **OK**. Word jumps back to the Odd Page Footer section and displays the number *1* in the footer space.

11 Click the Close Close button on the Header and Footer toolbar. The footer and the Header and Footer toolbar both close.

12 Ensure that Print Layout is the current view. Press Ctrl + Home and scroll through the complete document.

Tip The headers and footers display as dimmed text in the Print Layout view. There should be no numbers in the footer on the first two pages, Roman numerals on the next two pages, and Arabic numbers on the remaining pages. The text in the headers should appear on the right side of odd numbered pages and on the left side for even numbered pages starting on the first page after the outline.

13 Save the file.

Figure 4-44

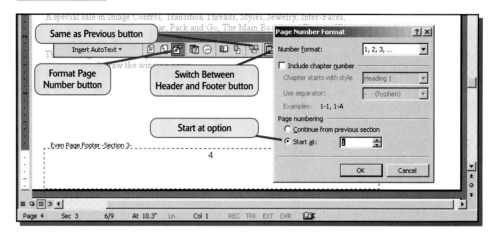

Tip

After you have broken the link with the previous header or footer, if you click the Same as Previous ⌨ button again, Word asks if you want to delete this header/footer and connect to the header/footer in the previous section. If you select Yes, the text of the current header/footer will be deleted and the text of the previous header/footer will be inserted. If you have deleted text accidentally with this process, click the Undo ⌨ ▾ button in the Standard toolbar and the header/footer space will close, restoring the original text.

Figure 4-45

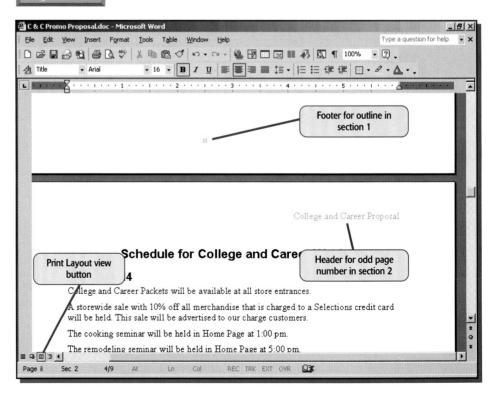

Modifying Headers and Footers

You can modify a header or footer at any time by choosing **View | Header and Footer**. However, if the header or footer is visible, you can double-click the header or footer space to open it.

Task 10:
To Modify a Header

1 Go to page 5 (the fifth page in the document) and double-click the header to open it.

2 Position the insertion point at the end of the text, type a space, a hyphen, and a space, and click the Insert Date button to insert the current date.

Figure 4-46

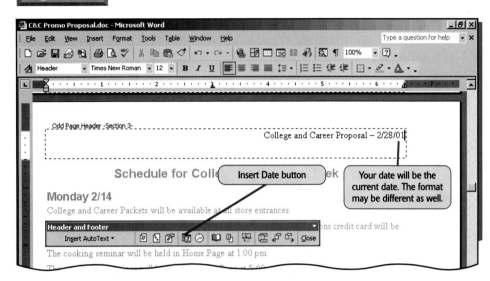

Troubleshooting If you try to go to page 5 by pressing Ctrl + G, typing a 5, and pressing Enter, you will actually go to the last page in the document because that page has the number 5 in the footer. The actual fifth page in the document is page 1 of section 3 and it has the number 1 in the footer.

3 Go to the next header (Even Page Header - Section 3). With the insertion point positioned before the existing text, insert the date followed by a space, a hyphen, and a space.

4 Close the header and save the file.

Figure 4-47

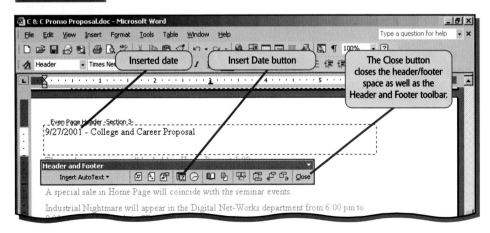

CHECK POINT

Do you remember how to set the format for the default date? Choose **Insert | Date and Time**, select the format, click **Default**, click **Yes,** and then click **OK**.

Creating Footnotes

A *footnote* is a comment or reference that appears at the bottom of the page. The reference in the text to which the footnote applies is generally shown as a raised number. The associated footnote displays the corresponding number. When you create a footnote, Word automatically numbers the footnote in the text and provides sufficient space at the bottom of the page for the footnote.

You can jump around and insert footnotes in any order on any page, and Word will number or renumber them consecutively throughout the document.

You can create multiple footnotes on the same page. If you group the footnotes together at the end of the document, they are called *endnotes*.

When you insert a footnote in Normal view, a footnote space opens. When you insert a footnote in Print Layout view, the insertion point moves to the bottom of the page where the footnote text actually appears. In the following task, you will use both methods.

Tip

According to the MLA guidelines, notes should use consecutive superscript Arabic numbers in the text. The notes themselves should be listed on a separate page under the title of Notes. Each note should be double-spaced, begin on a new line, and be numbered consecutively with superscript Arabic numbers.

Most academic style guidelines (including MLA and APA) recommend limited use of footnotes and endnotes because they can be distracting for the reader. Proper use of notes would include comments that evaluate or recommend a bibliographic source and explanatory notes that would seem digressive if included in the main text but might be interesting to readers.

Task 11:
To Create a Footnote

1 Ensure that the document is in Print Layout view. Find the phrase *slide show presentation*.

2 Position the insertion point after the word *presentation*.

3 Choose **Insert | Reference | Footnote** to open the Footnote and Endnote dialog box.

4 Verify that the settings in the dialog box match Figure 4-49. Click **Insert**. The insertion point moves to the bottom of the page.

Figure 4-48

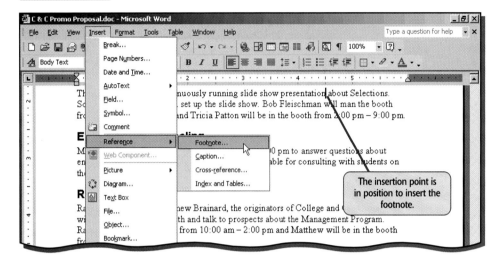

Figure 4-49

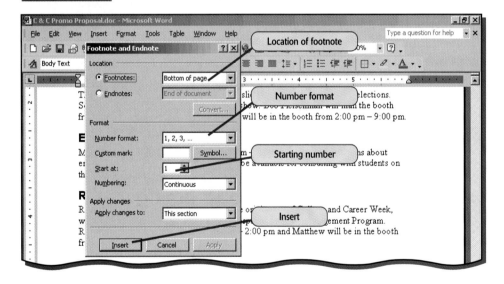

5 Type the sentence **Marketing will be responsible for creating this slide show.** and include the period.

Figure 4-50

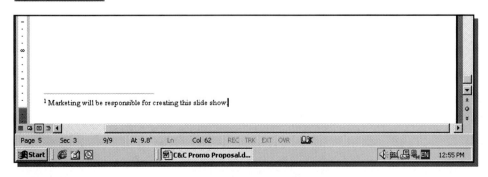

6 Click anywhere in the document and find the word *T-shirt*.

7 Switch to Normal view, and position the insertion point after the period that follows the word *t-shirt*.

8 Choose **Insert | Reference | Footnote**, and click **Insert**. The footnote page opens with the new footnote inserted before the existing footnote.

9 Type the sentence T-shirts will have the Selections logo on the back. and include the period.

10 Click the Close Close button on the footnote toolbar. The insertion point returns to the previous typing position automatically.

11 Save the file.

Figure 4-51

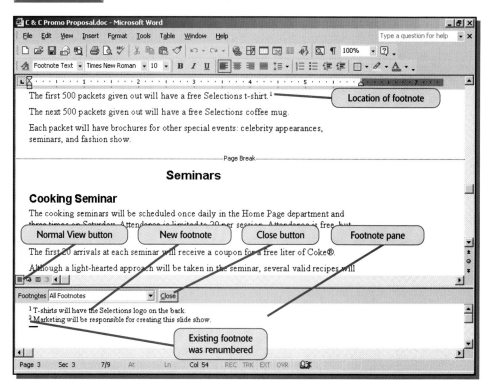

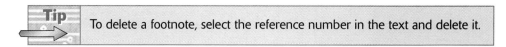

Tip
To delete a footnote, select the reference number in the text and delete it.

Using the Document Map to Navigate

The *Document Map* is a feature that lists all the document headings, similar to an outline, in a pane on the left. The headings are linked to the document so that you can click a heading and go directly to the text in the document. Additionally, the headings in the Document Map pane can be expanded and collapses like an outline so you can see more or less of the document hierarchy.

Task 12:
To Navigate with the Document Map

1 Click the Document Map 🔍 button. A pane opens on the left. The headings in the document are listed as hyperlinks in the new pane.

2 Click *Distribution* in the left pane. The corresponding section in the document is displayed.

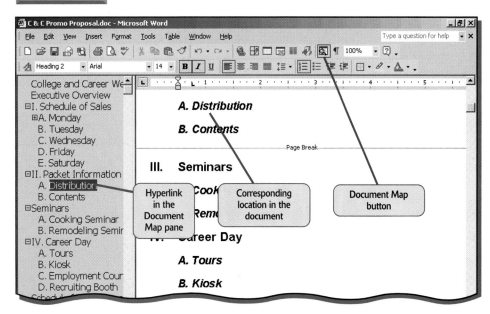

Figure 4-52

3 Click the minus sign beside *Seminars* in the left pane. The headings under the topic collapse.

4 Click the plus sign beside the same heading. The heading expands to show the subheadings.

5 Click all minus signs to collapse the headings.

6 Click *Kiosks* in the left pane. You are now on page 9.

7 Click the Document Map 🔍 button. The document returns to the original view.

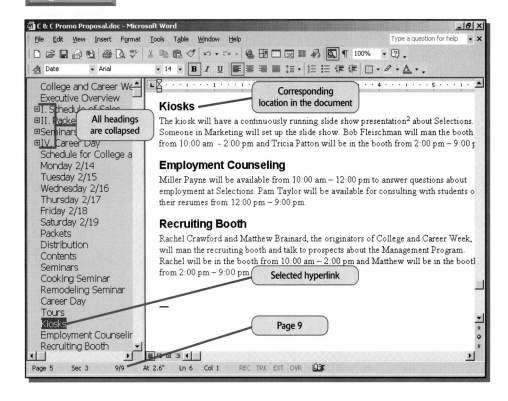

Figure 4-53

8 Save and close file.

> **Tip**
> When you drag the box in the vertical scroll bar, you can see the page number and the headings on the page in a Screen Tip. This works whether you are using the Document Map or not.

Printing Specific Pages

It is easy to print an entire document. You just click the Print 🖨 button. If you want to print specific pages in a document, you must use the Print dialog box, accessed by choosing **File | Print**. Table 4-2 lists the format that should be used in the Pages text box of the Print dialog box for printing sections and pages in sections.

> **Tip**
> You can move the insertion point to a single page you want to print and select **Current page** in the Print dialog box.

Table 4-2   Printing Specific Sections and Pages in Sections

To print:	Example	Type:
Entire section	All the pages in section 1	s1
Range of sections	All pages in section 1 and section 2	s1-s2
Noncontiguous sections	All pages in section 1 and section 3	s1, s3
Specific page in a section	Page 1 in section 2	p1s2
Range of pages in the same section	Pages 1-4 in section 2	p1s2-p4s2
Noncontiguous pages in the same section	Pages 1, 3 and 5 in section 2	p1s2, p3s2, p5s2
Range of pages that span contiguous sections	Page 2 in section 2 through page 2 in section 3	p2s2-p2s3
Noncontiguous pages in sections	Page 1 in section 2 and page 2 in section 3	p1s2, p2s3

SUMMARY AND EXERCISES

SUMMARY

- Word can compare two documents and mark the differences between them.
- Word can position text in the vertical center of the page.
- Section breaks divide a page or a document into independent parts that can have different page setups.
- The outline feature in Word numbers and renumbers each outline topic for you automatically.
- A header is text that prints at the top of every page in a section, and a footer is text that prints at the bottom of every page in a section.
- Each time you open the header or footer space, the Header and Footer toolbar appears automatically.
- When you create a footnote, Word automatically numbers the footnote in the text and provides sufficient space at the bottom of the page for the footnote.
- The Document Map is a feature that can be used to navigate a document that has headings.
- When printing pages in a document that has sections, you may have to specify the section number with the page number in the Print dialog box.

KEY TERMS & SKILLS

KEY TERMS

Document Map
  (p. 4-32)
duplex printing (p. 4-11)
endnotes (p. 4-30)
footer (p. 4-23)

footnote (p. 4-30)
header (p. 4-23)
outline numbering
  (p. 4-13)
section breaks (p. 4-11)

SKILLS

Collapse an outline topic (p. 4-19)
Compare documents (p. 4-6)
Create a footnote (p. 4-31)
Create a header or footer (p. 4-23)
Demote an outline topic (p. 13)
Display the outline (p. 4-13)
Expand an outline topic (p. 4-19)
Format a page number (p. 4-26)
Insert a date (p. 4-29)
Insert a page number (p. 4-26)
Insert a section break (p. 4-12)
Merge documents (p. 4-6)
Modify a header or footer (p. 4-29)
Print pages in a section (p. 4-34)
Promote an outline topic (p. 4-13)
Switch between header and footer
    (p. 4-23)
Use the document map (p. 4-33)

STUDY QUESTIONS

MULTIPLE CHOICE

1. Which of the following statements is true?
  a. A footnote is automatically renumbered if you insert another footnote after it.
  b. A footnote is automatically renumbered if you insert another footnote before it.
  c. A footnote displays a subscripted number.
  d. A footnote doesn't appear in Page Layout view.

2. The Document Map
  a. is an outline.
  b. lists all the document headings in a pane on the right.
  c. displays headings that are linked to the document.
  d. displays all the headers, footers, footnotes, and other objects that aren't actually part of the body of the text.

3. Which of the following statements is true?
  a. A section break always inserts a page break.
  b. A section break allows you to use a different page orientation for different pages in the same document.
  c. A section break is another name for a page break.
  d. A section break must be applied to even or odd pages.

4. "Same as Previous" indicates that
   a. the section break will be like the one before it.
   b. the footnote will be like the one
      before it.
   c. the page break will be like the one before it.
   d. the header will be like the one before it.

5. The vertical alignment option is located on the
   a. Line and Page Breaks tab of the Paragraph dialog box.
   b. Indents and Spacing tab of the Paragraph dialog box.
   c. Layout tab of the Page Setup dialog box.
   d. Margins tab of the Page Setup dialog box.

6. Which view shows headers and footers?
   a. Normal
   b. Print Layout
   c. Outline
   d. Web Layout

7. How do you promote a heading in an outline?
   a. Press Tab
   b. Press Ctrl + Tab
   c. Press Alt + Tab
   d. Press Shift + Tab

8. How do you demote a heading in an outline?
   a. Press Tab
   b. Press Ctrl + Tab
   c. Press Alt + Tab
   d. Press Shift + Tab

9. To turn off the formatting in Outline view,
   a. click the Show Formatting 🄰 button.
   b. click the Collapse ▬ button.
   c. click the Show/Hide ¶ button.
   d. choose **View | Normal**.

10. If you want the first page of a document to have portrait orientation and the next page to have landscape orientation, you must
   a. insert a page break.
   b. create two different documents.
   c. insert a section break.
   d. insert a footer.

SHORT ANSWER

1. Name at least three elements that can be inserted in a header or a footer.
2. How do you collapse a heading in the Document Map?
3. What's the difference between footnotes and endnotes?
4. Which section break does not carry a page break with it?
5. What would you type in the Pages: text box in the Print dialog box to print all the pages in section 5?
6. What would you type in the Pages: text box in the Print dialog box to print the first two pages in section 5?
7. What is body text in an outline?
8. How do you format a page number in a header or footer?
9. How do you collapse a heading in an outline?
10. How do you display the Document Map?

FILL IN THE BLANK

1. Outline number styles are located on the Outline _____ tab of the Bullets and Numbering dialog box.
2. When typing an outline, use _____ view.
3. The _____ section break divides a page into separate parts.
4. You can click text in the left pane in Document Map and go to the heading in the right pane because the headings are _____.
5. The number style I. A. 1. is a typical _____ numbering style.
6. A header is text that prints at the top of every page in a(n) _____.
7. You can modify a header or footer by choosing _____ , Header and Footer.
8. The Document Map is a feature that lists all the document _____ in a pane on the left.
9. When you drag the box in the _____ scroll bar, you can see the page number in a Screen Tip.
10. The text on a title page is generally _____.

FOR DISCUSSION

1. Discuss the advantages of inserting section breaks.
2. Discuss the benefits of using Word to create a long document with footnotes.
3. Explain why it is better to create headers and footers than to simply type what you want at the top or bottom of every page.
4. Discuss at least two methods of navigating in a long document.
5. Discuss the specifications that you have been given for writing papers in a specific class.

GUIDED EXERCISES

1 INSERTING FOOTNOTES

The Demographics document needs a few footnotes for clarification. In this exercise, you will add and delete footnotes.

1 Open *Demographics.doc*.

2 Find the text *Nancy Shepherdson,* and insert the footnote "Life's Beach 101." *American Demographics,* May 2000.

3 Switch to Normal view.

4 Find the text *Mindshare* and insert the footnote A Miami-based research firm.

5 Find the text *Ikea* and insert the footnote A Swedish home-furnishing retailer.

6 Delete the second footnote.

7 Save the file as *Demographics Edited* and close it.

2 NUMBERING PAGES IN THE FASHION SCHOLARSHIP PROPOSAL

The fashion scholarship proposal is ready to have the pages numbered. In this exercise, you will add page numbers in the footer.

1 Open *Fashion Scholarship Proposal Final.doc*.

2 Insert a Next page section break before the title *The Fashion Institute of Design & Merchandising (FIDM)*.

3 Press Ctrl + Home and then choose **View | Header and Footer**.

4 Go to the header for section 2 and click the Same as Previous 🔲 button.

5 Press Tab twice and type **Fashion Scholarship Proposal**. Drag the right tab for the header to 6.5" on the ruler.

6 Click the Switch Between Header and Footer 🔲 button and click the Same as Previous 🔲 button.

7 Press Tab and click the Insert Page Number 🔲 button.

8 Click the Show Previous 🔲 button.

9 Press Tab and insert a page number. Change the format of the page number to i, ii, iii and close the footer.

10 In Print Layout view, scroll through the document to see the headers and footers.

11 Use the Document Map feature to move through the document. Turn off Document Map when finished.

12 Save the file as *Fashion Scholarship Proposal Paginated* and close it.

3 CREATING AN OUTLINE

Matthew is busy planning for the sales event in the Fields of Play department. Figure 4-54 shows the outline that he is using to help him decide what should go on sale. In this exercise, you will create the outline for him.

Figure 4-54

I. Golfing Merchandise
   A. Golf Clubs
      1. The Burlington
      2. The Kensington
      3. The Wellington
      4. The Prince of York
   B. Golf Accessories
      1. Golf Balls
      2. Golf Bags
      3. Golf Gloves
      4. Golf Shoes
   C. Golf Clothing
II. Balls
   A. Footballs
   B. Baseballs and Softballs
   C. Soccer Balls
   D. Volley Balls
III. Skiing Merchandise
   A. Skis
   B. Ski Boards
   C. Ski Accessories
   D. Ski Clothing
IV. Bicycle Merchandise

   A. Bicycles
      1. Racing Bikes
      2. Street Bikes
      3. Road Bikes
   B. Seats
   C. Cycling Accessories
   D. Cycling Clothing

1 Create a new document and select the outline numbering style shown in Figure 4-54.

2 Switch to Outline view, turn off the formatting, and type the text shown in the figure.

3 Switch to Print Layout view and then switch back to Outline view.

4 Print the document.

5 Save the document as *Fields Sale* and close it.

4 EDITING THE C&C PROMO PROPOSAL

The College and Career plans are in full swing. In this exercise, you will use the Document Map to navigate to some areas that need editing in a document that outlines proposals for the promotion.

1 Open the *C&C Promo Proposal* file you created in this project.

2 Click the Document Map 🔲 button.

3 Click *Contents* (under the *Schedule for College and Career* heading) in the Document Map pane to go to that area of the document.

4 In the Contents section, insert a footnote after *discount coupons* that says **Ranging from 10% to 30%**.

5 Scroll to the bottom of the left pane and click the *Kiosks* heading in the Document Map. Point to the footnote in this section until you see the popup box with the text of the footnote.

6 Close the Document Map.

7 Go to page 7 and delete the page break above the title *Packets*. Insert a Next page section break.

8 Go to page 8 and delete the page break above the title *Seminars*. Insert a Next page section break.

9 Go to page 10 and delete the page break above the title *Career Day*. Insert a Next page section break.

10 Choose **View | Header and Footer**. Click the Show Previous 🔲 button until you get to the Odd Page Header for section 3. Type **Schedule** on the left side of the header.

11 Click the Show Next 🔲 button. Type **Schedule** on the right side of the header.

12 Click the Show Next ⟲ button to go to the Odd Page Header for section 4 and click the Same as Previous ⟲ button. Select *Schedule* and type **Packets**.

13 Click the Show Next ⟲ button to go to the Odd Page Header for section 5 and click the Same as Previous ⟲ button. Delete *Packets* and type **Seminars**.

14 Click the Show Next ⟲ button to go to the Odd Page Header for section 6 and click the Same as Previous ⟲ button. Delete *Seminars* and type **Career Day**. Click the Close ⟨Close⟩ button.

15 Scroll through the document in Print Layout view to see the headers and footers. Notice that the page numbers are incorrect.

16 Starting with the Odd Page Footer in section 3, make sure that Same As Previous is turned off for all remaining footers. Then, for each footer starting with the Even Page Footer for section 3, click the Format Page Number ⟨⟩ button and choose **Continue from previous section**. Close the footer.

17 Save the document as *C&C Promo Proposal Edited*. Close the file.

ON YOUR OWN

The difficulty of these case studies varies:
 are the least difficult; *are more difficult; and* *are the most difficult.*

1 CREATING A TITLE PAGE

Open *Demographics.doc* or *Demographics Edited.doc* (if you did Guided Exercise 1). Insert a Next page section break after the title at the top of the first page. Center the title vertically on the page. Save the file as *Demographics with Title*. Close the file or leave it open for the next exercise.

2 NUMBERING PAGES

Open *Demographics with Title*, if necessary. Insert page numbers centered at the bottom of the page, starting with the second page. Start the numbering with the number 1. Save the file as *Demographics Numbered*. Close the file.

3 WRITING AN OUTLINE FOR A LONG-RANGE PLAN

Refer to the MLA guidelines (or the guidelines prescribed by your school) and create an outline that describes the activities and plans you have for your college years, your first five years after you get out of college, the next five years, and then the next five years. Include your personal and career goals, salary goals, savings goals, investment goals, and so on. Save the document as *Long Range Plan*. Then close the document and try to stick to it!

4 EDITING THE LONG-RANGE PLAN

Now that you have an outline, let's flesh out the plan. Open the *Long Range Plan.doc* file and switch to Print Layout view. Add a title page. Then add text to each of the outline headings until the document is at least three pages long. Format the paper according to the MLA (or other) guidelines. Use the Document Map to navigate in the document. Save the file as *Long Range Plan2* and close the document or leave the document open for the next exercise.

⑤ ADDING HEADERS, FOOTERS, AND FOOTNOTES

Open the *Long Range Plan2.doc* file and add headers and footers to the paper. Add several footnotes. Then add another footnote after the first footnote. Edit the text of at least one of the footnotes. Move a sentence that contains a footnote reference to a new location in the document and notice how the footnote numbers adjust. Move the sentence back again. Save the file as *Long Range Plan 4 Final* and close the file.

⑥ CREATING A PROPOSAL

Imagine that you are going into business for yourself. Create a short proposal to give to the bank asking for a small-business loan to get you started. The proposal should include a title page, a short outline that lists what you need to start the business, and a short report that explains how much money you need, how much money you anticipate making annually, and when and how you expect to be able to pay back the loan. Create appropriate headers and footers. Save the file as *Business Proposal*.

Photospread credits pages 4-2 & 4-3
©CORBIS, ©Steve Chenn/ CORBIS; ©EyeWire; ©Tony Stone: ©Lonnie Duka; ©Pearson Education, © Lorraine Castellano

Glossary

Active window The window that you are working in.

Alignment The horizontal placement of text on a line.

Antonym A word that means the opposite of another word.

AutoComplete A feature that automatically completes many common words and phrases as you type.

AutoCorrect A feature that automatically corrects many common typographical errors.

AutoText entry An entry that has been saved with a specific name that can automatically insert text, formatting, and graphics.

Bar tab A tab that creates a vertical line.

Body text In an outline, text that has no outline level applied to it.

Bold A font attribute that makes the text appear darker so it stands out.

Border The top, bottom, left, and right lines you add to a table, a table cell, a paragraph, text, or a page.

Browse buttons Navigation buttons located at the bottom of the vertical scroll bar. They include the following default buttons (from top to bottom): Previous Page, Select Browse Object, and Next Page.

Bullet The character, such as a filled circle, that precedes the text in a bulleted paragraph.

Bulleted list A list set off with bullets.

Case The capitalization of text.

Cell In a table, the intersection of a column and a row.

Center To change the alignment of a paragraph so that an equal amount of white space appears on both sides of the text.

Center tab A type of tab that causes data to be centered on the tab stop.

Character style A collection of font attributes that is given a name and can be applied to text to format the text.

Click and Type The feature that allows you to type in areas that were previously considered "non-typing" areas.

Clip art A graphic provided in a file format such as tif, wpg, bmp, wmf, and so on. Office XP provides many clip art files and stores them in the Clip Art Gallery.

Close button The button that closes the window.

Collapse an outline heading To hide the level(s) under an outline heading.

Column A vertical group of cells in a table.

Column break A nonprinting character that causes the text in a column to go to the next column.

Cyclical diagram A diagram that illustrates a process that repeats itself (a cycle).

Date code A field that automatically updates the date to the current date.

Data Source document A document that contains the variable information that will be used to "fill in the blanks" in a mail merge document.

Decimal tab A type of tab that aligns text on a decimal.

Demote an outline level To convert an outline level to the next lower level.

Diagram A new feature in Office XP that allows you to create one of the following charts or diagrams: organization, cyclical, radial, Venn, pyramid, or target.

Document Map A tool that lists all the document headings, similar to an outline, in a pane on the left. The headings are linked to the document so that you can click a heading and go directly to the text in the document.

Document title bar The bar at the top of the document window that displays the document title and the Minimize, Maximize/Restore, and Close buttons.

Document window The window in which a Word file opens.

Endnotes The notes (comments or references) grouped together at the end of the document. The reference in the text to which the endnote applies is generally numbered, and the endnote displays the same number.

Enter The key you press to end short lines and paragraphs and create blank lines.

Expand an outline heading To display the level(s) under an outline level.

Field The variable information for each record in a Data Source document. Also, a code that inserts information automatically, such as the Date field.

Find A command that searches for specified text as well as formatting attributes.

First line indent An indentation in the first line of a paragraph.

Font A collection of letters, numbers, and symbols in a particular style, such as Times New Roman or Arial.

Font effects Attributes that alter the appearance of text. These include strikethrough, double strikethrough, superscript, subscript, shadow, outline, embossed, engraved, small caps, all caps, and hidden.

Footer Text that prints at the bottom of every page in a section.

Footnotes Comments or references that appear at the bottom of the page. The reference in the text to which the footnote applies is generally numbered, and the footnote displays the same number.

Formatting toolbar A toolbar that contains buttons commonly used for applying formatting attributes, such as bold, italic, underline, center alignment, font, font size, and so on.

Go To A command that moves the insertion point to a specific page, section, line, bookmark, comment, and so on.

Grammar Checker A feature that looks for incorrect spacing and punctuation, incorrect verb tense, disagreement between subjects and verbs, sentence fragments, incorrect use of that and which, passive voice, and so on.

Hanging indent A paragraph that has the first line extended farther to the left than the subsequent lines in the paragraph.

Header Text that prints at the top of every page in a section.

Highlight Shading that is applied to text using the Highlight feature. The color of the shading can be one of 15 different colors, but the default color is yellow.

HTML See Hypertext Markup Language.

Hyperlink A link to another file or page on the World Wide Web. When you click on a hyperlink, the linked file is displayed on the screen.

Hypertext Markup Language The standard language used to create pages for the World Wide Web.

Hyphenation A feature that automatically inserts hyphens in words that fall at the end of a line instead of wrapping the complete word to the next line.

I-beam The name of the mouse cursor when the mouse cursor is in the area of text.

Indent To change the alignment of lines of text. You can indent the first line or indent all the lines of a paragraph on the left or right.

Insertion point The blinking, vertical line that marks the position where a letter is inserted when you press a key.

Intranet A private network that uses Internet protocol.

Italic The style you apply to text to make the font appear slanted so that it stands out.

Justify To change the alignment of text so that it is spread evenly between the margins.

Landscape The orientation of text that prints using the long side of a piece of paper as the top of the document.

Leader Characters, such as periods, that appear before the tab. Any type of tab can have a leader.

Left-align To change the alignment of paragraphs in your document so that they are aligned at the left margin.

Left indent The position of a paragraph relative to the left margin.

Left tab A command that causes text to align on the left.

Line spacing The amount of space between lines of text.

Magnifier A button on the Print Preview toolbar that zooms in or out on the document that is displayed in the view.

Mail Merge Wizard The task pane that guides you through the process of creating a main document and a data source and then merging the two.

Mail merging A process in which you insert text from a file containing a list of information into a form file, such as a form letter. The process involves the following three steps: creating the file that contains the list of information, creating the form file and inserting the fields, and merging the two files.

Main document The document, usually a letter, with which you merge the list of names in the Data Source document when you use the mail merge feature.

Margin The white space around the edge of the page.

Menu bar The bar at the top of the window that contains menu options.

Newspaper columns The style of columns in which text flows from the bottom of one column to the top of the next.

Normal style A paragraph style on which many other styles are based.

Normal view A view of a document that does not show margins.

Numbered list A list set off with numbers, often to indicate a sequence of steps.

Office Assistant The Help feature that offers help on the task you are performing and looks up information in the Help files.

Office Clipboard In Office, the clipboard that can contain multiple items for pasting. You can select the items or paste all the items at once.

Organization chart A chart that illustrates the hierarchy (usually of personnel) of a company or other organization.

Orientation The direction in which text prints on a page. The default orientation is portrait.

Outline Text that is formatted with outline numbering styles.

Outline view The view that displays a document in a hierarchical format based on the headings that are applied to the text.

Outline numbering scheme The complete set of styles applied to each level of an outline.

Page break A break that separates pages of text. When a page fills up with text, Word automatically inserts a page break.

Page setup Adjustable options, including the margins, paper size, and orientation, that are preset in Word.

Paper size The size of the paper on which you will print. The default setting is 8.5" by 11".

Paper source The source from which paper is fed to the printer.

Paragraph spacing The spacing before and after a paragraph.

Paste Option button A new feature in Word 2002 that appears when you paste. The button contains options for pasting text with different attributes.

Print Layout view A view of a document that displays the document as it will look when it prints.

Print Preview A view that allows you to see the complete page or as many as 50 pages on the screen at the same time.

Promote an outline level To convert an outline level to the next higher level.

Pyramid diagram A diagram that illustrates a hierarchy using a pyramid.

Radial diagram A diagram that illustrates relationships to a core element.

Record All the information, such as a name, address, city, state, zip code, and so on, in the fields for one set of data in a Data Source document.

Right-align To change the alignment of paragraphs in your document so that they are aligned at the right margin.

Right tab A command that causes text to align on the right.

Row A horizontal group of cells in a table.

Ruler The feature that displays the settings for the margins, tabs, and indents. The ruler also can be used to make these settings.

Scroll bars The vertical and horizontal bars in a window that enable you to move the contents viewed in the window.

Select Browse Object The button at the bottom of the vertical scroll bar that displays a palette of buttons used for browsing through a document by particular elements, such as tables, pages, endnotes, and footnotes.

Selection bar The area on the left side of the screen in which you can use the mouse to select portions of text.

Section A physical division in a document that can be formatted differently.

Section break A nonprinting character that creates a section.

Select Browse Object button A button you use to change the navigation buttons.

Shading Various percentages of gray and colors you add to draw attention to important text.

Signature block The text at the bottom of a letter that contains the sender's name and a complementary closing statement such as "Sincerely."

Special character A character that does not have a key on the keyboard, such as an em dash.

Spelling Checker The feature that checks the spelling in a document.

Spelling and Grammar Status icon An icon on the status bar that displays an X if there is a spelling or grammar error in the document.

Standard toolbar A toolbar that contains buttons for common tasks such as opening, saving, and printing a file.

Status bar The bar at the bottom of the window that displays information about the current document, including the page number and the position of the insertion point.

Status indicator In the status bar, the letters REC, TRK, EXT, and OVR that are either dimmed or not dimmed to signal whether the feature is active or not.

Style A collection of character and/or paragraph settings that are saved with a name and can be applied to text.

Symbol A character that cannot be entered from the keyboard, such as © or ®.

Synonym A word that has the same meaning as another word.

Tab The feature on the ruler or command on the Format menu that aligns text.

Tab stop The location on the ruler where a tab is set.

Table A grouping of columns and rows (like a spreadsheet).

Target diagram A diagram that illustrates steps toward a goal.

Template A pattern for creating a document.

Thesaurus Word's feature that finds and inserts synonyms.

Title bar The bar at the top of a window that displays the name of the program and the name of the open file (if there is one).

Title case Uses uppercase and lowercase as you would in capitalizing words in a title—e.g., lowercase for articles and prepositions, uppercase for nouns and verbs.

Toggle case Reverses the capitalization of the existing text.

Toolbar A bar that contains buttons for accomplishing commands.

Underline The rule added under text so that it stands out.

Venn diagram A diagram that illustrates areas of overlap.

Vertical ruler A ruler that appears only in the Print Layout view and only if the option to display it is selected. It displays the top and bottom margins.

View buttons The buttons in the horizontal scroll bar that change the views. These include Normal, Web Layout, Print Layout, and Outline.

Web Layout view A view that wraps all text to fit the width of the window. Use this view when you are viewing a document on screen or on the Web.

Web Page Preview The view of a document that is displayed as a Web page in Internet Explorer.

Wrap The feature in Word that causes the text that won't fit on a line to automatically be moved to the beginning of the next line.

Writing style An option that determines what is included in grammar checking.

Zoom The feature that increases or decreases the size of the text on the screen.

Index